National Council for the Social Studies

8555 Sixteenth Street • Suite 500 • Silver Spring, Maryland 20910 • socialstudies.org

ISBN 978-0-87986-150-6

Revolution of Ideas: A Decade of C3 Inquiry

Introduction: Looking Back

The publication of the *College, Career and Civic Life (C3) Framework for Social Studies State Standards* has become a watershed moment for social studies, a revolution of ideas. But, it didn't begin that way.

We vividly remember the anticipation and anxiety that accompanied the day the C3 Framework went live on the NCSS website—Constitution Day, September 13, 2013. Social studies is known for getting tangled up in history and culture wars, and we worried the C3 Framework would end up as a punching bag on a partisan news segment or as a talking point for politicians that could shut it down before it even got started.[1] A year before publication, Chester Finn of the Fordham Institute wrote a negative op-ed about the C3 as a "hodgepodge" and a disappointing "jumble."[2]

Truth be told, while we hoped for a bit of good buzz after the actual publication, we prepared for an onslaught of negative press. In fact, neither occurred. Yes, there was a short article in *Education Week* that reported on the substance of the document and included more reactions from Finn that "one could build good stuff on this framework" or "one could also build trash."[3] This was followed a day later by a scathing blog post by Frederick Hess of the American Enterprise Institute (AEI), who complained about the lack of content.[4]

And, then, nothing. Unlike the Common Core, which came out like a lion, the C3 Framework dropped like a feather. Looking back, it seems that the silence we heard was a key to its success.

Despite the national-level silence, the C3 Framework started making some noise. State departments of education began to pay it some mind as their social studies standards came up for revision. Connecticut, Hawaii, and Maryland led that charge.[5] Then, the New York Toolkit project was published in 2015 with the C3-inspired Inquiry Design Model (IDM) front and center.[6] With these actions, a revolution of ideas gained some ground.

Since that time, even more state departments have used the C3 Framework as the basis for reforming their social studies curriculum: As of today, thiry-eight states have revised their social studies standards in part or in whole based on the C3 Framework.[7] The New York Toolkit project—which featured nearly one hundred K–12 IDM-based curriculum inquiries—had a multiplier effect as additional states, districts, and cultural institutions adopted the Inquiry Design Model as a preferred way of articulating their curriculum goals.

But to burn brightly, revolutions need fuel. To stoke the inquiry revolution, other ideas and actions had to have come into play. C3Teachers (c3teachers.org), a website devoted to all things inquiry and C3 related, launched with curricular resources, educator blogs, and a bank of free, downloadable inquiries.[8] Alex Cuenca led a revision of the *National Standards for the Preparation of Social Studies Teachers*, placing inquiry in general and the C3 Framework in particular, squarely in the forefront of teacher education.[9] Michael Simpson collaborated with us to establish the "Teaching with the C3 Framework" columns in each of the NCSS publications: *Social Education*, *Middle Level Learning*, and *Social Studies and the Young Learner*.

Even more recently, the C3 Framework and IDM are playing a key role in terms of assessment. The testing company Pearson is launching a new line of formative assessments for social studies that center on a sequence of eight inquiry skills within a set of content frameworks. And the Virginia Department of Education is offering school districts an alternative to the traditional multiple-choice state test that employs an IDM approach.

Of course, no one of these efforts, in and of itself, is sufficient to sustain a revolution. Taken together, however, they clearly point to a gathering of the inquiry forces. But it is a gathering unlike any curriculum effort in the past.

First, it is an effort that has lacked any major funding or legislative mandate that typically accompanies widespread policy changes. Our sister disciplines of math and English Language Arts flaunted the Race to the Top legislation that tied gazillions of dollars to the adoption of the Common Core standards. As a result, forty-six states adopted the Common Core standards almost overnight.[10] With seemingly unlimited funds from the National Science Foundation (NSF), the science community produced the *Next Generation Science Standards*—an effort that included a slick website and accompanying instructional materials with professional learning opportunities to any state that requested it.[11] We used to joke that the C3 got made by paying compliments to its contributors.

Second, it is an effort devoted to the idea of a big tent, one where everyone in social studies can find utility for the C3. States have a solid framework for upgrading their standards and a persuasive argument for "Why social studies?" Cultural and curricular organizations and educational publishers have a unified approach and an inquiry vernacular to use when preparing instructional materials and professional learning experiences. Teachers have an inquiry manifesto and mission statement that reinforces what they already knew to be true about teaching good social studies. And, most importantly, students have an invitation and a promise. No longer the most boring subject in school, social studies invites them to engage with real-world problems that require their agency and grit and a promise that this is a new day in their social studies classes.

And third, it is an effort based in the power of ideas—*really* good ideas about inquiry. The roots of the C3 Inquiry Arc can be traced back to John Dewey, the constructivist curricula of *Man: A Course of Study* (MACOS), and Fred Newmann's Authentic Intellectual Work (AIW).[12] *Dimension 2: Applying Disciplinary Concepts and Tools* of the C3 could not have been possible without years of research spent nailing down historical thinking, geographic reasoning, deliberation, and economic decision-making skills that are distinct but complementary approaches for disciplinary *and* interdisciplinary inquiry. The glue that continues to hold the social studies together is its commitment to civic engagement and action. Drawing on the important work of researchers and practitioners in civic education, we built a language for Taking Informed Action as the ultimate expression of inquiry-based engagement. The C3 Framework has reflective intellectual properties that resonate with past work and point towards a more coherent future for the field.

We produced this book because we thought this revolution of ideas should be televised. We wanted to chronicle what we have seen over the last decade and note how the C3 have made their way into so many facets of social studies: standards, curriculum, instruction, assessment, and teacher education. We draw primarily from the "Teaching the C3 Framework" columns in *Social Education* to tell the C3 story. Ultimately, we selected twenty-seven published articles that we think stand out over the decade. As in any revolution based on ideas, there is still more to do. We leave suggestions for the next ten years in the conclusion.

This book is about celebrating the improbable victories and to recognize how far we have come as a social studies community. *¡Viva la inquiry revolución!*

Notes

1. Ronald W. Evans, *The Social Studies Wars: What Should We Teach the Children?* (New York: Teachers College Press, 2004); David Warren Saxe, *Social Studies in Schools: A History of the Early Years* (New York: State University of New York Press, 1991).

2. Chester Finn, Jr., "Social Studies Follies," The Thomas Fordham Institute, November 20, 2012, https://fordhaminstitute.org/national/commentary/social-studies-follies.

3. Catherine Gerwertz, "New Social Studies Framework Aims to Guide Standards," *Education Week*, September 17, 2023.

4. Frederick Hess, "A Content-Free Framework for K–12 Social Studies Standards," American Enterprise Institute, September 18, 2013, www.aei.org/education/a-content-free-framework-for-k-12-social-studies-standards/.

5. Kathy Swan, "The C3 Framework: One Year Later," *Social Education* 78, no. 4 (2014): 172–174.

6. Kathy Swan, John Lee, and S. G. Grant, "The New York State Toolkit and the Inquiry Design Model: Anatomy of an Inquiry," *Social Education* 79, no. 5 (2015): 316–322.

7. S. G. Grant, John Lee, and Kathy Swan, "The State of the C3 Framework: An Inquiry Revolution in the Making," *Social Education* 87, no. 6 (2023): 361–366.

8. John Lee, Kathy Swan, and S. G. Grant, "By Teachers, For Teachers: The NYS Toolkit and C3 Teachers," *Social Education* 79, no. 5 (2015): 325–328.

9. Alex Cuenca, "Inquiry-Based Core Practices for Social Studies Teacher Education," *Social Education* 85, no. 6 (2021): 382–386.

10. Michele McNeil, "46 States Agree to Common Academic Standards Effort," *EdWeek*, June 1, 2009, www.edweek.org/policy-politics/46-states-agree-to-common-academic-standards-effort/2009/06.

11. Next Generation Science Standards, https://www.nextgenscience.org/

12. John Dewey, *Democracy in Education: An Introduction to the Philosophy of Education* (1916; reis., London: Telegraph Books, 1986); Fred Newmann, M. Bruce King, and Dana Carmichael, *Authentic Instruction and Assessment: Common Standards for Rigor and Relevance in Teaching Academic Subjects* (Des Moines, IA: Iowa Department of Education, 2007), http://psdsped.pbworks.com/w/file/fetch/67042713/Authentic-Instruction-Assessment-BlueBook.pdf.

List of Contributors

Christy Byrd, Associate Professor of Educational Psychology, North Carolina State University

James Carlson, Social Studies Instructional Coach, Branford Public Schools, Connecticut

Christy Cartner, Social Studies Teacher, Bryan Station High School in Lexington, Kentucky and Doctoral Student at the University of Kentucky

Lauren Colley, Assistant Professor of Secondary Social Studies Education, University of Cincinnati

Ryan M. Crowley, Associate Professor of Social Studies Education, University of Kentucky

Alexander Cuenca, Associate Professor of Social Studies Education, Indiana University

Andrew Danner, Doctoral Student, University of Kentucky

Laura Darolia, Associate Professor of elementary social studies education, University of Kentucky

Beau Dickenson, K–12 Social Studies Supervisor, Rockingham County Public Schools, Virginia

Jennifer Fraker, Assistant Vice President, Government Relations and K-12 Policies and Programs, Kentucky Council on Post Secondary Education

S. G. Grant, Professor of Social Studies Education, Binghamton University

Susan Griffin, Past Executive Director, National Council for the Social Studies

Meghan Hawkins, Social Studies Teacher and Department Chair, Normal Community High School, Illinois

Joel Hinrichs, Social Studies Teacher and Coach, Branford, Connecticut public school system

John Hobson, Assistant Principal, Murray Elementary School, Virginia.

LaGarrett J. King, Associate Professor of Social Studies Education, University of Buffalo

Patricia Krizan, Educational Consultant, Rockland County Board of Cooperative Educational Services (BOCES)

John Lee, Associate Dean for Faculty and Academic Affairs and Professor in the Department of Teacher Education and Learning Sciences in the College of Education, North Carolina State University

Bonnie Lewis, Assistant Professor of Social Studies Education, University of Delaware

Ryan Lewis, Department Chair and Social Studies Teacher, Woodford High School

Arine Lowery, Clinical Practice Coordinator, University of North Carolina Pembroke

Paula McAvoy, Associate Professor of Social Studies Education, North Carolina State University

Alicia McCollum, Doctoral Student, University of Kentucky

Rebecca Mueller, Associate Professor of Social Studies Education, University of South Carolina Upstate

Carly Muetterties, Founder, CommonGoodEd

Ryan New, Instructional Lead for Social Studies, Jefferson County Public Schools

Nick Stamoulactos, Director of Social Studies Education, Syracuse City School District, New York

Grant Stringer, Research Analyst, National Association of Independent Schools (NAIS)

Gerry Swan, Associate Professor of Instructional Systems Design, University of Kentucky

Kathy Swan, Professor of Social Studies Education, University of Kentucky

Emma S. Thacker, Associate Professor of Social Studies Education, James Madison University

Josephine L. Valentine, Elementary Teacher, Southeast Raleigh Elementary School, North Carolina

Nada Wafa, Assistant Teaching Professor of Social Studies Education, North Carolina State University

MaryBeth Yerdon, Assistant Professor of Social Studies Education, State University of New York, Cortland

Section 1: Standards

Section 1: The C3 Framework and Standards

The educational standards movement, now in its fortieth year, continues unabated. Beginning with the 1983 *Nation at Risk* report, the motivation to set down academic goals, particularly at the national and state levels, remains strong. Whether those many efforts can claim real effects is problematic. However, the shelf-life of most standards documents is so short as to defy empirical evidence of any benefit.

There is an exception to this rule. *The College, Career, and Civic Life (C3) Framework for Social Studies State Standards*[1] held its 10th anniversary on Constitution Day, November 2023. Since the Framework's publication, most state departments of education have revised their social studies standards; several professional disciplinary organizations have done the same (e.g., Center for Civics Education). True to its origin, the C3 Framework has not been *adopted* as the Common Core for English Language Arts was (and was then unadopted by several states). Instead, the Framework has been used by state-level policy makers as a guide to revise their social studies standards. And, in that regard, the C3 Framework can be credibly cited as leading a revolution of ideas.

In this section, we present five articles from the "Teaching the C3 Framework" archive in *Social Education* that describe and contextualize the origins, development, and impact of the Framework. In some ways, a lot has happened since 2013, and yet the central elements of the Framework—academic rigor, relevance to students' lives, teacher agency, and a commitment to inquiry-based teaching and learning—are as powerful as ever.

* * * * *

The first article in the section, "Beating the Odds: The College, Career, and Civic Life (C3) Framework for Social Studies State Standards" by Kathy Swan and Susan Griffin, sets the context for the conception of the C3 Framework in 2013. They detail the challenges that the Common Core for English Language Arts posed for the field of social studies. Swan and Griffin argue that, by addressing social studies in an appendix, the Common Core English Language Arts Standards became "the de facto standards for social studies" (p. 13). Social studies and language arts *should* be natural allies, but the authors of the Common Core treated social studies as an add-on.

Against this background, Swan and Griffin describe the origins of the C3 Framework in a meeting of two groups: social studies experts in state departments of education and representatives of professional organizations devoted to the disciplinary fields representing social studies. Through a series of meetings, and in spite of severe financial challenges, the two groups found common ground around a set of standards that "maintain disciplinary integrity but should be rooted in an interdisciplinary inquiry approach" (p. 16). Thus, from the beginning, inquiry has been the central theme of the C3 Framework.

The story of how the C3 Framework came to be continues in Kathy Swan's article, "The Importance of the C3 Framework." Through an interview format, Swan describes why the standards are important in general, why the C3 Framework was created, why it matters to social studies teachers and students, and how it is different from previous efforts. She presents two features that define the ambitious nature of the C3 Framework: its approach to the disciplines that make up social studies and its commitment to informed action.

Squabbles about disciplinary prominence and positioning have dogged the field. Carving a new path, the C3 Framework takes seriously the twin notions of disciplinary integrity (i.e., the importance of discipline-specific content and skills in civics, economics, geography, and history) *and* disciplinary interrelationships (i.e., the many ways that disciplinary boundaries can cross when trying to understand and act on social problems). The Framework also takes seriously the need for opportunities in which students can engage in informed civic action. Social studies is about knowing and understanding the past; it is also about knowing, understanding, and doing in the present.

In "The C3 Framework: One Year Later," Kathy Swan offers the first look back at the impact the Framework has had. By keying in on the difference between "implementation" and "adoption," Swan notes that the Framework "allows states to determine the appropriate content to be taught at each grade level" (p. 24). Describing the C3 movement as "grassroots and organic," she argues that it is defined as much by what it is not—i.e., "a top-down or one-size-fits-all effort" (p. 24)—as it is by what it stands for—an inquiry-based approach leading to student agency.

Swan goes on to name four issues relevant to implementing the C3 Framework—(a) challenges such as attending to both content *and* skills, (b) the need for new teacher/student relationships, (c) the importance of professional development, and (d) the power of assessment.

The fourth article in this section, "The State of Social Studies Standards: What Is the Impact of the C3 Framework?" by Ryan New, Kathy Swan, S. G. Grant, and John Lee, is the first attempt to assess the influence of the framework on state-level social studies standards. New et al. conducted a content analysis of the current standards in each state and the District of Columbia 8 years after the C3 Framework launch. That analysis yielded 4 levels of impact:

> Level N/A: States that had not undergone standards revision since 2013;
>
> Level 1: States that did not cite the Framework as an influence;
>
> Level 2: States the cited, endorsed, or excerpted elements of the Framework; and
>
> Level 3: States that framed, modeled, or adopted the Framework.

The findings were as surprising as they were welcome: "In all, 32 of 51 standards documents include, at a minimum, a reference to the C3 Framework. These 32 states represent 61% of all children enrolled in public schools in the United States" (p. 31).

Three years later, that headline is even more impressive. In "The State of the C3 Framework: An Inquiry Revolution in the Making," S. G. Grant, Kathy Swan, and John Lee update the New et al. (2021) study. A new analysis of social studies standards in the 50 states and District of Columbia shows that the influence of the C3 Framework is both stable and growing: "With the 10-year-anniversary of the C3 Framework, we were tickled to see that six more states have joined the inquiry fold. In effect, that means that approximately 35 million, or nearly 70% of American students have the opportunity to engage in more ambitious social studies teaching and learning than ever before."

* * * * *

1. Kathy Swan and Susan Griffin, "Beating the Odds: The College, Career, and Civic Life (C3) Framework for Social Studies State Standards," *Social Education* 77, no. 6 (2013): 317–321.
2. Kathy Swan, "The Importance of the C3 Framework," *Social Education* 77, no. 4 (2013): 222–224.
3. Kathy Swan, "The C3 Framework: One Year Later," *Social Education* 78, no. 4 (2014): 172–174.
4. Ryan New, Kathy Swan, John Lee, and S. G. Grant, "The State of Social Studies Standards: What Is the Impact of the C3 Framework?" *Social Education* 86, no. 4 (2021): 239–246.
5. S. G. Grant, John Lee, and Kathy Swan, "The State of the C3 Framework: An Inquiry Revolution in the Making," *Social Education* 87, no. 6 (2023): 361–366.

Note

1. National Council for the Social Studies, *The College, Career, and Civic Life (C3) Framework for Social Studies State Standards* (Silver Spring, MD: National Council for the Social Studies, 2013).

Social Education 77, no. 6 (2013): 317–321

Beating the Odds: The College, Career, and Civic Life (C3) Framework for Social Studies State Standards

Kathy Swan and Susan Griffin

When the College, Career, and Civic Life (C3) Framework for Social Studies State Standards project began, there really was nowhere else to go but up. The project was up against great odds—a dearth of funding, a history of incivility amongst the disciplines within social studies, a knack for ending up in media battles over what should be taught in a social studies curriculum, a lack of disciplinary and interdisciplinary coherence within previous social studies standards documents, and the list went on.[1] In the first couple of months, one of the more optimistic colleagues on the C3 project gave the work about a 30 percent chance of success. He wasn't that far off.

But fear is a great motivator. At the time this project began, the Common Core State Standards reform movement was sweeping the country.[2] The majority of states had formally adopted the new standards in English Language Arts and Mathematics emphasizing a "fewer, higher, clearer" approach to K-12 education.[3] That action created tremors within the social studies community that we could be further squeezed out of the curriculum.

As the Common Core Standards gained momentum, the need for a framework for state social studies standards became increasingly evident. Many in the social studies community feared that the effect of the Common Core Standards on social studies would be to emphasize English Language Arts, and make the English Language Arts Standards the de facto standards for social studies. It was essential to reassert the importance of social studies subjects, especially as the Common Core Standards acknowledge the necessary contribution of history and other social studies subjects to literacy in grades 6–12. The Common Core Standards also include a substantial emphasis on informational text, much of which is drawn from social studies disciplines, in the English Language Arts Standards for grades K–5.[4] As state departments of education faced greater budget cuts, and in the absence of a clear consensus around the purpose and outcomes of social studies education, many in the social studies community feared that social studies would be marginalized further. Where once disciplinary quarrels and boundary disputes might have sunk any attempt at constructing social studies standards, the potential elimination of social studies as a viable school subject created a more constructive environment.

A Social Studies Alliance Forms

By January 2010, a few months before the Common Core Standards were officially published, two groups were meeting concurrently to discuss the critical state of social studies education. The Social Studies Assessment, Curriculum, and Instruction (SSACI) is a state collaborative within the Council of Chief State School Officers (CCSSO) made up of state-level social studies consultants, assessment experts, and administrative personnel who are on the front lines of adoption and implementation of standards within their states. The SSACI collaborative membership structure allows the group to meet six times a year (three face-to-face meetings and three virtual meetings). These meetings provide a forum for examining the current needs and issues facing the states and allow state education agencies to draw from a greater pool of experience. After much discussion about the ways in which the Common Core standards implementation was eclipsing social studies in their respective departments, SSACI decided to work toward the creation of a resource for members to assist them in upgrading their respective social studies standards.

At the same time SSACI was meeting, the National Council for the Social Studies (NCSS) joined with the Campaign for the Civic Mission of Schools (CMS) to sponsor a summit of 15 national organizations representing civics, economics, geography, and history education. Within a half-day meeting, the organizations had agreed that social studies could not be further marginalized, and they must work together to elevate the field. They cemented their partnership that day by crafting a working definition of social studies that focused social studies on the four disciplines named in the *No Child Left Behind Act of 2001* by recognizing the interdisciplinary focus of citizenship education, and by acknowledging the role of literacy education within and across the disciplines:

> The social studies is an interdisciplinary exploration of the social sciences and humanities, including civics, economics, geography, and history in order to develop responsible, informed and engaged citizens and to foster civic, economic, global, and historical literacy.

It was agreed that the initiative would focus on state standards on the four disciplines identified in the No Child Left Behind framework as the "core" social studies subjects—civics, economics, geography, and history.

Through the grapevine, we heard about each other's work and after a series of phone calls and summer meetings, SSACI extended an invitation to form the Task Force of Professional Organizations (See Sidebar A) to unite with SSACI to collectively work on a common resource for social studies.

Initially, the group decided to follow in the footsteps of English Language Arts and Mathematics by creating a uniform set of standards that states could opt into. At the time, we referred to the work as the Common State Standards for Social Studies Project and hoped that a state-led initiative would improve the chances of acceptance by state policymakers and mitigate the possibilities for corrosive political controversy. Although the ethos of the project remained intact, over the course of the project, *standards would necessarily turn into a framework for development of standards* as a more flexible document focusing on social studies skills and concepts had the greatest appeal to a wider

Sidebar A. Task Force of Professional Organizations

American Bar Association	National Council for Geographic Education
American Historical Association	National Council for History Education
Association of American Geographers	National Council for the Social Studies
Campaign for the Civic Mission of Schools	National Geographic Society
Center for Civic Education	National History Day
Constitutional Rights Foundation/Chicago	Street Law, Inc.
Constitutional Rights Foundation/USA	World History Association
Council for Economic Education	

range of states. For example, while some of the SSACI states were on the eve of standards creation (e.g., Kentucky), many states had either just created and adopted new social studies standards (e.g., Kansas and North Carolina). A framework would assist all states in utilizing the document as either a companion to existing standards, as a foundation for new standards, or as a mandate to initiate a conversation about the importance of social studies in their state.

Also influencing the framework decision was the enduring tension of skills versus content. While the document would focus on disciplinary processes and skills as well as vital conceptual content, it would avoid historically divisive prescriptions of curricular content (e.g., names, dates, places, historical eras). However, it is important to note that the group did not want the work to devolve into the old debate of knowledge versus skills, forcing educators to fall into two opposing camps. Instead, the group recognized that a robust and complete social studies education includes an understanding of essential content knowledge, but the decisions around curricular content would need to be determined at the state or local level.

At first glance, the voluntary, state-led effort to develop what would become the C3 Framework faced long odds as it hinged on professional collaboration between and among a loosely arranged coalition of state departments of education and professional organizations. If the past is any kind of predictor (e.g., history wars of the 1990s), social studies educators seemed like the last content area group who should be betting on a cooperative movement. Further, while CCSSO had initially agreed to host these meetings, they were clear that their commitment to the Common Core initiative did not extend to taking a leadership role in the development of state social studies standards. At the time, Chris Minnich, now executive director of CCSSO, expressed the tacit support his organization was willing to offer:

> Our board has been very clear that they're not interested in leading the social studies work in the same way we've led the common core in Math and English Language Arts. We're hopeful that states working together can write social studies standards as they would like to. Some states are interested in upgrading their standards, and that is what we are interested in helping support. We are not part of the development as we were with the common standards [in math and English Language Arts].[5]

While our group had a "living room," we knew the residence would be temporary,[6] and that there was the possibility of eviction if the work became too precarious. Against this tenuous backdrop, the group forged ahead.

Building a Foundation for the C3 Framework

Work on the C3 Framework began in the fall of 2010 with the development of a conceptual guidance document written by individuals from the Social Studies Assessment, Curriculum and Instruction state collaborative and representatives from the Task Force. In the section that follows, we summarize a number of these foundational ideas that provided a common frame of reference for the group and became a guide to the writers of the C3 Framework.

- *Social studies prepares the nation's young people for college and career, and equally important, civic life.*

The ideas, concepts, skills and understandings gained in a study of the social studies disciplines prepare young people to be more effective citizens and provide students with the tools to understand, interpret, and effectively meet challenges in our ever-changing twenty-first century world.

- *Social studies should maintain disciplinary integrity but should be rooted in an interdisciplinary inquiry approach.*

Social studies is an organizational structure which brings together unique ways of knowing from the disciplines of political science or civics, economics, geography, history, and behavioral sciences. Social studies should include a strong emphasis on disciplinary knowledge and the structures of specific disciplines but, at the same time, social studies should provide students with opportunities to apply disciplinary knowledge and skills as they examine enduring questions related to human experiences. Students must develop the creative and adaptive habits of mind that come with interdisciplinary thinking so as to apply those ways of thinking to real-world problems in college, career and citizenship.

- *Social studies should prioritize deep and enduring understandings using concepts and skills from the disciplines.*

Social studies should emphasize deep and enduring understandings over surface level learning. This represents a shift in the current status of teaching and learning in social studies. The C3 Framework focuses on inquiry skills and key

Sidebar B: C3 Writing Team

Kathy Swan, Ph.D. (Lead Writer), Associate Professor, Social Studies Education, University of Kentucky

Keith C. Barton, Ed.D., Professor of Curriculum and Instruction and Adjunct Professor of History, Indiana University

Stephen Buckles, Ph.D., Senior Lecturer (formerly Professor) in Economics, Vanderbilt University

Flannery Burke, Ph.D., Associate Professor of History, Saint Louis University

Jim Charkins, Ph.D., Professor Emeritus of Economics at California State University, San Bernardino; Executive Director of the California Council on Economic Education

S.G. Grant, Ph.D., Founding Dean of the Graduate School of Education, Binghamton University

Susan W. Hardwick, Ph.D., Professor Emeritus of Geography at the University of Oregon

John Lee, Ph.D., Associate Professor of Social Studies Education, North Carolina State University

Peter Levine, D.Phil., Lincoln Filene Professor of Citizenship & Public Affairs and Director of the Center for Information and Research on Civic Learning and Engagement (CIRCLE), Tufts University's Jonathan Tisch College of Citizenship and Public Service

Meira Levinson, D.Phil., Associate Professor of Education, Harvard University

Anand Marri, Ph.D., Associate Professor of Social Studies Education, Teachers College, Columbia University

Chauncey Monte-Sano, Ph.D., Associate Professor of Educational Studies, University of Michigan

Robert Morrill, Ph.D., Professor Emeritus of Geography, Virginia Polytechnic Institute and State University

Karen Thomas-Brown, Ph.D., Associate Professor of Social Studies Education and Multiculturalism, University of Michigan-Dearborn

Cynthia Tyson, Ph.D., Professor of Social Studies Education, The Ohio State University

Bruce VanSledright, Ph.D., Professor of History and Social Studies Education, University of North Carolina at Charlotte

Merry Wiesner-Hanks, Ph.D., Distinguished Professor and Chair of the Department of History, University of Wisconsin-Milwaukee

concepts, and guides the choice of curricular content necessary for a rigorous social studies program. While curricular content is critically important to the disciplines within social studies, the C3 Framework illustrates the disciplinary ideas, such as political structures, economic decision-making, spatial patterns, and chronological sequencing that lead to deep and enduring understanding.

- *Social studies shares in the responsibility for literacy education.*

As a core area in the K–12 curriculum, social studies shares in the responsibility for literacy education, including the development of reading, writing, speaking and listening, and language skills. Because many of the states involved in the C3 Framework project had recently adopted the Common Core State Standards for English Language Arts and Literacy in History/Social Studies, it was imperative for the Framework to seek to define disciplinary literacy for social studies.

With consensus on this set of core ideas, SSACI and the Task Force recruited a team of writers who represented the individual disciplines as well as social studies education (see Sidebar B). The writers built the C3 Framework around four dimensions that weave together several important threads: inquiry, disciplinary integrity, common core literacy, and civic engagement. In the articles that follow in this special issue, our writers and participants illustrate these foundations in greater detail focusing on aspects of the document including the Inquiry Arc, Taking Informed Action, and Literacy in the C3 Framework.

The Writing Process for the C3 Framework

As important as what the document says is how it was constructed. Collaboration and community were central tenets of the work. There was a conscious effort to bring stakeholders who had never all talked together into the same room for an extended period of time. Our job was to manage the discourse within and across the individual stakeholder groups, making sure that a range of voices were heard and that the writing process moved forward.

The team of writers, hired in the summer of 2011, initially met in disciplinary teams to map out the key practices and processes of the individual disciplines. The writing team wanted the four disciplines to be represented as distinctive but complementary, with equal weight given to each. The products of these conversations, which are featured in Dimension 2 of the C3 Framework, spurred additional deliberations around the broader social studies practices that bind these unique disciplines together. Dimensions 1, 3, and 4 were built to frame the disciplinary processes and concepts, to provide an interdisciplinary structure to social studies inquiry, and to help define and elaborate approaches to disciplinary literacy in the social studies.

As the writing team worked, they received editorial guidance from a team of teachers and state education personnel (Sidebar C). These individuals on the Editorial Committee helped translate the occasionally academic prose of the writing team into language more useful for the broader social studies community. As the document moved through the editorial team, it was vetted by individuals representing 23 SSACI member states and affiliates, the directors of the 15 Task Force professional organizations, and a group of 42 elementary and secondary teachers—the Teacher Collaborative Council—chosen by the state education department personnel. Feedback loops across these groups occurred every few months and continued for approximately a year and a half. After each round of review, the writers would look for consensus in the comments as well as individual insights that would improve each draft.

Once the C3 Framework took a more final form, additional voices representing K-12 educators, university faculty, state education personnel, professional organization representatives, educational publishers, and cultural organizations were asked to weigh in during a series of targeted reviews in the spring of 2013. By May 2013, more than 3,000 individuals had reviewed the C3 Framework draft, and the great majority of the numerous comments sent to the Writing Team found the document compelling. One of our favorite comments during the reviews said, "I hope it will be a document that will bring at least 70% positive comments." We were happy to report back this past summer that the document received over 90% positive feedback in the last round of review. Energized by overwhelming response to the document, the writers spent the summer finalizing the document, paying close attention to suggestions that bubbled up in the spring.

One of the most prominent suggestions made during the reviews of the draft was to move beyond the original focus of the project on the four federally defined "core" areas of social studies by including more social and behavioral sciences in the final publication. The American Psychological Association, the American Sociological Association, and the American Anthropological Association responded favorably to an invitation to contribute and worked steadily in the late spring and summer months of 2013 to produce companion documents, which are Appendices B, C, and D, respectively, of the C3 Framework.

Despite great odds and retaining a collaborative model of development, the C3 Framework was published online by National Council for the Social Studies on behalf of the Task Force on Constitution Day, September 17, 2013.

The Grand Challenge of the C3 Framework

As daunting as it seems, the publication of the C3 Framework was really just the beginning. From its inception, the participants in the C3 project knew that to usher in an ambitious new era in social studies education, more than just standards were required. State-wide and classroom-based assessments need to evolve to overcome current shortcomings; instructional materials and resources need to be either aligned or developed to assist teachers in promoting inquiry and facilitating students in taking action; new teacher standards need to recognize the C3 approach to teaching and learning; and, in order to move the needle, funding for professional development around the C3 Framework needs to be plentiful. Additionally, we need to continue to widen the C3 tent to include other partners and stakeholders who can provide further insight into cross-subject matter connections and special student populations.

The success of the C3 Framework will lie in its implementation. The Task Force and writing team do not seek adoption (like the Common Core Standards initiative). Successful implementation requires educators to use all their networks, such as state social studies specialists, social studies supervisors, national and state council conferences, meetings sponsored by other Task Force members, workshops, and webinars.

Our guess is that those who take up the C3 banner will face the challenge to reform social studies with the same gusto and energy as those who worked to develop the C3 Framework. The challenges awaiting social studies educators are considerable, but the stakes are high. So, what can you do right now to help implement the C3 Framework?

- Support your students as they begin to ask questions and conduct academic inquiries.
- Examine your own strengths and weaknesses around facilitating student inquiry. And then, experiment instructionally with aspects of the inquiry arc!
- Push for more rigorous and authentic assessment that measure inquiry and not just names, dates, and places—even if it's in your own classroom!
- Find ways to incorporate and support the Common Core Standards for literacy in social studies using the C3 as a companion document.
- Be a leader in your school and/or your Professional Learning Community (PLC) around the C3.
- Be creative and aggressive in locating funding for new projects in social studies.
- Meet with an administrator about using the C3 to measure good social studies instruction.
- Advocate for the C3 Framework in your state, given your unique needs.

In the end, we encourage you to find what our colleague Walter Parker calls "wiggle room," and further the C3 project within your current context.[7] Will it seem insurmountable at times? Yes, but we are social studies—we invite grand challenges!

Notes

1. Tracy C. Rock, et al., "One State Closer to a National Crisis: A Report on Elementary Social Studies Education in North Carolina Schools," *Theory and Research in Social Education* 34, no. 4 (2006): 455-483; Ronald W. Evans, *The Social Studies Wars: What Should We Teach the Children?* (New York, N.Y.: Teachers College Press, 2004); S.G. Grant, "Locating Authority Over Content and Pedagogy: Cross-Current Influences on Teachers' Thinking and Practice," *Theory and Research in Social Education* 24, no. 3 (1996): 237- 272; James C. McKinley Jr, "Texas Conservatives Win Curriculum Change," *The New York Times* (March 12, 2010), www.nytimes.com/2010/03/13/education/13texas.html; E. Wayne Ross, *Social Studies Curriculum: Purposes, Problems, and Possibilities* (Albany, N.Y.: State University of New York Press, 2006).
2. The Common Core State Standards Initiative website (https://corestandards.org/) has a map that shows how the Common Core State Standards have been adopted in the U.S. and its territories.
3. Stephen Sawchuck, "More Than Two-Thirds of States Adopt Common Core Standards," *Education Week* (August 6, 2010), www.edweek.org/ew/articles/2010/08/06/37standards.h29.html?qs.
4. National Governors Association Center for Best Practices (NGA) and Council of Chief State School Officers (CCSSO), *Common Core State Standards for English Language Arts and Literacy in History/ Social Studies, Science, and Technical Subjects* (Washington, D.C.: NGA and CCSSO, 2010).
5. Catherine Gewertz, "Specialists Weigh Common Social Studies Standards," *Education Week* (May 18, 2011), www.edweek.org/teaching-learning/specialists-weigh-common-social-studies-standards/2011/05
6. Catherine Gewertz, "Chiefs Group Terminates Role in Social Studies Framework," *Curriculum Matters* (blog), June 7, 2013, http://blogs.edweek.org/edweek/curriculum/2013/06/chiefs_group_terminates_role_i.html.
7. Walter C. Parker, "Constructing Public Schooling Today: Derision, Multiculturalism, Nationalism," *Educational Theory* 61, no. 4 (2011): 413-432.

Social Education 77, no. 4 (2013): 222–224.

The Importance of the C3 Framework

The C3 Framework for Social Studies State Standards will soon be released under the title *The College, Career, and Civic Life (C3) Framework for Social Studies State Standards: State Guidance for Enhancing the Rigor of K–12 Civics, Economics, Geography, and History*. The C3 Project Director and Lead Writer was NCSS member Kathy Swan, who is associate professor of social studies education at the University of Kentucky. In an e-mail interview, Kathy responded to the following questions about the C3 Framework from Social Education.

There are already so many standards out there: what is different about these?

There are definitely a lot of standards documents floating around! From disciplinary standards to 50 different state social studies standards documents to the NCSS curriculum standards, and the Common Core Standards—it's a veritable stew of standards out there!

The C3 Framework pulls from the best of what has been done—especially in the disciplines—and presents a vision of social studies for the 21st century classroom.

The C3 Framework features the idea of disciplinary integrity—the idea that the tools, concepts, and habits of mind within civics, economics, geography, and history play a critical role in developing young people's understanding of the world around them, and help to make them college, career, and civic ready. Dimension 2 of the Framework lays out these tools of disciplinary literacy alongside one another.

The C3 Framework also creates a relationship within and among the disciplines by anchoring social studies in the process of inquiry. Dimensions 1, 3, and 4 envelop the disciplines in an active exploration of questions that both intrigue students and have intellectual merit. Taken together, the four Dimensions act as the Inquiry Arc, which provides the backbone to the Framework and set an intellectual quest for K–12 social studies students.

The other important feature, and some would say the most important feature, is the emphasis on civic action as a fund mental outcome of a meaningful social studies experience. In Dimension 4, the C3 Framework closes the Inquiry Arc with a section of indicators under the heading "Taking Informed Action." We see this as the most ambitious part of the C3 Framework, and our greatest aspiration for students is that their social studies classrooms provide opportunities to learn actively about citizenship.

What do you consider the most important single contribution of C3?

I think the greatest contribution of the C3 Framework is the addition of civic readiness to the national conversation around student preparedness for college and career. Instead of narrowing the purposes of K–12 education, the authors and contributors to the C3 Framework agreed that social studies reminds educators of this essential mission.

The C3 Framework prepares students for civic life in important ways. First, it encourages the civic act of inquiry by asking students to develop evidence-based arguments and to share their findings in a variety of modalities—including writing, oral and visual means—to diverse audiences. Threaded throughout the Framework is the notion that students will be working in collaborative environments, either individually with their teachers or with others, to develop questions, to adopt disciplinary perspectives, make claims, and formulate conclusions. And lastly, the C3 Framework makes taking informed action an essential skill that should be practiced by all social studies students in a vibrant democracy.

In what way could the implementation of this Framework change social studies education in this country?

We certainly approached the C3 Framework as an important resource to impact state social studies standards. Many states are already utilizing the document as either a companion to existing standards, as a foundation for new standards, or as a mandate to initiate a conversation about the importance of social studies in their state.

It is important to note that the writers, participants, and reviewers of the C3 Framework see this document as more than a standards document. Certainly, standards are an important step in influencing social studies policy. But the social studies educators who have worked on the C3 Framework see it as a mission statement for a robust social studies experience. In fact, there are already efforts underway to use the C3 as a foundation for teacher development initiatives and as a template for better instructional materials. We think the ideas and key tenets of the document are timeless and should be the foundation for all aspects of building strong social studies teachers and students.

The next conversations about C3 will need to be around assessments. Without thoughtful, realistic, and ambitious sets of assessments, the C3 efforts might be in vain. As a community, we need to roll up our sleeves and have the difficult but necessary conversations about building a better assessment system in social studies and this includes both classroom based and statewide assessments. By outlining the key interdisciplinary and disciplinary skills and concepts, the C3 Framework should be a starting place for talking about what exactly we want these assessments to measure and tell us about student's understanding.

Ultimately, we want the C3 Framework to reverberate within the social studies community and to challenge us to work together to usher in a new era of social studies reform. But this effort is grass roots—meaning it will be up to our teachers, curriculum specialists, professional organizations, teacher educators, and policymakers to make it happen. In essence, we have to practice civic action and model that for our students.

How and why was the C3 initiative taken?

The C3 Framework began three years ago as the Common Core standards were released. There was a palpable concern among state departments of education and professional organizations that social studies would be further marginalized if we didn't act as a community to elevate the role of social studies in K–12 curriculum.

Initially, the Council of Chief State School Officers (CCSSO) hosted a series of meetings between 23 states and 15 professional organizations. These groups worked together to create a structure for developing the C3 Framework. A team of writers with disciplinary and interdisciplinary expertise was hired in 2011, and they worked over an 18-month period to draft the C3 Framework. The writing process involved feedback loops with the states, professional organizations, and a collaborative of 50 teachers.

Once the C3 Framework took a more final form, additional voices representing K–12 educators, university faculty, state education personnel, professional organization representatives, educational publishers, and cultural organizations were asked to weigh in during a series of targeted reviews in the spring of 2013. By May 2013, over 3,000 individuals had reviewed the C3 Framework draft and found the document compelling.

The writers spent this past summer working to finalize the document and to incorporate suggestions made during the spring review. One of those suggestions was the need to include the social and behavioral sciences in the final draft. The national anthropology, psychology and sociology associations had been engaged in the early spring of 2013 and worked steadily over the late spring and summer months to produce companion documents, now featured in the appendices of the C3 Framework.

We are delighted that the C3 Framework will soon be published by the National Council for the Social Studies.

What is the connection between the C3 Framework and the Common Core standards?

Because most of the states involved in the C3 Framework project had recently adopted the Common Core Standards for English Language Arts and Literacy in History/Social Studies, it was imperative the Framework should seek to define disciplinary literacy for social studies. The C3 Framework builds on the foundation provided by the Common Core by elevating the purpose of literacy to be in the service of academic inquiry and civic action. We like to say "literacy for a social studies purpose," as social studies content provides the context and inspiration for wanting to read, write, and communicate with others. The C3 Framework also expands the disciplinary context of social studies by placing civics, economics, geography and history on an equal footing and by recognizing that social studies includes the social and behavioral sciences.

In the document, we represent these ideas and connections through a series of narratives and tables that explicitly demonstrate the relationship between the C3 indicators and the Common Core anchor standards for English Language Arts and Literacy in History/Social Studies. We intentionally use language and concepts from the Common Core to further make these connections. For example, the terms argument and explanation; claim and counterclaim; information and evidence; and point of view and opinion appear regularly in the Common Core and throughout the Dimensions of the C3 Framework.

The Framework seizes the opportunity that the Common Core has provided to define literacy in the context of social studies. Many see this as particularly important for elementary teachers who have struggled to make room for social studies instruction. The C3 is a road map for all teachers, but especially elementary teachers, for promoting meaningful literacy skill development within a social studies framework of inquiry.

What kinds of assessments are needed to support the C3 Framework?

Because of its emphasis on skills and concepts, the C3 Framework clearly lends itself to performance-based assessments that best measure students' understandings of disciplinary perspective taking, inquiry, and civic understanding and action.

But this does not mean that we have to abandon all other types of assessments. While the C3 avoids historically divisive prescriptions of curricular content— names, dates, places, historical eras— the document recognizes that a robust and complete social studies education includes an understanding of essential content knowledge. While performance-based assessment can measure content knowledge, there are a range of assessments that do so as well.

What we do need to do as a community is ask the tough question, "How do we know what students know and can do?" If we can begin answering this question, we might be able to build a more balanced assessment approach that is valid, varied, feasible, and meaningful. The C3 Framework creates the impetus for these important conversations about our purpose and approach to social studies assessment.

Social Education 78, no. 4 (2014): 172–174, 178

The C3 Framework: One Year Later

On September 17, 2013 (Constitution Day), the C3 Framework was released under the title *The College, Career and Civic Life (C3) Framework for Social Studies State Standards: Guidance for Enhancing the Rigor of K-12 Civics, Economics, Geography, and History.* The C3 Project Director and lead writer was NCSS member Kathy Swan, who is associate professor of social studies education at the University of Kentucky. Kathy evaluated the progress of the C3 Framework in its first year in a recent e-mail interview with *Social Education.*

One year later, what are the prospects of the C3 Framework being adopted nationwide?

Adoption has always been a tricky word with the C3 Framework. Unlike the Common Core and the Next Generation Science Standards, the C3 document was never intended to be adopted, but instead integrated into existing standards documents or used as a foundation for new standards. I think we should speak the language of local "implementation," not "adoption."

The C3 Framework honors local contexts and allows states to determine the appropriate content to be taught at each grade level. It's not your grandmother's Common Core! As long as there is a commitment to the key tenets of the document, including inquiry, disciplinary literacy, student agency, and civic engagement, I think standards and implementation could vary from state to state.

I have always seen the C3 movement as one that is grassroots and organic. I often say it's like the slow food movement and should be driven by local needs. It should not be a top-down, one-size-fits-all effort. It is important that we emphasize the notion of student agency throughout the document— agency around the questions that are asked, agency around the ways in which evidence-based arguments are communicated, and agency around action.

The ethos of the document, and quite frankly of social studies in general, is around individuals or collections of individuals making a difference. To me, the implementation of C3 should honor these foundations.

We have seen incredible progress on the C3 Framework in different states. A number of states (e.g., New York) have officially hard-wired the C3 into current standards documents through the Inquiry Arc and in ways that should inform how content standards are created and taught. Other states (e.g., Connecticut, Kentucky) have either begun or are about to begin the process of writing new standards and are using the C3 Framework in doing so.

What have been the most positive developments of the last year for the C3 Framework?

Well, I think there are many. In addition to the way in which the C3 Framework is making its way into official state policy documents, we see many other impressive developments that use C3 as a framework rather than a set of standards. For example, districts like Rockwood in St. Louis, Missouri, Clark County in Nevada, the District of

Columbia, and others are working to develop curriculum that embraces the Inquiry Arc of the C3 Framework. We see this kind of work percolating throughout the country through C3 professional development that focuses on the use of inquiry and innovative assessments.

Curricular organizations are also joining in. John Lee and I collaborated with 15 curricular partners this year to edit the upcoming NCSS Bulletin, *Teaching the C3 Framework: A Guide to Inquiry Based Instruction.* We worked individually with these organizations to create lessons that incorporated the entirety of the Inquiry Arc in one to five days worth of instruction. We are pleased that the book will be a resource for teachers, but equally pleased that these organizations have embraced C3 as a key resource for their educational outreach.

For example, this fall, the Smithsonian National American History Museum (NAMH) is offering a Massive Online Open Course (MOOC) for secondary social studies teachers that features C3 and object-based instruction at the museum. This work has mushroomed into other requests by our curriculum partners (e.g., Federal Reserve, Library of Congress, Ford's Theater, National Museum of the American Indian) who are developing new educational materials that feature the Framework.

We also see individual teachers taking informed action. Check out C3 Teachers (c3teachers.org) and hear from master teachers as they wrestle with the big ideas and instructional implications of the C3 Framework. In collaboration with NCSS, this online community of approximately 500 teachers from around the country are sharing their instructional experiences as they tinker with the dimensions of the Inquiry Arc. I encourage the readers of *Social Education* to sign up—it's both free and inspiring—and puts the locus of educational reform where it should be, in the hands of teachers.

Lastly, but definitely not least, the state of New York has recently stepped into the C3 limelight with a commitment to building a toolkit of instructional resources that would fuse the C3 Inquiry Arc with the newly published New York Social Studies Framework. The most exciting part of this project is that this toolkit will be published in July 2015 with a creative commons license and thus will be available for other states to use or modify according to their own state standards. So, stay tuned!

What do you think are the biggest problems facing the implementation of C3?

One of the biggest challenges that we face in C3 implementation is the perennial debate over content and skills. In the C3 Framework, we left the selection of curricular content up to states but stated very clearly that this content is essential for animating the Inquiry Arc. Without content, what would we inquire about?

The greatest challenge that states are currently facing, then, is to what degree should states articulate curricular content and how should they approach curricular content in standards? For example, at what point does standards writing become curriculum writing with a fully articulated scope and sequence? What responsibility should districts and teachers hold in fleshing out this content?

In states where there is local control of content, we see teachers struggling with issues that are more pedagogical in nature. For example, how much content should be "pre-loaded" before approaching an inquiry? Or said differently, does content become fully developed within the inquiry or should there be some direct teaching before the inquiry begins? These are good questions and ones that teachers struggled with long before C3. I would argue that the Dimensions have an intentional sequence, but should not be approached too rigidly.

What is an obstacle for teachers implementing the C3?

I think many educators are scared to get it wrong. I get weekly emails and calls asking for advice on how to use the C3 Framework in ways that perhaps went unstated in the document. I am always encouraged by these conversations, as our community wants to get inquiry right. I am often saying that, while I really love the C3, it was intended to guide what students should know and be able to do. As a result, although there are instructional implications in the C3, very little is said about how teachers might support students within an inquiry.

So, for example, should teachers create compelling questions? Absolutely! It would be too challenging to develop a curricular scope and sequence without some direction and modeling. The key is to offer students an opportunity to practice their own questioning skills. Another issue that has come up is whether it is all right to abridge the Inquiry Arc? Again, absolutely! Of course, I think students should practice the process of inquiry from questioning to communicating conclusions as often as possible, but it may be that a unit allows for experiences with only Dimension 2 and 3.

In the end, the Inquiry Arc is a model whose tires can be kicked a bit by teachers. I think it's an excellent model, but I don't think teachers should fear innovating around it, or get paralyzed if they think they are breaking a C3 rule or covenant. We should be a community that is open to interpretation, context, and innovation and I encourage teachers and district leaders to be flexible in interpreting the C3.

My C3 co-authors, S.G. Grant and John Lee, and I wrote a short document called the "C3 Instructional Shifts" as a way for teachers to begin thinking about how they might best support students within a C3 inquiry (www.c3teachers.org/c3shifts/).

What kind of teacher-student relationship is implied by C3?

One of the C3 writers, S.G. Grant, wrote about this in *Social Education* last year soon after the C3 Framework was published:

> Trust matters. The Inquiry Arc reflects a level of trust between teachers and students that is not part of the traditional pattern of schooling. Good teachers know that students will blunder sometimes as they embrace the greater responsibilities an inquiry approach demands, but they also know that students will not become the kind of life-long learners that we desire if they are not trusted to take an active role in their education.*

I can't improve on that explanation— trust matters and it's at the very heart of the C3 teacher-student relationship.

How do you think C3 can change social studies classrooms?

I want to start by saying that we did not invent inquiry or the other important components within the C3 document. What we did do is package them in a way that we hope structures and enriches students' social studies experience. C3 offers a model for practicing the elements of inquiry alongside civic participation. In this way, I think it is a road map for doing all the things we believe are fundamental tenets of social studies.

Ultimately, the C3 Framework is not going to change anything unless teachers want to change classroom pedagogies that are not inquiry-based. Teachers need to be comfortable with any such change. I like to think of teachers moving along a professional journey and constantly improving. We should encourage teachers to be reflective about their own practice and to begin experimenting with the C3 where they see areas for growth. For example, while I helped write the C3 Framework, I do not think I ever had students create a compelling question. I wrote them; I asked students to answer them. But, I never created enough instructional space for students' own questions to drive their inquiries. Doing so is a shift for me and I have begun the uncomfortable exercise of modifying my own instructional practice. Teachers get beaten up from all sides these days, and I would hate to think of the C3 Framework being used as a punishing ideal.

If a state developed new standards, or accomplished an overhaul of existing standards just before the C3 Framework was published, and it does not want to go through the process again, what can supervisors and teachers in that state do to advance C3?

There are a number of states that are in this very situation: North Carolina, Kansas, Oklahoma, Nebraska, and others. What I have seen many states do when state standards cannot be revised is look to professional learning networks to examine the ways in which the Inquiry Arc could help animate their current standards. Additionally, some states are looking at curriculum models that infuse the C3 Dimensions into the heart of new units or lessons. An additional area is teacher evaluation. Many states are looking at alternative ways to evaluate teachers using new metrics and student growth models. I have seen social studies departments and districts use the C3 indicators as targets for measuring student growth over time.

In the end, the C3 movement is about flexible implementation that meets the needs of states and their capacity for reform. For supervisors and teachers, I would look to the ways in which the C3 Framework could inform professional learning communities, curriculum development, teacher education, and, of course, assessment. There is no prescription for this—only encouragement to follow their instincts and look to concrete ways in which they could start a dialogue. A first step would be mirroring the C3 project and pulling together a local community that could begin brainstorming approaches. The C3 effort benefitted greatly from the wide range of expertise and perspectives. For example, we pulled together academics, teachers, state department social studies consultants, professional organization leaders, and others for a national conversation around college, career, and civic readiness. I would recommend creating a similar community that would focus on C3 implementation at the state or local level.

Does implementation of the C3 Framework require an overhaul of existing social studies assessments?

The short answer is yes. Current assessments, particularly high-stakes assessments, lack the architecture to measure the kinds of skills and conceptual knowledge that the C3 Framework states are vital for college and career readiness.

Some individuals and organizations are already generating new thinking about assessment. For example, Stanford's *Beyond the Bubble* project is beginning to make inroads using classroom-based performance assessments called History Assessments of Thinking or HATs. Other scholars are also working in the assessment space. For example, Bruce VanSledright just published a book last year, titled *Assessing Historical Thinking and Understanding: Innovative Designs for New Standards*. And the College Board is also working to redesign many of its content exams to align them to new standards and ways of thinking about the disciplines.

Social studies educators should also follow the efforts of two assessment consortia, in which groups of states are working together to develop assessments—the Partnership for Assessment of Readiness for College and Careers (PARCC), and Smarter Balanced—and the degree to which they will create literacy performance assessments that are valid and scaled. Their success or failure to do so will greatly inform how states proceed with social studies. If the aims of C3 are to be realized, states will need to make room for more authentic assessments. Some states are already moving in this direction. For example, Virginia just recently announced that in an effort to reduce testing load on students at the end of year, it would cut the number of tests in half by removing social studies and science tests. The glass half full on this proposal is that there may be an opportunity to move social studies in the direction of the C3 Inquiry Arc and have students demonstrate competency by working proficiently through inquiry and, if we are really lucky, practicing informed action.

The C3 Framework emphasizes preparation for civic life. It is easy to pay lip service to this ideal. What more should schools be doing to put it into practice, and what can individual teachers in schools do to advance this objective?

There is a danger of losing the civic purposes that ground our academic inquiries. One of the victories of the C3 Framework has been the inclusion of Dimension 4—preparing students for collaborative conversations and for taking informed action. I think we need to demystify taking informed action and create a continuum of experiences that either blur the lines between communicating conclusions and action or make action much more doable than many teachers currently see. In the instructional shifts document I mentioned, we talk about teachers providing tangible spaces for action. My hope is that as curriculum is developed, we do not lose this incredible opportunity to define action within and as a result of academic inquiry.

There are many curricular organizations that are leading the way in defining and illustrating action within the social studies. For example, Mikva Challenge has been working with Chicago youth to mobilize them as meaningful actors in the political process. Other organizations like National History Day and C-Span have created public spaces for students to communicate their conclusions from academic inquiries in ways that are in keeping with Dimension 4 of the C3. Still other efforts, like the Speak Truth to Power video competition sponsored by the Robert F. Kennedy Center for Justice and Human Rights, provide a focus for middle and high students to become engaged in human rights issues through video production.

In an article in last year's November/December issue of this journal, Meira Levinson and Peter Levine presented many ways of taking informed action to engage students in civic life.** It would be fantastic to read about how teachers are interpreting their ideas and preparing their students to take informed civic action.

---

*   S.G. Grant, "From Inquiry Arc to Instructional Practice: The Potential of the C3 Framework," *Social Education* 77, no. 6, (November/December 2013): 351.

**   Meira Levinson and Peter Levine, "Taking Informed Action to Engage Students in Civic Life," *Social Education* 77, no. 6, (November/December 2013): 339–341.

The NCSS book *Social Studies for the Next Generation* includes the published hard copy of the C3 Framework plus important explanatory chapters that introduce the C3 Framework and the Inquiry Arc, explain the links between C3 and the Common Core Standards and national social studies standards, and discuss approaches to assessments. It can be ordered at www.socialstudies.org/standards/c3.

Social Education **86**, no. 4 (2021): 239–246.

The State of Social Studies Standards: What Is the Impact of the C3 Framework?

Ryan New, Kathy Swan, John Lee, and S.G. Grant

On Constitution Day 2013, the National Council for the Social Studies (NCSS) published the *College, Career and Civic Life (C3) Framework for Social Studies State Standards*. The document was written by a team of academics with specialties in social studies education and its disciplines in consultation with state education agencies, professional organizations, and teachers from across the country.[1] This collaboration produced a watershed moment for social studies. Publication of the C3 Framework demonstrated that social studies educators could get along and work ambitiously toward a common goal and that they could produce a framework reconciling the "turf wars" that have hampered previous social studies standards and reform efforts.[2]

Up until the publication of the C3 Framework, most social studies state standards provided an inventory of content and/or broad concepts for students to either memorize or analyze.[3] These standards made few people happy.[4] Although some standards documents may have received an "A" or "B" from the Fordham Institute for their attention to historical detail, others were critiqued for their lack of enduring ideas that cut across and bind together the study of social studies.[5] Simultaneously, the broad adoption of the Common Core Standards for English Language Arts struck fear in the hearts of social studies educators because it stripped away all content and concepts and focused solely on the disciplinary processes that enable historical study.[6]

And yet, the collaborators on the C3 Framework did not blink. They took on the literacy aims of the Common Core as well as the perennial content-versus-skills tension in our field and integrated them into the Inquiry Arc. The Inquiry Arc frames social studies with four distinct, but interrelated dimensions: (1) developing questions and planning inquiries; (2) applying disciplinary concepts and tools; (3) evaluating sources and using evidence; and (4) communicating conclusions and taking informed action. Together, these dimensions link content, concepts, and skills and marshal them toward the core purposes of social studies: college, career, and most importantly, *civic life*. Although no standards effort will satisfy everyone, the C3 Framework effort showed promise.

It has been eight years since the publication of the C3 Framework. The intent of the document was to provide states with "voluntary guidance for upgrading existing social studies standards."[7] We thought it was time to see how the C3 is being used by states and what its impact has been on state standards. Unlike the Common Core, the C3 Framework clearly stipulated that it was a framework and not a set of standards to be adopted whole cloth. The authors wrote on the first pages:

> This Framework does not include all that can or should be included in a set of robust social studies standards, and intentionally preserves the critical choices around the selection of curricular content taught at each grade level as a decision best made by each state.... The concepts expressed in the C3 Framework illustrate the disciplinary ideas, such as political structures, economic decision making, spatial

patterns, and chronological sequencing, that help organize the curriculum and content states select.[8]

In other words, state education agencies would need to take the broad disciplinary concepts and tools laid out in Dimension 2 (e.g., Constitution, economic scarcity, geographical modeling, and chronological sequence) and add specificity to that content (e.g., how a bill becomes a law or the difference between a map and a globe).

In this article, we report on a content analysis of the 50 social studies state standards documents, and the social studies standards of the District of Columbia, by asking our own compelling question: What has been the impact of the C3 Framework on state social studies standards? As part of our analysis, we examine standards that use the C3 Framework and identify the ways in which the authors approached the use of the Inquiry Arc, its dimensions, and the indicators within. Because of the decentralized nature of departments of education and the soft language of "implementation" in the C3 Framework itself, we expected to see a wide variation in approaches when states sought to update their social studies standards, particularly among states that chose to use the C3 Framework but then adapted it for their local context.

Method

In this work, we used content analysis methods to examine the extent to which states and the District of Columbia have incorporated the C3 Framework into their standards. Content analysis is a research method by which we can engage in a "systematic, objective, quantitative analysis of message characteristics" that are present in a defined body of content.[9] We defined the content being analyzed as 51 state standards documents. State standards reflect unique priorities, political contexts, and legal requirements within each state. These factors have resulted in a patchwork of documents that vary widely in length, tone, specificity, and formatting. Some states include appendixes and ancillary materials within the standards document, while others publish such materials separately. State-wide initiatives may also have been considered in constructing new social studies standards. For example, some states (e.g., Nevada, Iowa) must account for financial literacy within the social studies and so their documents add financial literacy to the standards. Other states must give attention to state history (e.g., Kentucky, Illinois) and have thus included this content in their standards. Additionally, each state has its own approach to developing writing teams and writing standards. Given the variety of processes that states use and the unique contexts that shape their work, we focused on the standards themselves and did not analyze ancillary materials, whether published as appendixes or separate documents.

We began our content analysis by examining social studies standards documents for all 50 states and the District of Columbia as of June 1, 2021. Our process of analysis involved an initial sorting of the standards into three broad categories reflecting: (1) no evidence of a connection to the C3 Framework; (2) some connection; or (3) considerable connection. We then fine-tuned these categories through recursive analysis, and moved from the initial three-category sorting to a more nuanced classification system in which we examined the standards documents for evidence of alignment with the C3 Inquiry Arc and the four Dimensions of the C3 Framework. We also took into account new or novel approaches to representing the ideas within the C3 Framework in the state standards documents. Our analysis resulted in the development of four final analytic categories, which we have termed "levels" as a way of reflecting the extent to which each state has incorporated ideas from the C3 Framework within its standards. We also created nine categories nested within the four levels to further clarify differences between state approaches to using the C3 Framework:

- Level N/A: States that have not undergone (n=5) or are currently undergoing (n=6) comprehensive social studies standards revision
- Level 1: States that did not cite (n=8) the C3 Framework as part of their social studies standards document
- Level 2: States that cited (n=2), endorsed (n=2), or excerpted (n=12) the C3 Framework in their social studies standards document
- Level 3: States that framed (n=4), modeled (n=11), or adopted (n=1) the C3 Framework in their social studies standards document.

In addition to classifying all 51 standards documents in one of the nine categories and four levels, we selected one or two states whose standards document exemplify each category and described how the document reflects the characteristics of that category. States in Levels N/A and 1 were relatively simple to classify. Levels 2 and 3 required more careful consideration. The categories that were most challenging to code were the subcategories within Level 3. In this analysis, we stayed focused on several major factors: (1) the treatment of the four dimensions of the Inquiry Arc (e.g., where it appears in the document, whether it stayed intact, and renaming of the dimensions); (2) the inclusion of specific indicators and the extent to which they were differentiated for grade level; and, (3) any innovations to the presentation of the standards document (e.g., modifications in language, addition of skills). In the next section, we present Table 1, which accounts for all 50 states and the District of Columbia's social studies standards documents, explains each category, and specifies how each state document was categorized.

Findings

In this section, we report on the findings of our content analysis of state social studies standards featuring four levels, each with one or more categories to delineate the various ways in which states did and did not use the C3 Framework to inform state social studies standards (Table 1 and Figure 1). The distribution of states across the four levels is fairly consistent, but a majority of states fell into Levels 2 and 3. In all, 32 of 51 standards documents include, at a minimum, a reference to the C3 Framework. These 32 states represent 61% of all children enrolled in public schools in the United States (see Table 2).[10] Twenty-seven of those 32 states actually included ideas from the C3 Framework, incorporated the structure of the C3 Framework, or modeled or replicated aspects of the C3 Framework. One state, Vermont, went so far as to adopt the C3 Framework writ large.

Level N/A: States that have not undergone (n=5) or are currently undergoing (n=6) comprehensive social studies standards revision

Five states (Alabama, Florida, Louisiana, New Mexico, and Pennsylvania) **have not undergone** a comprehensive social studies standards revision process since the publication of the C3 Framework and thus have not had an opportunity to consider how the document might influence their social studies standards.

Five states (Minnesota, Montana, New Hampshire, Rhode Island, and Virginia) and the District of Columbia are **currently undergoing** social studies standards revision and have not officially adopted new standards at the time of data collection on June 1, 2021. We chose not to place these states into categories despite early drafts in several states that clearly show the influence of the C3 Framework. For example, in the first draft of Minnesota's new social studies standards, the writers acknowledge that the C3 Framework "guided the writing of standards and benchmarks

... and will be based upon the C3 Framework's Dimensions."[11] However, shifts and changes often occur as standards move through committees, public comment periods, and internal reviews with stakeholders so we coded these states according to their current standards and labeled them as N/A.

Level 1: States that did not cite (n=8) the C3 Framework as part of their social studies standards document

Eight states (Alaska, Delaware, Georgia, Idaho, Indiana, Ohio, Texas, and Wyoming) **do not cite** the C3 Framework in

Table 1: Use of the *C3 Framework* by State as of June 1, 2021

Level (# of states in level)	Category Description	Number of States	States in Each Category*
N/A (n=11)	States that **have not undergone** comprehensive social studies standards revision since the publication of the C3 Framework.	5	New Mexico (2009), Pennsylvania (2009), Alabama (2010), Louisiana (2011), Florida (adopted in 2014, but prepared earlier)
	States that are **currently undergoing** social studies standards revision and have not formally adopted new standards as of June 1, 2021.	6*	New Hampshire (2006), *Washington DC (2006), Rhode Island (2008, 2012), Virginia (2015), Minnesota (Draft 2021), Montana (Draft 2021)
Level 1 (n=8)	States that **do not cite** the C3 Framework in social studies standards or in any accompanying documents, including works cited/references.	8	Alaska (2016), Georgia (2016), Idaho (2016), Delaware (2018), Ohio (2018), Texas (2018), Wyoming (2018), Indiana (2020)
Level 2 (n=16)	States that **cited** the C3 Framework as one of the documents consulted in a standards writing and adoption process.	2	Mississippi (2018), Maine (2019)
	States that **endorsed** the use of the C3 Framework by presenting it as a complementary resource for implementing their social studies standards.	2	California (2016), New York (2016)
	States that **excerpted** one or more ideas (e.g., questions, taking informed action) from the C3 Framework.	12	South Dakota (2015), Missouri (2016), Utah (2016), Tennessee (2017), Oregon (2018), Nebraska (2019), North Dakota (2019), Oklahoma (2019), Washington (2019), Colorado (2020), Kansas (2020), South Carolina (2020)
Level 3 (n=16)	States that **framed** their social studies document with a version of the C3 Framework's Inquiry Arc.	4	West Virginia (2016), Massachusetts (2018), Maryland (2020), New Jersey (2020),
	States that **modeled** their social studies standards on the C3 Framework by differentiating and integrating the Inquiry Arc at grade-band/level.	11	Arkansas (2014), Connecticut (2015), Illinois (2016), Iowa (2017), Hawaii (2018), Nevada (2018), Wisconsin (2018), Arizona (2019), Kentucky (2019), Michigan (2019), North Carolina (2021)
	States that **adopted** the C3 Framework as their social studies standards.	1	Vermont (2017)

* States are listed by year of the most recent standards adoption, then listed alphabetically.

recently adopted state social studies standards or in any accompanying documents, including works cited pages. Social studies standards in these states typically focus on the content ideas within the disciplines of history, civics, geography, and economics. Some of the state standards reference disciplinary skills (e.g., historical thinking, spatial thinking, economic decision making) and, in some cases, general critical thinking or literacy skills. For example, Delaware's state social studies standards include the Common Core Literacy Standards for History/Social Studies to address broad reading and writing skills in social studies.[12]

Level 2: States that cited (n=2), endorsed (n=2), or excerpted (n=12) the C3 Framework in their social studies standards document

Two states (Maine and Mississippi) **cited** the C3 Framework as one of the documents consulted in a recent standards

Figure 1: Use of the C3 Framework by State as of June 1, 2021

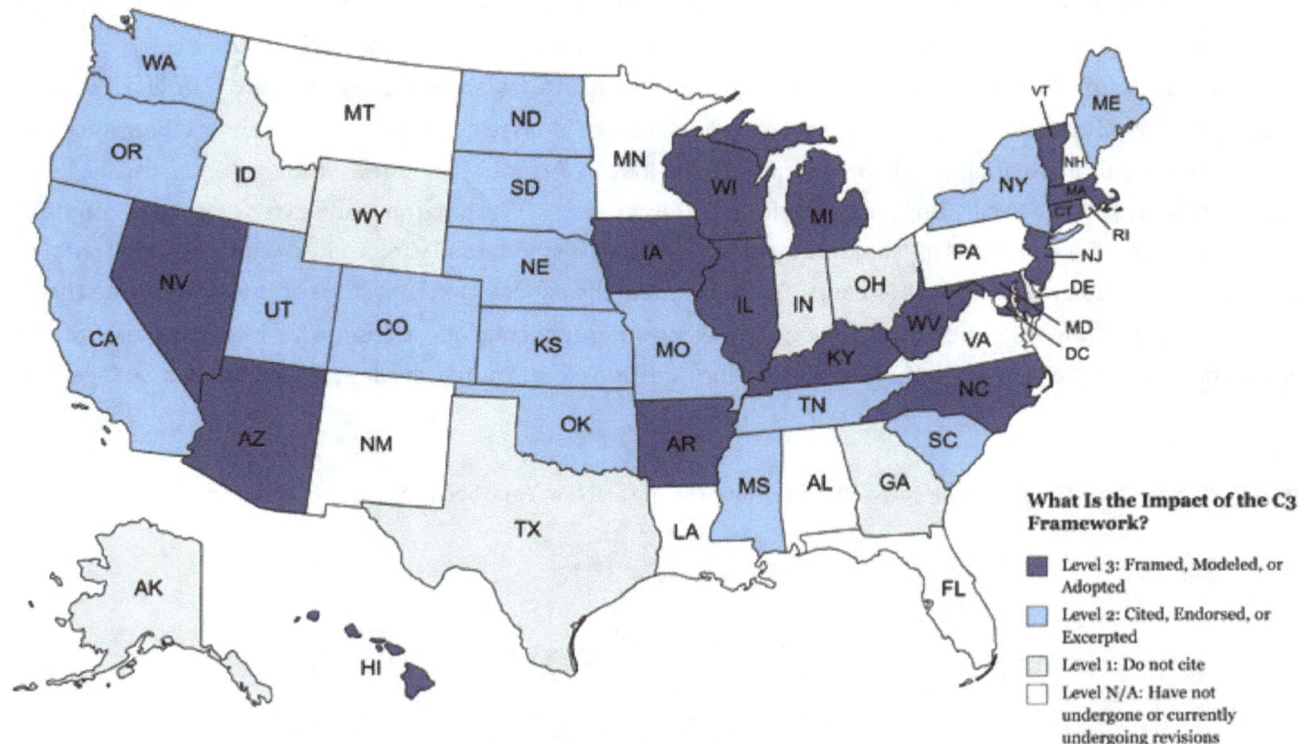

Table 2: Distribution of Students based upon C3 Framework Level

C3 Framework	Total States (including DC)	Total Students	Percentage
Level N/A	11	9,121,300	18%
Level 1	8	10,629,400	21%
Level 2	16	17,441,500	34%
Level 3	16	13,462,000	27%
Totals	51	50,654,200	100%

writing and adoption process. These citations are found in the document's introduction, appendices, and/or works cited page. For example, Mississippi's social studies standards noted the C3 Framework along with other national and state standards documents to gain "sufficient understanding of the direction of social studies education."[13] The reference to the C3 Framework as a key document to inform standards deserves recognition, even if the language and structure of the Inquiry Arc are absent within the state social studies standards.

Two states (California and New York) **endorsed** the use of the C3 Framework by presenting it as a complementary resource for implementing their social studies standards. California's History-Social Science Framework identified the C3 Framework as an "important step forward in our ongoing commitment to ensure that all California students are prepared for college, twenty-first century careers, and citizenship."[14] The writers of New York's K-12 Social Studies Framework integrated the C3 Framework's Inquiry Arc into a graphic presented below (see Figure 2) that illustrates the components of the New York Framework and places the C3 Inquiry Arc as the highest level organizing component, with other components (e.g., key ideas and conceptual understandings and content specifications) all nesting within the Inquiry Arc.[15] While there are no other specific ideas from the C3 Framework in the New York standards document, it is important to note that these standards were adopted in 2014, a few short months after the publication of the C3 Framework, which may have made a more integrated approach to the Framework impossible.

Twelve states (Colorado, Kansas, Missouri, Nebraska, North Dakota, Oklahoma, Oregon, South Carolina, South Dakota, Tennessee, Utah, and Washington) **excerpted** one or more ideas (e.g., compelling questions, taking informed action) from the C3 Framework but did not incorporate the Inquiry Arc into their social studies standards. These states varied broadly when excerpting ideas within the C3 Framework. Washington made extensive use of compelling questions by embedding hundreds of "sample questions" within the standards.[16] Colorado's Academic Standards in Social Studies include what they call "Inquiry Questions," and the expectation that students will "determine the kinds of sources that will be helpful in answering compelling and supporting questions, taking into consideration the different opinions people have about how to answer the questions."[17] In South Carolina's Social Studies College-and

Figure 2: Diagram that articulates the social studies practices in the New York Social Studies Framework

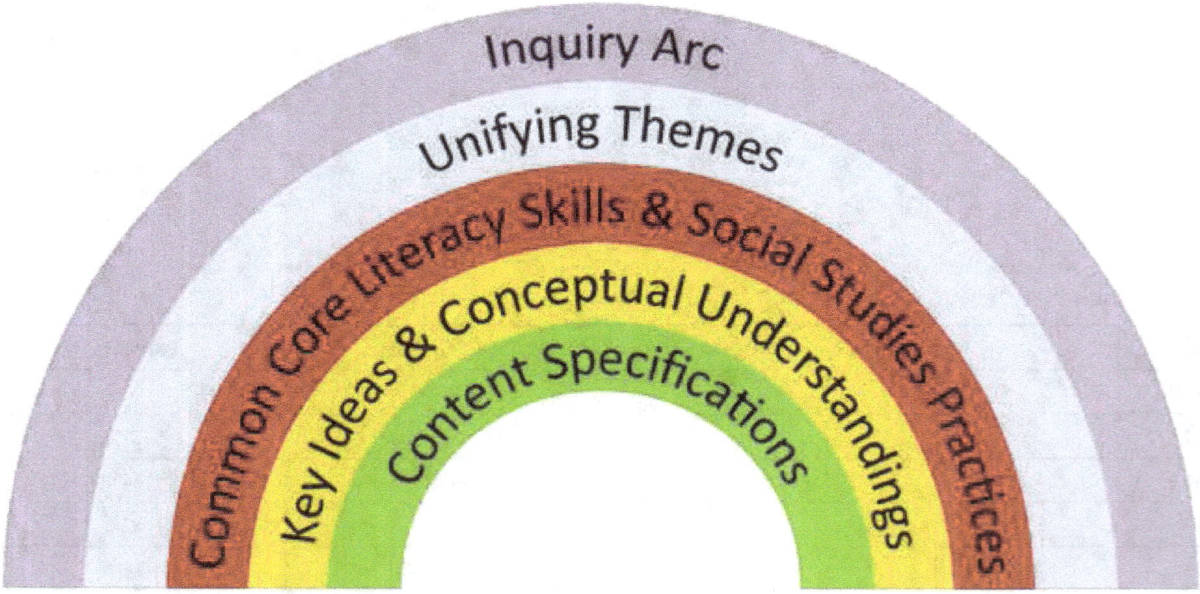

Career-Ready Standards, there are consistent references to the idea of inquiry situated broadly within the study of the four core social studies disciplines that make up the C3 Framework's Dimension 2 (civics, economics, geography, and history). For example, each individual content standard within the document is accompanied by an explanatory statement that "encourages inquiry" into the ideas presented within the standard.[18]

Level 3: States that framed (n=4), modeled (n=11), adopted (n=1) the C3 Framework in their social studies standards document.

Four states (Maryland, Massachusetts, New Jersey, and West Virginia) **framed** their social studies standards using the C3 Framework's Inquiry Arc. West Virginia's College and Career Readiness Standards for Social Studies represent the four dimensions of the C3 Framework at each grade level in four "College and Career Readiness Indicators"[19] including: (1) Develop questions through investigations; (2) Apply disciplinary concepts and tools; (3) Evaluate sources and use evidence; and (4) Communicate conclusions and take informed action. Although these indicators are not differentiated by grade band, they are presented as bulleted ideas at the beginning of each grade level to frame disciplinary standards. The Massachusetts' History and Social Science Frameworks have seven practices which reflect the Inquiry Arc of C3 Framework, although with more variation and detail.[20] Like West Virginia, these practices stay consistent across grades in the social studies standards:

1. Demonstrate civic knowledge, skills, and dispositions.

2. Develop focused questions or problem statements and conduct inquiries.

Figure 3: Diagrams that articulate the *C3 Framework's* Inquiry Arc Dimensions and the *Kentucky Academic Standards for Social Studies* four social studies practices.

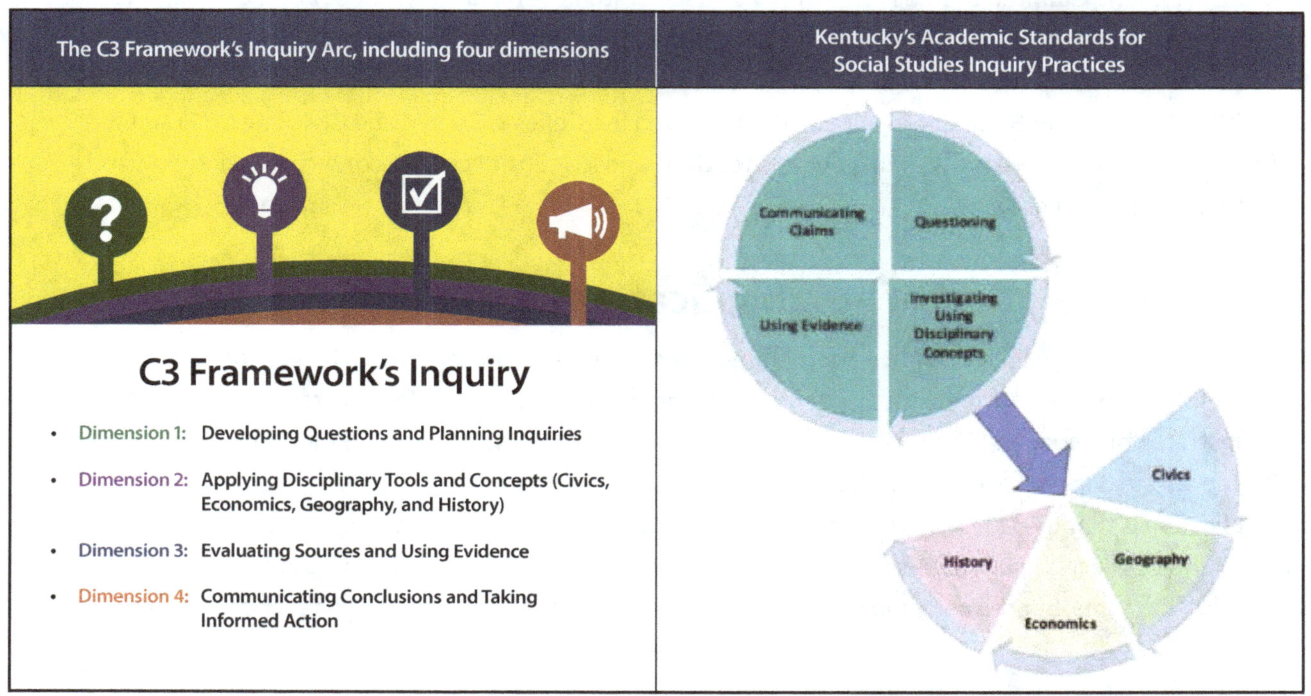

3. Organize information and data from multiple primary and secondary sources.

4. Analyze the purpose and point of view of each source; distinguish opinion from fact.

5. Evaluate the credibility, accuracy, and relevance of each source.

6. Argue or explain conclusions, using valid reasoning and evidence.

7. Determine next steps and take informed action, as appropriate.

Eleven states (Arizona, Arkansas, Connecticut, Hawaii, Illinois, Iowa, Kentucky, Michigan, Nevada, North Carolina, and Wisconsin) **modeled** their social studies standards on the C3 Framework's Inquiry Arc, differentiating these skills into grade-band indicators. In Kentucky's Academic Standards for Social Studies, all four dimensions of the C3 Framework's Inquiry Arc are included intact, but are renamed as inquiry practices with shortened titles.[21] See Figure 3.

Kentucky's four inquiry practices are further described in the document where each practice is differentiated at grade level. For example, Kindergarten students are expected to "ask compelling questions about their community," and in the 12th grade, students are expected to "generate compelling questions to frame thinking, inquiry and/or understanding of key disciplinary concepts."[22] Although students are not expected to develop supporting questions in Kindergarten, by high school the standards state that students would be expected to "generate supporting questions to develop knowledge, understanding and thinking relative to key concepts framed by compelling questions."[23] Similarly, the North Carolina standards include grade-banded inquiry strands reflective of the C3 Framework that describe specific inquiry skills expected of students. Like Kentucky, these indicators are differentiated, increasing in sophistication and scope. For example, in Kindergarten, students are expected to "demonstrate an understanding of facts, opinions, and other details in sources."[24]By high school, students are expected to "differentiate between facts and interpretation of sources."[25] These efforts around differentiation, integration, and explanation were key attributes for state standards in this category, distinguishing the standards from Level 3A.

One state (Vermont) **adopted** the C3 Framework as its social studies standards without any modifications to the document:

> In 2017, the Vermont State Board of Education adopted the College, Career, and Civic Life C3 Framework for Social Studies Standards (C3) to guide the teaching and learning of civics, economics, geography, and history within Vermont.[26]

Implications

Measuring the impact of one document on another (much less 51 others) presents a challenge. The term "impact" implies a range of effects—from none to full adoption. Our analysis above clearly demonstrates that outcome. But it also demonstrates the more and less subtle ways that the C3 Framework has influenced the standards-based content and skills represented in well over half of the states.

One implication is that the C3 Framework has actually had an impact. By the numbers alone, the C3 Framework has influenced state-level social studies policies.[27] That said, the impact is as varied as there are states. No two states' standards look the same, but the commonalities and distinctions (as evident in the findings section) are equally illuminating.

A common feature of the states that attended to the C3 Framework is their use of Dimension 2 (Applying Disciplinary Concepts and Tools). State standards writers took seriously the focus on disciplinary concepts and skills exemplified in the NCSS document. States personalized these standards to reflect their various priorities, but attention to the C3 Framework approach to describing content and skills is evident.

Our findings also highlight the different state-level treatments of the C3 Framework. Some states simply nodded in the direction of the C3 Framework, while others pulled selectively from the ideas and/or language expressed in the C3 Framework; nearly one-third of the states, however, made a significant effort to incorporate major elements into their standards.

A third implication of this study is that, although standards are a clearly recognized element of a state's social studies policy, they are not all that matters. At this point, several states have supplemented their state standards with a range of other materials. Those materials range from the curriculum exemplars in the New York State Toolkit to the state-level curriculum hubs on C3Teachers.org.[28] Probably even more important are the state-level testing programs that exist in approximately half of the states (n=22).[29] Those programs range from tests based on the civics portion of the US Naturalization Service Test to comprehensive exams that assess all areas of social studies. State-level standardized tests are often cited as a profound influence on teachers' practices; the empirical evidence for that claim, however, is disputed.[30]

One last implication of this study is that policy matters. The relationship between policy and practice, state standards, and the pedagogy of teachers, is uncertain at best.[31] The decentralized nature of American schooling, the generally vague wording of standards documents, and the mixed messages that standards and state-level tests can send mean that teachers have considerable autonomy over their classroom practices. They may embrace a new set of standards, they may pick and choose among those standards, or they may ignore those standards on the assumption that another new set will arrive in a few years.

That the relationship between standards and practices is fickle need not mean that standards are irrelevant—particularly if those standards push in an ambitious direction. Prior to the C3 Framework, most state social studies standards reflected a wide and disparate set of people, places, events, and ideas that may or may not have had skills attached to them. Such standards offered cover for every teaching practice on the spectrum. By placing inquiry squarely and substantially at the center of standards revision efforts, the C3 Framework, and the states that embraced it, push in two important directions. First, those standards give even more support and encouragement to teachers who are trying to ratchet up the power of their pedagogy. Ambitious teachers in the past have too often faced derision and resistance from colleagues and administrators who are content to accept conventional schooling outcomes. With state standards that promote inquiry-based teaching and learning, those teachers stand on far firmer ground. And that means that teachers who resist any change to their traditional practices could now find themselves on far shakier ground.

Administrators who understand and embrace the ideas represented in their C3-inspired state standards have a leverage point with which to encourage change. There are no guarantees in education, however, and a host of factors could intervene allowing traditional teachers to maintain their practices. But if the impact of the C3 Framework on state standards grows, then the potential for substantive change in social studies classrooms multiplies.

Notes

1.   Kathy Swan and Susan Griffin, "Beating the Odds: The College, Career, and Civic Life (C3) Framework for Social Studies State Standards," *Social Education* 77, no. 6 (2013): 317–317.

2. Ronald W. Evans, *The Social Studies Wars: What Should We Teach the Children?* (New York: Teachers College Press, 2004).

3. S.G. Grant, Kathy Swan, and John Lee. *Inquiry-Based Practice in Social Studies Education: Understanding the Inquiry Design Model* (New York: Routledge, 2017).

4. Kenneth E. Vogler and David Virtue, "'Just the Facts, Ma'am': Teaching Social Studies in the Era of Standards and High-Stakes Testing," *The Social Studies* 98, no. 2 (2007): 54–58.

5. Jeremy A. Stern et al., *State of State Standards for Civics and U.S. History in 2021* (Washington D.C.: Thomas B. Fordham Institute, June 2021), https://fordhaminstitute.org/national/research/state-state-standards-civics-and-us-history-2021.

6. John Lee and Kathy Swan, "Is the Common Core Good for Social Studies? Yes, but...," *Social Education* 77, no. 6 (2013): 327–330.

7. National Council for the Social Studies (NCSS), *The College, Career, and Civic Life (C3) Framework for Social Studies State Standards: Guidance for Enhancing the Rigor of K–12 Civics, Economics, Geography, and History* (Silver Spring, Md.: NCSS, 2013), 6.

8. C3 Framework, 6.

9. K. A. Neuendorf, *The Content Analysis Guidebook* (Thousand Oaks, Calif.: Sage Publications, 2017).

10. Calculated using the National Center for Education Statistics, "Enrollment in Public Elementary and Secondary Schools, by Region, State, and Jurisdiction," projected for fall 2020.

11. Minnesota Department of Education, *2020 Minnesota K–12 Academic Standards in Social Studies, First Draft* (Roseville, Minn.: Department of Education, 2020).

12. Delaware Department of Education, "Delaware State Standards for Social Studies," last modified September 17, 2018, www.doe.k12.de.us/Page/2548

13. Mississippi Department of Education, *2018 Mississippi College and Career Readiness Standards for the Social Studies* (Jackson, Miss.: Department of Education, 2018).

14. California Department of Education, History–Social Science Framework (Sacramento, Calif.: Department of Education, 2016), www.cde.ca.gov/ci/hs/cf/documents/hssframeworkwhole.pdf.

15. New York State Education Department, "K–12 Social Studies Framework," accessed June 1, 2021, www.nysed.gov/curriculum-instruction/k-12-social-studies-framework.

16. Washington State Department of Education, *Washington K–12 Social Studies Learning Standards* (Olympia, Wash.: Department of Education, 2019), www.k12.wa.us/sites/default/files/public/socialstudies/standards/OSPI_SocStudies_Standards_2019.pdf.

17. Colorado Department of Education, *Colorado Academic Standards: Social Studies* (Denver, Colo.: Department of Education, 2020), www.cde.state.co.us/cosocialstudies/2020cas-ss-p12

18. South Carolina Department of Education, *South Carolina Social Studies College and Career-Ready Standards* (Columbia, S.C.: Department of Education, 2020), www.cde.state.co.us/cosocialstudies/2020cas-ss-p12.

19. West Virginia Department of Education, *West Virginia's College and Career Readiness Standards for Social Studies* (Charleston, W.Va.: Department of Education, 2016), https://apps.sos.wv.gov/adlaw/csr/readfile.aspx?DocId=27577&Format=PDF.

20. Massachusetts Department of Elementary and Secondary Education, *History and Social Science Framework: Grades Pre-Kindergarten to 12* (Malden, Mass.: Department of Elementary and Secondary Education, 2018), www.doe.mass.edu/frameworks/hss/2018-12.pdf.

21. Kentucky Department of Education, *Kentucky Academic Standards: Social Studies* (Frankfort, Ky., 2019), https://education.ky.gov/curriculum/conpro/socstud/Pages/default.aspx

22. Ibid.

23. Ibid.

24. North Carolina State Board of Education, "K–12 Social Studies Standards," accessed June 1, 2021.

25. Ibid.

26. State of Vermont Agency of Education, "Global Citizenship," accessed June 1, 2021, https://education.vermont.gov/student-learning/content-areas/global-citizenship.

27. By contrast, the Common Core State Standards were adopted whole cloth by 46 states. Since then, 12 states have sought to repeal the standards and five have withdrawn them.

28. In addition to state-level supplementary materials, many school districts—either individually or in collaboration—have developed resources for their teachers that support and extend their state standards.

29. "State Education Practices (SEP)," National Center for Education Statistics (NCES) Home Page, a part of the U.S. Department of Education, https://nces.ed.gov/programs/statereform/tab2_16.asp (accessed July 17, 2021).

30. See, for example, S.G. Grant, ed., *Measuring History: Cases of State-Level Testing in the United Statesv.* (Greenwich, Conn.: Information Age, 2010) and Paul Fitchett and Tina Heafner, "A National Perspective on the Effects of High-Stakes Testing and Standardization on Elementary Social Studies Marginalization," *Theory and Research in Social Education* 38, no.1 (2010): 114–130.

31. S.G. Grant, *op. cit.* (2010) and S.G. Grant, "An Uncertain Lever: The Influence of State-Level Testing in New York State on Teaching Social Studies," *Teachers College Record* 103, no. 3 (2001): 398–426.

Social Education 87, no. 6 (2023): 361–366.

The State of the C3 Framework: An Inquiry Revolution in the Making

S.G. Grant, John Lee, Kathy Swan

When leading professional development, we sometimes joke that the C3 Framework launched a "revolution" in social studies.[1] But if one element of a successful revolution is widespread support, we may not be joking much longer.

In 2020, with our colleague Ryan New, we published "The State of Social Studies Standards: What Is the Impact of the C3 Framework."[2] In that report, we detailed evidence that the C3 Framework was having a profound effect on the substance of state-level social studies standards. We revealed that of 50 states (and the District of Columbia), 32 made use of the C3 Framework in one way or another. With the 10-year-anniversary of the C3 Framework, we were delighted to see that six more states have joined the inquiry fold. In effect, that means that approximately 35 million, or nearly 70 percent of American students have the opportunity to engage in more ambitious social studies teaching and learning than ever before.

In this article, we update our 2020 analysis and contend that the potential for an inquiry revolution is growing. We begin, however, with a bit of history.

The Birth of the C3 Framework

In the decades before the *College, Career and Civic Life (C3) Framework for Social Studies State Standards* was launched in 2013, social studies standards and curriculum efforts tended to privilege content over skills and failed to capture any notice on a national scale.[3] Larger concerns further eclipsed those efforts, and the United States began a sustained focus on literacy and mathematics. Two waves of reform that promoted those school subjects—No Child Left Behind and the Common Core curricula—cemented public and teachers' attention. The low point was when the Common Core English-Language Arts curriculum reduced social studies to an appendix.

With little left to lose, a small group of state-level social studies specialists and leaders of cultural institutions held a series of meetings to discuss the fate of social studies. In a pivotal moment, the group decided to avoid the pitfalls of developing one more set of content standards. Instead, sponsored by the National Council for the Social Studies and led by Kathy Swan and then-NCSS executive director Susan Griffin, the group chose to (a) privilege state-developed standards over a national effort and (b) focus on the broad concepts and tools of social studies in each of four disciplinary areas—civics, economics, geography, and history. To affect these ideas, the group decided to construct a framework or guidance document social studies leaders could use when their states developed new standards and curriculum.

The *College, Career and Civic Life (C3) Framework for Social Studies State Standards*, or C3 Framework, went live on Constitution Day 2013. The document has four sections. The introduction lays out the process by which the document was produced and the nearly 100 writers and reviewers who produced it, as well as the 15 organizations that participated and the 25 organizations invited to review it. The second section offers a reader's guide to the framework including links to the Common Core English Language Arts standards. The bulk of the C3 Framework is presented in the third section. Here, the Inquiry Arc is described and the four Dimensions of the framework are delineated. Those four dimensions are (1) Developing Questions and Planning Inquiries, (2) Applying Disciplinary Concepts and Tools (i.e., civics, economics, geography, and history), (3) Evaluating Sources and Using Evidence, and (4) Communicating Conclusions and Taking Informed Action. The final section of the framework offers a disciplinary matrix, a scholarly rationale for the effort, and three companion documents featuring the disciplines of psychology, sociology, and anthropology.

Methodology of the Survey

In the original study,[4] we conducted a content analysis on the extent to which each of the 50 states and the District of Columbia used the C3 Framework in their social studies standards. This seemingly simple task soon became complicated due to the considerable variation in how states define standards and surround them with supporting materials. As a result, in order to compare roughly equivalent documents, we decided to focus on whatever each state labeled as its standards document; we did not include ancillary documents.[5]

As our analysis developed, we saw the states' efforts falling into nine categories that could be described on four levels:

- Level N/A: States that have not undergone (n=5) or are currently undergoing (n=6) comprehensive social studies standards revision;
- Level 1: States that did not cite (n=8) the C3 Framework as part of their social studies standards document;
- Level 2: States that cited (n=2), endorsed (n=2), or excerpted (n=12) the C3 Framework in their social studies standards document;
- Level 3: States that framed (n=4), modeled (n=11), or adopted (n=1) the C3 Framework in their social studies standards document.[6]

The level that proved most challenging to categorize was Level 3. In our earlier paper, we noted that:

> In this analysis, we stayed focused on several major factors: (1) the treatment of the four dimensions of the Inquiry Arc (e.g., where it appears in the document, whether it stayed intact, and renaming of the dimensions); (2) the inclusion of specific indicators and the extent to which they were differentiated for grade level; and (3) any innovations to the presentation of the standards document (e.g., modifications in language, addition of skills).

For this follow-up study, we began by looking at the 19 states that fell into Level N/A and Level 1 as these were the cases most likely to represent any change toward the C3 Framework. With that review complete, we spot-checked the Level 2 and Level 3 states to see if there was any significant movement toward or away from the C3 Framework in any revised documents.

Findings

Whereas the shelf life of most curriculum reforms is only a few years, at most, we found that time has not diminished interest in the C3 Framework. In fact, it continues to be the go-to source when states revise their standards.

Our updated survey of state standards and the C3 Framework support two trends: (a) states that employed the C3 Framework continue to use it, and (b) states that have revised their standards since 2020 have used the C3 Framework to a significant degree.

Figure 1. State Social Studies Standards Categorized by Use of the C3 Standards

Level (# of states in level)	Category Description	Number of States	States in Each Category*
N/A (n=4)	A. States that **have not undergone** comprehensive social studies standards revision since the publication of the C3 Framework.	3	Pennsylvania (2009), Alabama (2010), New Hampshire (2006)
	B. States that are **currently undergoing** social studies standards revision and have not formally adopted new standards as of June 1, 2021/2023	1	Alaska (2016)
Level 1 (n=9)	A. States that **do not cite** the C3 Framework in social studies standards or in any accompanying documents, including works cited/references.	9	Delaware (2018), Florida (2014, 2023), Georgia (2016, 2023), Idaho (2016), Indiana (2020, 2023), Ohio (2018), South Dakota (2015, 2023), Texas (2018, 2023), Wyoming (2018)
Level 2 (n=20)	A. States that **cited** the C3 Framework as one of the documents consulted in a standards writing and adoption process.	2	Mississippi (2018, 2022), Maine (2019)
	B. States that **endorsed** the use of the C3 Framework by presenting it as a complementary resource for implementing their social studies standards.	2	California (2016), New York (2016),
	C. States that **excerpted** one or more ideas (e.g., questions, taking informed actions) from the C3 Framework.	16	Virginia (2015, 2023), New Mexico (2009, 2022), Louisiana (2011, 2022), Washington, DC (2006, 2023), Rhode Island (2012, 2023), Missouri (2016), Utah (2016, 2023), Tennessee (2017), Oregon (2018), Nebraska (2019), North Dakota (2019), Oklahoma (2019), Washington (2019), Colorado (2020), Kansas (2020), South Carolina (2020)
Level 3 (n=18)	A. States that **framed** their social studies standards with the C3 Framework's Inquiry Arc.	5	Minnesota (2011, 2022), West Virginia (2016), Massachusetts (2018), Maryland (2020), New Jersey (2020)
	B. States that **modeled** their social studies standards on the C3 Framework.	12	Montana (2017, 2021), Arkansas (2014, 2022), Connecticut (2015), Illinois (2016), Iowa (2017, 2023), Hawaii (2018), Nevada (2018), Wisconsin (2018), Arizona (2019), Kentucky (2019), Michigan (2019), North Carolina (2021)
	C. States that **adopted** the C3 Framework as their social studies standards.	1	Vermont (2017)

* Note: The first year listed after each state reflects the latest version when its state social studies standards were surveyed in 2020. States with a second year listed have subsequently revised their standards.

Figure 2. The Rhode Island Anchor Standard Constructs and Concepts for Social Studies K-12

Civics & Government

1. **Rules and Laws**
   Authority & Equity; Participation & Equality

2. **Power**
   Political Processes & Structures; Positionality & Privilege; Decision-Making & Consequences

3. **Rights and Responsibilities**
   Freedom & Control; Individuals & Society; Belonging & Citizenship

History

4. **Interpretation**
   Facts, perspectives, and biases; Sources & representation

5. **Change/Continuity**
   Past & Present; Causation; Social Action & reactions

6. **Individuals/Groups**
   Identity & Social Roles; Class; Gender, Ethnicity, Race, Religion; Community & Culture

Geography

7. **Human and Physical Interactions**
   Modification & Adaptation; Naming Environments; Resources (Distribution and Access)

8. **Populations**
   Movement; Density & Distribution; Cultures

9. **Spatial Considerations**
   Landforms; Locations; Climate & Weather

Economics

10. **Scarcity/Abundance**
    Choices & Consequences; Trade-offs; Economic Systems & Opportunities

11. **Producers/Consumers**
    Goods & Services; Means of Exchange; Technology

12. **Economics/Government**
    Roles; Interdependence; Influence

Continuing with the C3 Framework

Of the 32 states that incorporated the C3 Framework in our 2020 survey at Levels 2 or 3, all have continued their use of the document with one exception. In some ways, this result is no particular surprise as 28 of these states have not revised their standards in the last three years. But, of the four states that did undergo a standards revision effort, three (Arkansas, Iowa, and Mississippi) retained their use of the C3 Framework as an important influence on their standards.

The one exception to the trend of continuing use of the C3 Framework is South Dakota. In the 2015 social studies standards, the drafting committee "used C3 Framework skills … to inform standards and outcomes."[7] Inquiry was also listed as one of the four dimensions of the South Dakota standards along with communication, problem solving, and critical thinking. In the 2023 revision, all mention of these dimensions is gone as is any reference to the C3 Framework. Based on the Trump administration-supported *1776* curriculum, the new standards are heavily centered around content with only lower-level skills (e.g., identifying, telling stories, and explaining) listed. (To learn more about South Dakota's standards controversy, see Stephen Jackson's article on page 355 of this issue.)

Given the turbulent times, we were surprised that nearly all states that used the C3 Framework in 2020, with its commitment to inquiry-based teaching and learning, continue to endorse that document.

Growth and Strength of the C3 Framework

The continued influence of the C3 Framework is heartening. We were surprised and gladdened by the fact that of the states that did revise their social studies standards since our 2020 survey, nearly 70 percent did so in ways that reflect attention to the C3 Framework.

In total, 16 states have adopted new standards since 2020; 11 did so by incorporating elements of the C3 Framework. As noted above, four of those states used the C3 Framework according to our initial survey; three of the four continue to do so. Six states (Virginia, New Mexico, Louisiana, Washington DC, Rhode Island, and Utah) built the Framework into their new standards at one of the Level 2 categories. In the Level 2 categories, states alternatively cited, endorsed, or excerpted elements from the C3 Framework. The other four states (Minnesota, Montana, Arkansas, and Iowa) embraced the Framework at Level 3A or 3B. Reflecting greater attention to the C3 Framework, these Level 3 states framed or modeled their standards after the Framework.

Five states (Florida, Georgia, Indiana, South Dakota, and Texas) revised their standards after 2020, but show no influence of the inquiry-based principles of the C3 Framework. As noted in the South Dakota example, the new standards in these states tilt heavily toward content specifications; any attention given to social studies skills typically reflects lower-level thinking.

Thus, when given the opportunity to develop new standards for social studies, the vast majority of states opted to incorporate the C3 Framework. Even more important, those states went beyond simply citing the framework as an influence or endorsing it as a complementary resource. In short, virtually all of the revised state standards reflect a more ambitious use of the C3 Framework.

One example is the new Rhode Island social studies standards.[8] Consisting of 12 anchor standards and dozens of content standards, Rhode Island teachers and students will see the C3 Framework baked into the mix. The anchor standards, which are intended for use across the K-12 curriculum, are built around three key constructs in each of four academic disciplines: civics/government, economics, geography and history. Each construct represents a range of interrelated concepts many of which are directly related to the C3 Framework. (See Figure 2)
Each of those constructs and concepts are then expressed through a four-part hierarchy of inquiry-rooted skills: Identify, Explain, Analyze, and Argue. For example, the Individuals and Groups construct under history looks like this:

Individuals / Groups (H.IG)

Students act as historians as they...

1. *Identify* peoples, events, technologies, and ideas involved in historical and social change in various geographical and temporal locations.

2. *Explain* how historical and social change have been and continue to be accomplished in relation to systems of power, identity, and resistance.

3. *Analyze* historical change through the intersectional identities and lived experiences of people who have accomplished social change throughout history in relation to systems of power, identity, and resistance.

4. *Argue* how all individuals can act as local, national, and/or global agents of social change by using lessons learned form history.

In this example, we can see how K-12 teachers in Rhode Island can use the same standard to explore the content relevant to each grade level at a much higher level of rigor than in most content-only standards. And, in doing so, they push through to the level of evidence-based argumentation, a key feature of the C3 Framework.

Conclusion

Uncertain times can breed a revolution. By 2013, the No Child Left Behind legislation, the Race to the Top funding priorities, and the Common Core for English-Language Arts had created all kinds of uncertainty for the future of social studies in schools. But that uncertainty spurred a new vision for the field, one that embraced the central elements of an inquiry-based C3 Framework—compelling questions, robust sources, evidence-based arguments, taking informed action. That the document has remained viable for the past 10 years is notable; that it is growing in influence may well prove revolutionary.

Notes

1. National Council for the Social Studies, *The College, Career, and Civic Life (C3) Framework for Social Studies State Standards* (Washington, DC: National Council for the Social Studies, 2013).
2. Ryan New, Kathy Swan, S.G. Grant, John Lee, "The State of Social Studies Standards: What is the Impact of the C3 Framework," *Social Education* 86, no. 4 (2021), 239–246.
3. The exception to this claim was the uproar over the National History Standards developed in 1994. See Gary B. Nash, Charlotte Antoinette Crabtree, Ross E. Dunn, *History on Trial: Culture Wars and the Teaching of the Past* (Vintage Books, 2000).
4. New, Swan, Grant, and Lee, "The State of Social Studies Standards."
5. Readers interested in a more detailed description of our methodology, should refer to New et al., 2021.
6. New, Swan, Grant, and Lee, "The State of Social Studies Standards," 240.
7. See https://doe.sd.gov/contentstandards/documents/SS-Standards-2015.pdf.
8. See https://ride.ri.gov/sites/g/files/xkgbur806/files/2023-03/RhodeIsland_SocialStudiesStandards_FULL.pdf

Section 1: Conclusion

Observers of education in the United States learned long ago that change happens in fits and starts, surfaces and fades, makes sense ... and doesn't. As Tyack and Cuban note, American schools have been engaged in an endless process of "tinkering toward utopia."[1] So, although we are thrilled with the influence the C3 Framework is having on state-level standards, we know that the *real* impact will occur as inquiry-based teaching and learning is implemented in K–12 classrooms.

To that end, in the next section, we offer a set of six articles from the "Teaching the C3 Framework" column that delve into the key area of curriculum.

Note

1. David Tyack and Larry Cuban, *Tinkering Toward Utopia: A Century of Public School Reform* (New York: Harvard University Press, 1997).

Section 2: Curriculum

Section 2: Curriculum

Publishing the C3 Framework was exhilarating. Getting to the standards end zone, we spent September 2013 doing a victory dance before realizing that the Framework was really just the beginning. The Inquiry Arc proved a useful first step in delineating a process for social studies inquiry and in coming to a consensus about what students should know (disciplinary ideas) and be able to do (construct questions, form evidentiary arguments, and take informed action). But, there was more to do if a real inquiry revolution was to take place.

An opportunity to think about next steps came with the New York Social Studies Toolkit, a three-million-dollar project to (re)imagine teaching materials that would accompany New York's new social studies standards that call upon the C3 Inquiry Arc.[1] Led by S. G. Grant, the toolkit project allowed us to immediately begin prototyping what ultimately became the Inquiry Design Model (IDM) featuring a one-page blueprint that articulated three curricular components of inquiry: Questions, Tasks, and Sources (QTS).

We see these QTS elements as distinct but mutually reinforcing. Questions, both compelling and supporting, help frame the "why" of reading and interpreting sources. Students use those sources to investigate the inquiry questions and then complete formative and summative performance tasks. Sources become the "how" of performance assessments within an inquiry. The student-generated products (e.g., claims, arguments, actions) that result from formative and summative performance tasks become the "what" of an inquiry. It is impossible to remove either questions *or* tasks *or* sources from an inquiry—we argue that they are the *essence* of inquiry.

In the spirit of the C3 Framework, the IDM blueprint is meant to be malleable, enabling teachers to construct questions, tasks, and sources that animate their course content and instructional practice such that it meets their students' needs. We underscore that flexibility with a Creative Commons license. Teachers are encouraged to openly share their ideas and for other teachers to adapt those ideas for their own contexts. In other words, our hope is to enable a common-good ethos around IDM where social studies teachers can share their great inquiry work, and those contributions benefit the entire C3 inquiry commonwealth.

Since the New York Toolkit project, we have worked to *flex* the blueprint, shrinking it to one day (i.e., a focused inquiry), expanding it to encompass an entire unit of study (i.e., a jigsaw inquiry), and handing it over to students to create their own inquiry experience (i.e., a student-guided inquiry). Further, we have looked across a course of study and designed a variety of loops to demonstrate what the spine of an inquiry-based curriculum might look like. We then flexed that idea even further by developing a *conceptual* inquiry-based curriculum where the inquiries are held together with a powerful concept.

Our colleagues in K–12 classrooms and universities have been instrumental in the various iterations and perspectives that guide the work of the IDM. In the following section, we present six articles from the "Teaching the C3 Framework" archive in *Social Education* that establish the origin story of the IDM, demonstrate its flexibility and change over time, and highlight the creative artistry of its users.

* * * * *

The first article in the section, "From Inquiry Arc to Instructional Practice: The Potential of the College, Career, and Civic Life (C3) Framework" by S. G. Grant, set the charge for the IDM in 2013. Grant writes that teaching with an inquiry approach is going to require "necessary scaffolding so that even young children can examine issues of substance and interest" (p. 55). Grant goes on to name the things that *matter* when shifting towards inquiry teaching and learning: (a) questions, (b) students' questions, (c) language, (d) resources, (e) writing, and (f) trust. In the last line of the article, Grant recognizes that inquiry-based teaching is not for the "faint hearted" (p. 55). Over the years, we are learning about the grit it takes in making inquiry come to life.

The birth of the Inquiry Design Model is chronicled in Kathy Swan, John Lee, and S. G. Grant's article, "The New York State Toolkit and the Inquiry Design Model: Anatomy of an Inquiry." Published two years after the C3 Framework, we detail the blueprint for the first time by asking and answering our own compelling question, "What does inquiry look like?" (p. 56). This new inquiry theory is illustrated with a 7th-grade structured inquiry on *Uncle Tom's Cabin* where each component of the blueprint—questions, tasks, and sources—is explained. To avoid the trap of over-prescription, we argue that this new approach "reflects a specific, conscious decision not to produce fully developed and comprehensive" lessons or units encouraging teachers to "mold around their particular students' needs and the contexts in which they teach" (p. 63). In doing so, the blueprint becomes just that—a plan for inquiry that leaves open the possibilities that teachers and students bring to it.

The original IDM blueprint begins to flex in Kathy Swan, John Lee, and S. G. Grant's article titled "Questions, Tasks, Sources: Focusing on the Essence of Inquiry." In this piece, we address one of the main issues teachers experience when shifting to inquiry teaching—time. Inspired by Picasso's work around abstraction, we step back from the original blueprint with 3–4 supporting questions to identify the *essence* of inquiry—as long as a blueprint has the components (compelling and supporting questions, formative and summative performance tasks, and disciplinary sources), the number of each is less important than the structure. We write, "abbreviating inquiry into a 1- to 2-day lesson means some ideas are going to be left on the cutting room floor. But that is true for curriculum in general" (p. 69). This was a major step forward for the IDM and kicked off new riffs and interpretations of the blueprint.

One of the more significant interpretations of the blueprint arrived in the article written by Ryan Crowley and LaGarrett King, "Making Inquiry Critical: Examining Power and Inequity in the Classroom." Crowley and King suggest that "critical inquiries should be designed to identify and to challenge master narratives that legitimate systems of oppression and power" (p. 73). In doing so, blueprint designers should craft *questions* that explicitly critique systems of oppression and power, select *sources* that include perspectives of marginalized and oppressed groups, and develop *tasks* that allow students to confront injustice. The critical inquiry blueprint re-invention was a seminal moment for the IDM showing, once again, that it could flex to include important theoretical frameworks in social studies while the original theory of questions, tasks, and sources remained intact.

In the fifth article in this section, "Blueprinting an Inquiry-Based Curriculum: Planning with the Inquiry Design Model" by Kathy Swan, S. G. Grant, and John Lee, we move beyond the single blueprint (or what we now refer to as the "Coke Classic") to create an elastic typology of five additional kinds of blueprints that flex in terms of time and teacher scaffolding. Using the imagery of a house, we identify three parts:

1. The foundational elements of inquiry—questions, tasks and sources;
2. Rooms that include five different types of blueprints—structured, embedded action, focused, guided, and student-directed; and,
3. A roof that includes a plan for inquiry that is consistent and regular.

Harkening back to the preamble of the C3 Framework, we argue that students must be given opportunities to take up the inquiry reins and that, most importantly, students "must possess the capability and commitment to repeat that process as long as is necessary … in order to traverse successfully the worlds of college, career, and civic life" (p. 82). By collapsing or expanding and, in some cases, shifting the authorship of a blueprint, we illustrate how the IDM can operate as a curricular framework that flexes to meet the contextual needs of teachers.

The final article in this section, "Power, Injustice, Costs and Benefits: Looping Curriculum Concepts with the Inquiry

Design Model" by Kathy Swan, S. G. Grant, John Lee, Andrew Danner, Christy Cartner, and Grant Stringer, is the first in a series of articles about curricular loops. Kathy Swan and team define a curricular loop as a coherent plan to regularly engage students in inquiry throughout a course. In this article, they go on to describe three curricular loops with the help of practicing teachers who have co-designed these loops for a U.S. Government course, a U.S. history course, and an economics course. Each of the curricular loops are anchored in an essential social studies concept (e.g., power, injustice, cost/benefit) thereby showing how inquiry can be planned in such a way that students examine and then re-examine an important idea iteratively in a variety of contexts. The authors conclude that looping inquiries provides students with an opportunity "to learn more deeply and find connections among what might otherwise seem to students to be just, 'one damn thing after another'" (p. 90).

* * * * *

1. S. G. Grant, "From Inquiry Arc to Instructional Practice: The Potential of the College, Career, and Civic Life (C3) Framework," *Social Education* 77, no. 6 (2013): 322–326, 351.

2   Kathy Swan, John Lee, and S. G. Grant, "The New York State Toolkit and the Inquiry Design Model: Anatomy of an Inquiry," *Social Education* 79, no. 6 (2015): 316–322.

3. Kathy Swan, John Lee, and S. G. Grant, "Questions, Tasks, Sources: Focusing on the Essence of Inquiry," *Social Education* 82, no. 3 (2018): 133–137.

4. Ryan M. Crowley and LaGarrett J. King, "Making Inquiry Critical: Examining Power and Inequity in the Classroom," *Social Education* 82, no. 1 (2018): 14–17.

5. Kathy Swan, S. G. Grant, and John Lee, "Blueprinting an Inquiry-Based Curriculum: Planning with the Inquiry Design Model," *Social Education* 84, no. 6 (2020): 377–383.

6. Kathy Swan, S. G. Grant, John Lee, Andrew Danner, Christy Cartner, and Grant Stringer, "Power, Injustice, Costs and Benefits: Looping Curriculum Concepts with the Inquiry Design Model," *Social Education* 85, no. 3 (2021): 167–172.

Note

1. New York State Education Department, "New York State K–12 Social Studies Toolkit Featured in Special Section of Flagship Social Studies Journal," press release, November 15, 2015, www.nysed.gov/Press/New-York-State-K-12-Social-Studies-Toolkit-Featured-In-Special-Section-of-Flagship-Social-Studies-Journal.

Social Education 77, no. 6 (2013): 322–326, 351

From Inquiry Arc to Instructional Practice: The Potential of the C3 Framework

S. G. Grant

Students are clear: They do not like social studies.[1] What they dislike, however, is not the civic, economic, geographic, and historical ideas they encounter so much as the instructional practices they experience. And instructional experiences matter: Students who read more than textbooks, who write more than end-of-the-chapter questions, and who have more rather than fewer opportunities to discuss ideas out-perform their peers in more traditional classroom settings.[2] Smith and Niemi argue that "if faced with a choice of only one 'solution' to raise history scores, it is clear that instructional changes have the most powerful relationship to student performance."[3]

Although numerous attempts have been made to revitalize social studies, the bulk of them have focused on curricular reforms rather than on instruction.[4] The Inquiry Arc featured in the C3 Framework is a form of guidance for social studies curriculum writers.[5] It also represents an approach to instructional planning that moves away from traditional textbook coverage to a model that is more consistent with the research on ambitious social studies teaching.[6]

Overview of the Inquiry Arc

"We begin with the hypothesis," asserts Jerome Bruner, "that any subject can be taught effectively in some intellectually honest form to any child at any stage of development."[7]

Bruner's quote is not cited in the C3 Framework, but its spirit runs throughout the document in general and the Inquiry Arc in particular. Defined as a set of interlocking and mutually reinforcing elements, the four dimensions of the Inquiry Arc speak to the intersection of ideas and learners. Those four dimensions are:

1. Developing questions and planning inquiries;
2. Applying disciplinary concepts and tools;
3. Evaluating sources and using evidence; and
4. Communicating conclusions and taking informed action.

Key to the Inquiry Arc is the use of questions. As noted in the Scholarly Rationale of the C3 Framework, "children and adolescents are naturally curious, and they are especially curious about the complex and multifaceted world they inhabit."[8] Curiosity drives interest and interest drives knowledge, understanding, and engagement. At heart, social studies is about understanding the things people do. Whether those things are brave, ambitious, and inventive or cowardly, naïve, and silly, social studies is about using questions to direct our investigations into the world around us. Dimension 1, then, features the development of questions and the planning of inquiries.

If social studies is about understanding why people do the things they do, then Dimension 2–Applying Disciplinary Concepts and Tools—is a fundamental step in the Inquiry Arc. With a robust instructional question in mind, teachers and students determine the kind of content they need in order to create a plan to address their questions. This process is an artful balancing act; teachers must preload some disciplinary content when developing questions with their students. At the same time, teachers must provide students with enough content to propel their inquiries without quashing their curiosity or, worse yet, doing their work for them.

Children will naturally begin proposing solutions to instructional questions based on their lived experiences. Rich social studies teaching, however, offers students opportunities to answer those questions more thoroughly through disciplinary (civic, economic, geographical, and historical) and multi-disciplinary venues. Dimension 2 sets forth concepts from the disciplines, such as the historian's habit of accounting for how perspectives of people in the present shape their interpretations of the past. This practice from history and the distinctive habits of thinking from other disciplines inform students' investigations and contribute to an instructional framework for teaching social studies.

Instructional questions posed may demand content representing a single discipline. For example, a question like "Which will you buy—lunch or a new video game?" would have teachers and students draw primarily from the concepts of economics. A question that asks, "Has the definition of 'Americans' changed over time?" would feature concepts from civics/political science. Many questions, however, can best be explored through the use of multiple disciplines. For example, a contemporary environmental question such as "Should transcontinental pipelines be banned?" demands the use of economic, geographical, historical, and political lenses.

With a question in hand and a sense of the relevant concepts and ideas, the Inquiry Arc turns toward the matter of sources and evidence. Social studies, like science, is an evidence-based field. The disciplinary concepts represented in Dimension 2 provide a solid base from which students can begin constructing answers to their questions. Equally important, however, is knowing how to fill in the gaps in their knowledge by learning how to work with sources and evidence in order to develop explanations and to make persuasive arguments in support of their conclusions.

Evidence can come in many forms, including historical and contemporary documents, data from direct observation in environments, graphics, economic statistics, and legislative actions and court rulings. Digital sources are now also more readily available than ever via the Internet. That said, not all sources are equal in value and use. Sources do not, by themselves, constitute evidence. Rather, evidence results from the choices made by teachers and students to appropriate information from sources in support of an explanation or argument. Helping students develop a capacity for gathering, evaluating, and then using sources in responsible ways is a central feature of Dimension 3.

For example, a question like "Was the Civil Rights Movement of the 1960s a success?" demands that students examine more than one or two sources. A wide range of perspectives is available in both primary and secondary form, and so having students gather, evaluate, and use a subset of those sources offers teachers opportunities to make key instructional points about the nature of evidence. Those activities also offer students opportunities to demonstrate their abilities to develop explanations and to make and support arguments in answer to their questions.

Breaking the power of the multiple-choice test, developing explanations and making and supporting arguments can take the form of individual essays, group projects, and other classroom-based written assessments, both formal and informal. But they need not be limited to those options for there are any number of ways that students can express the evolution of their ideas. Although there is no substitute for thoughtful and persuasive writing, Dimension 4 of the Inquiry Arc supports expanding the means by which students communicate their findings and conclusions. It also expands the venues in which students participate. Classroom and school sites are important arenas for students as they work through their ideas. But if students are to take informed action—the second aspect of Dimension 4—then they will need to be able to interact in other arenas as well—from cross town to across the globe. Defining questions, seeking the best knowledge available, examining and using source material, and constructing and communicating conclusions are the hallmark qualities of thoughtful and engaged students. Helping students prepare for civic life demands new means of expressing themselves and new settings in which to do so.

In one sense, Dimension 4 closes the Inquiry Arc. Every good teacher knows, however, that teaching and learning play off one another—new sources can lead to new disciplinary and multi-disciplinary concepts, new concepts can lead to new questions, and new questions can lead to new audiences. The Inquiry Arc, then, offers teachers multiple opportunities to involve students in powerful learning opportunities and to develop as thoughtful, engaged citizens.

The C3 Framework in general and the Inquiry Arc in particular were designed to help state and local curriculum writers retool their social studies standards. To that purpose, I would offer a second—the Inquiry Arc as an instructional arc, a lesson and unit planning approach that foregrounds the use of teacher- and student-developed questions.

Compelling Questions

Pushed into the classroom, the Inquiry Arc challenges some basic and long-held instructional practices. Perhaps the most challenging element, however, is designing lessons and units around questions.

Teachers have long used questions as part of their pedagogical repertoire. But there is a big difference between using questions to check for student understanding and using questions to frame a teaching and learning inquiry. Good questions can be difficult to create, but they can also help teachers and their students focus their inquiries and produce powerful learning outcomes.

Questions, as envisioned in the Inquiry Arc, are of two types— compelling and supporting. *Compelling questions* address "problems and issues found in and across the academic disciplines that make up social studies."[9] They "deal with curiosities about how things work; interpretations and applications of disciplinary concepts; and unresolved issues that require students to construct arguments in response."[10] In short, compelling questions are provocative, engaging, and worth spending time on.

Compelling questions must satisfy two conditions. First, they have to be intellectually meaty. That means that a compelling question needs to reflect an enduring issue, concern, or debate in social studies and it has to draw on multiple disciplines. For example, "Was the American Revolution revolutionary?" works as a compelling question because it signals a continuing argument about how to interpret the results of the Revolution. And, although it sounds like a history question, to address it fully demands that one must look at it through a range of disciplinary lenses—Did the Revolution yield dramatic political change? Economic? Social? All of the above?

The second condition defining a compelling question is the need to be student-friendly. By student-friendly, I mean a question that reflects some quality or condition that teachers know students care about and that honors and respects students' intellectual efforts. The American Revolution question above seems to fit these qualifications as well: It brings students into an authentic debate and it offers the possibility that adults may be confused—how could the American Revolution not be revolutionary? The latter is a condition that students tend to find especially fascinating.

Quiz time: Which of the following examples fit the criteria for a compelling question?

1. Why do we need rules?
2. What are the five largest sources of oil for U.S. markets?
3. Why is Albany the capital of New York?
4. Who are our community helpers?
5. Can Canada and the U.S. be friends forever?
6. Who won the Cold War?

I would argue that numbers 1, 3, 5, and 6 fit the bill as compelling questions. For example, "Can Canada and the U.S.

be friends forever?" satisfies the student-friendly criteria in that it keys off the idea that young people find the notion of friendship intriguing. On the substantive side, the notion of U.S.-Canada relations can be explored on multiple disciplinary dimensions. Think about it: If the U.S. and Canada compete on an economic level, can they still maintain good relationships on the political and/or social level? Similarly, the question, "Who won the Cold War?" qualifies as a compelling question because it meets the intellectually meaty criteria of highlighting a genuine dispute and the student interest criteria because it presumes that students can offer a useful perspective on the question through the arguments they make.

By contrast, "What are the five largest sources of oil for U.S. markets?" and "Who are our community helpers" may be useful in developing a larger inquiry, but on their own, they do not carry the day either in terms of substantive or student interest engagement.

Supporting Questions

From an instructional perspective, if a compelling question helps frame a unit of study, supporting questions can provide the infrastructure for lesson planning.

Supporting questions are "intended to contribute knowledge and insights to the inquiry behind a compelling question." Furthermore, they "focus on descriptions, definitions, and processes on which there is general agreement."[11] In other words, supporting questions help scaffold students' investigations into the ideas and issues behind a compelling question.

For the question about the revolutionary elements of the American Revolution, supporting questions could include the following: What were the regulations imposed on the colonists under the Stamp and Townshend Acts? How did colonists respond? What were the arguments for and against the Revolution? What were the political conditions in America before and after the Revolution? What were the economic conditions before and after the Revolution? What were the social conditions before and after the Revolution? Supporting questions like these offer important pedagogical support, but typically lack either the intellectual heft or the student connections necessary to be considered a compelling question.

Returning to the list of questions in the preceding sections, I would argue that "What are the five largest sources of oil for U.S. markets?" and "Who are our community helpers" could work as supporting questions. For example, identifying the sources of oil would be helpful if students were tackling a compelling question like, "What path should a new transcontinental oil pipeline take?" In similar fashion, "Who are our community helpers" would aid an inquiry into a question such as "Should our community grow?"

Implications for Practice: Thinking about What Matters

The College, Career, and Civic (C3) Framework for Social Studies State Standards offers a different way of thinking about curriculum development. Instead of advocating for the creation of long lists of names, dates, and places, the C3 Framework pushes curriculum writers to think about how the meaningful concepts and skills of civics, economics, geography, and history play out across an inquiry arc. Equally important, however, may be the push the C3 Framework offers to teachers who are interested in employing an inquiry approach in their instructional practice.

Taking such an approach calls for a kind of mindfulness that echoes standard teacher practice, but pushes well beyond it. In teaching through inquiry, these six distinct, but inter-related elements matter:

1. *Questions matter*. Successful teaching and learning inquiries are built around powerful questions of two sorts—compelling and supporting. Most teachers and students have extensive experience working with supporting-style questions. Compelling questions, however, can be a challenge for teachers to create, especially for those who work with younger students. But if the compelling questions offered meet the conditions outlined above, teachers will find that student effort and engagement will soar.

2. *Students' questions matter*. The C3 Framework argues that questions— both compelling and supporting— can originate from teachers and/or students. It does not advocate turning over the question-developing responsibility to kindergartners, but it does promote the idea that students should play an increasingly prominent role in defining inquiry questions over the course of their school lives. Needless to say, teachers play a key role in helping students identify compelling questions that will work for instructional purposes.

3. *Language matters*. If we are going to take Bruner's quote at the beginning of this article seriously, then we need to realize that one of the biggest challenges teachers and students will face is at the level of language. This issue has two dimensions. First, although students can grasp almost any social studies construct through their lived experience, they do not always have the language or vocabulary to participate fully in classroom discourse. (Imagine, for example, a student who misses the point of a discussion because he or she does not understand the difference between guerrilla and gorilla warfare.)

The second challenge lies more on the teacher's side: One of the trickiest parts of being an inquiry-based teacher is learning how to "hear" the kernels of rich ideas in what seems like the fumbling, inarticulate, and confusing things that students of all ages say. Students can be useful partners in constructing compelling questions, but only if we can help them articulate their ideas.

4. *Resources matter*. Again, if we are going to take Bruner's view seriously, we need to realize the challenges teachers and kids face at the resource level. Students bring considerable life experience to their understanding of social studies ideas. To help them grow beyond the limits of their own experiences requires a range of high-quality and accessible resources.

5. *Writing matters*. Whether it is in the form of an oral report, an essay, a debate, or a blog, good social studies teaching and learning demands the capacity to write well. Explanations and arguments are at the heart of the ways in which students present their ideas.

6. *Trust matters*. The Inquiry Arc reflects a level of trust between teachers and students that is not part of the traditional pattern of schooling. Good teachers know that students will blunder sometimes as they embrace the greater responsibilities an inquiry approach demands, but they also know that students will not become the kinds of life-long learners that we desire if they are not trusted to take an active role in their own education.

Conclusion

Teaching through an inquiry approach demands the skilled use of questions to frame units of study and to develop the necessary scaffolding so that even young children can examine issues of substance and interest. It is not a teaching approach for the faint hearted, but the research evidence gathered to date that supports the C3 Framework, suggests that students will embrace it.[12]

Notes

1. T. Epstein, *Interpreting National History: Race, Identity, and Pedagogy in Classrooms and Communities* (New York: Routledge, 2009); M. Schug, R. Todd, and R. Beery, "Why Kids Don't Like Social Studies," *Social Education* 47, no. 5 (1984), 382-387.
2. A. Beatty, C. Reese, H. Persky, and P. Carr, U.S. *History Report Card* (Washington, D.C.: U.S. Department of Education, Office of Educational Research and Improvement, 1996); D. Hess, *Controversy in the Classroom: The Democratic Power of Discussion* (New York: Routledge, 2009).
3. J. B. Smith and R. Niemi, "Learning History in School: The Impact of Course Work and Instructional Practice on Achievement," *Theory and Research in Social Education*, 29 (2001), 38.
4. S. G. Grant, K. Swan, and J. Lee, "Lurching toward Coherence: An Episodic History of Curriculum and Standards Development in Social Studies." Featured presentation of the Research in Social Studies SIG at the annual conference of the American Educational Research Association, Vancouver, BC, April 2012.
5. National Council for the Social Studies (NCSS), *The College, Career, and Civic Life (C3) Framework for Social Studies State Standards: Guidance for Enhancing the Rigor of K-12 Civics, Economics, Geography, and History* (Silver Spring, Md.: NCSS, 2013), 16-64.
6. S. G. Grant, *History Lessons: Teaching, Learning, and Testing in U.S. High School Classrooms* (Mahwah, N.J.: Lawrence Erlbaum Associates, 2006); eds. S. G. Grant and J. M. Gradwell, *Teaching History with Big Ideas: Cases of Ambitious Teachers* (New York: Rowman & Littlefield, 2010).
7. J. Bruner, *The Process of Education* (Cambridge: Harvard University Press, 1960), 33.
8. *The College, Career, and Civic Life (C3) Framework for Social Studies State Standards: Guidance for Enhancing the Rigor of K-12 Civics, Economics, Geography, and History*, 83.
9. Ibid., 97.
10. Ibid., 23.
11. Ibid.
12. Grant, *History Lessons*; Grant and Gradwell, Teaching History with Big Ideas; S. Van Hover, "Teaching History in the Old Dominion: The Impact of Virginia's Accountability Reform on Seven Secondary Beginning History Teachers," in *Measuring History: Cases of State-Level Testing across the United States*, ed. S. G. Grant (Greenwich, Conn.: Information Age Publishing, 2010), 195-220; B. VanSledright, *In Search of America's Past: Learning to Read History in Elementary School* (New York: Teachers College Press, 2002).

Social Education **79**, no. 6 (2015): 316–322

The New York State Toolkit and the Inquiry Design Model: Anatomy of an Inquiry

Kathy Swan, John Lee, and S. G. Grant

What does inquiry look like? Though often used, the concept of "inquiry" is typically ill defined and only rarely developed coherently and consistently through curriculum. The Inquiry Design Model (IDM) attempts to give legs to this alluring, but elusive construct.

IDM is a distinctive approach to creating instructional materials that honors teachers' knowledge and expertise, avoids over-prescription, and focuses on the key elements envisioned in the C3 Inquiry Arc. Unique to the IDM is the *blueprint* based on these key C3 elements—a one-page presentation of the questions, tasks, and sources that define a curricular inquiry. The blueprint offers a visual snapshot of an entire inquiry such that the individual components and the relationship among the components can all be seen at once.

Each of the 84 inquiries within the New York State Toolkit features a blueprint and a description of how the inquiry might be taught. The inquiries are explicitly linked to the Key Ideas as well as to the related Conceptual Understandings, Content Specifications, and Social Studies Practices of the New York State K-12 Social Studies Framework. Although the inquiries align with standards, they are not intended to be comprehensive content units, nor are they intended to be a series of prescribed lesson plans. They are intended to serve as pedagogically rich examples of content and skills built out in inquiry-based fashion.

In this article, we illustrate the IDM structure by unpacking one of the Toolkit inquiries. In the *Uncle Tom's Cabin* inquiry, seventh-grade students explore how words can affect public opinion through an examination of Harriet Beecher Stowe's novel.[1] Here, we highlight the compelling and supporting *questions* that frame and organize the inquiry; the assessment *tasks* that provide opportunities for students to demonstrate and apply their understanding; and the disciplinary *sources* that allow students to practice disciplinary thinking and reasoning. (See the blueprint for the *Uncle Tom's Cabin* inquiry on page 58.)

Questions

From Socrates on, the value of questions in general, and their central role in teaching and learning in particular, has been well established. In Plato's *Protagoras*, Socrates claims, "My way toward truth is to ask the right questions." Answers are important, but a well-framed question can excite the mind and give real and genuine meaning to the study of any social issue. The C3 Inquiry Arc and the Inquiry Design Model feature compelling questions as a way to drive social studies inquiry.

The key to crafting compelling questions is hitting the sweet spot between the qualities of being intellectually rigorous and personally relevant to students. Intellectually rigorous questions reflect an enduring issue, concern, or debate in social studies and speak to the big ideas of history and the social sciences. For example, the compelling question "Can Words Lead to War?" asks students to grapple with the power of words generally, and the causes of the Civil War specifically by examining the impact of the publication of *Uncle Tom's Cabin*. Historians continue to tease out the profound complexity and the chains of action and reaction that caused this turning point in U.S. history. In the inquiry described in this article, students enter the ongoing historical discussion by investigating the impact of Harriet Beecher Stowe's words.

Compelling questions need to be worth investigating from an academic angle, but they also need to be worth exploring from a student angle. Recall Jerome Bruner's claim that "Any subject can be taught effectively in some intellectually honest form to any child at any stage of development."[2] To take this point seriously does not mean that we have to dumb down the curriculum. In fact, it means just the opposite: Teachers *should* teach intellectually ambitious material. The key is to see within the ideas to be taught those elements that teachers know their students care about. It is not the case that students are uninterested in the Civil War. But it is the case that teachers need to pull relevant connections from those ideas to students' lives.

In examining the compelling question "Can Words Lead to War?", the student-friendly elements of the question quickly emerge. First, the question pulls on a thread that all students care about—words. Words are a powerful medium to which all students can relate. Students surely have said something they regret, repeated a word that has gotten an adult incensed, or watched as others have been hurt by an insult. Second, the question is free of jargon and is written in a way that is highly accessible for students. Students should be able to hold compelling questions in their heads in ways that are illuminating rather than merely decorative.

If compelling questions frame an inquiry, supporting questions sustain it. Supporting questions (SQs) build out the compelling question by organizing and sequencing the main ideas. Supporting questions follow a content logic or progression that becomes increasingly more sophisticated over the inquiry experience. For example, in the *Uncle Tom's Cabin* inquiry, the sequence of the supporting questions is:

- **SQ1**: How did Harriet Beecher Stowe describe slavery in *Uncle Tom's Cabin*?
- **SQ2**: What led Harriet Beecher Stowe to write *Uncle Tom's Cabin*?
- **SQ3**: How did Northerners and Southerners react to *Uncle Tom's Cabin*?
- **SQ4**: What was the impact of *Uncle Tom's Cabin* on abolitionism?

Taken together, the compelling question and supporting questions provide the architecture for the inquiry as they highlight the ideas and issues with which teachers and students can engage. There is no one right compelling question for a topic, nor is there only one way to construct and sequence supporting questions. The question "Can Words Lead to War?" has been vetted and found to be compelling by a range of teachers and academics, but that is not to say that others might not develop equally engaging questions on the antebellum period. Similarly, the supporting questions in this inquiry have won the teachers' endorsement. Others, however, might rearrange the sequence, insert additional questions, or even substitute a whole new series. All 84 inquiries are published in Word and PDF so that teachers wanting to modify questions can easily do so.

Formative and Summative Performance Tasks

The Inquiry Design Model blueprint features a variety of performance tasks that provide students with opportunities for learning and teachers with opportunities to evaluate what students know and are able to do. Based on the idea that assessments serve instructional as well as evaluative purposes, the IDM features both formative and summative performance tasks as well as extension activities, and opportunities for taking informed action.

Can Words Lead to War?

New York State Social Studies Framework Key Ideas & Practices	**7.7 REFORM MOVEMENTS**: Social, political, and economic inequalities sparked various reform movements and resistance efforts. Influenced by the Second Great Awakening, New York State played a key role in major reform efforts. ☑ Gathering, Using, and Interpreting Evidence ☑ Chronological Reasoning and Causation ☑ Comparison and Contextualization
Staging the Question	Consider the power of words and examine a video of students using words to try to bring about positive change.

Supporting Question 1	Supporting Question 2	Supporting Question 3	Supporting Question 4
How did Harriet Beecher Stowe describe slavery in *Uncle Tom's Cabin*?	What led Harriet Beecher Stowe to write *Uncle Tom's Cabin*?	How did people in the North and South react to *Uncle Tom's Cabin*?	How did *Uncle Tom's Cabin* affect abolitionism?
Formative Performance Task	**Formative Performance Task**	**Formative Performance Task**	**Formative Performance Task**
Write a summary of the plot of *Uncle Tom's Cabin* that includes main ideas and supporting details from Stowe's description of slavery in the book.	List four quotes in the sources that point to Stowe's motivation and write a paragraph explaining her motivation.	Make a T-chart comparing viewpoints expressed in newspaper reviews of *Uncle Tom's Cabin* and make a claim about the differences.	Participate in a structured discussion regarding the impact *Uncle Tom's Cabin* had on abolitionism.
Featured Source	**Featured Source**	**Featured Source**	**Featured Source**
Source A: Summary of *Uncle Tom's Cabin* **Source B:** Excerpts from *Uncle Tom's Cabin* **Source C:** Illustrations from *Uncle Tom's Cabin*	**Source A:** Harriet Beecher Stowe's concluding remarks to *Uncle Tom's Cabin*. **Source B:** Letter from Harriet Beecher Stowe to Lord Thomas Denman	**Source A:** Review of *Uncle Tom's Cabin* published in the *Boston Morning Post* **Source B:** Review of *Uncle Tom's Cabin* published in the *Southern Press Review*	**Source A:** Excerpt from Charles Sumner's Senate speech **Source B:** Article by John Ball Jr. published in *The Liberator* **Source C:** Sales of *Uncle Tom's Cabin*, 1851–1853

Summative Performance Task	**ARGUMENT** Can words lead to war? Construct an argument (e.g., detailed outline, poster, essay) that discusses the impact of *Uncle Tom's Cabin* using specific claims and relevant evidence from historical sources, while acknowledging competing views.
	EXTENSION Create an educational video of the argument that responds to the compelling question "Can words lead to war?"
Taking Informed Action	**UNDERSTAND** Identify and describe a human rights issue that needs to be addressed (e.g., child labor, trafficking, or poverty). **ASSESS** Create a list of possible actions that involve words. This may include letters, editorials, social media, videos, and protests. **ACT** Choose one of the options and implement it as an individual, small group, or class project.

The complete inquiry is available to all teachers at https://c3teachers.org/inquires

Following the C3 Inquiry Arc, IDM begins with a compelling question (Dimension 1) that is consistently answered in the form of an evidence-based argument (Dimension 4). In this way, the structure of the students' summative product is *convergent*—that is, each of the 84 inquiries in the Toolkit results in the construction of an evidence-based argument that answers the compelling question. Students have opportunities for *divergent* thinking through the extension activities and exercises in taking informed action.

Although the extension activities and exercises in taking informed action in the 84 inquiries allow students to express their arguments creatively, the heart of each inquiry rests between two points— the compelling question and the argument that defines the summative performance task. What comes between (e.g., supporting questions, formative performance tasks, and sources) is designed to prepare students to move constructively between the compelling question and the summative argument. In the seventh-grade *Uncle Tom's Cabin* inquiry, for example, the summative performance task begins with the compelling question followed by the phrase, "construct an argument." The verb *construct* was purposefully chosen to indicate that not all arguments must take the form of an essay.

In order to make a strong argument, students must engage with content and skills throughout an inquiry. Dimensions 2 and 3 of the C3 Framework help to provide clarity about the skills and conceptual knowledge that move students from question to argument. The formative performance tasks within the inquiry are designed as *exercises* intended to move students toward success in constructing a coherent, evidence-based argument. Although these tasks do not include all of what students might need to know, they do include the major ideas that provide a foundation for their arguments. In this way, teachers avoid "gotcha" assessments—tasks that catch students off guard or without the proper preparation for success on the summative performance task.

Sales of *Uncle Tom's Cabin*

Date	Sales
June 5, 1851–April 1, 1852	A serial publication in the *National Era* magazine has a circulation of about 8,000
March 20, 1852–April 1, 1852	The first printing of 5,000 copies of *Uncle Tom's Cabin* sells out in two weeks.
April 2, 1852–April 15, 1852	The second printing of 5,000 copies of *Uncle Tom's Cabin* also sells out in two weeks.
May 1852	Sales of the first edition reach 50,000
September 1852	Sales of the first edition reach 75,000
October 1852	Sales of the first edition reach 100,000
Holiday season, 1852	3,000 copies of a special illustrated edition are sold
January 1853	30,000 copies are sold of a new "Edition for the Million"
February 1853	The first foreign language version is printed in German
1852	Another 100,000 copies of a special edition printed in England are sold
Early 1853	Sales of various editions reach 310,000
End of 1853	Sales reach 1 million worldwide

Chart showing printing and sales figures for the book *Uncle Tom's Cabin*, 1851–1853. The chart is used as a source in the inquiry.

The formative performance tasks are framed by the supporting questions within the inquiry. In this way, the formative performance tasks and the supporting questions have a similar relationship to that of the summative argument and the compelling question. Moreover, the formative performance tasks increase in complexity so that students can build and practice the skills of evidence-based claim making.

In the *Uncle Tom's Cabin* inquiry, these formative performance tasks provide opportunities to develop the knowledge (e.g., an understanding of the book and its historical context) and practice the skills (e.g., reading sources and supporting claims with evidence) necessary to construct a coherent, evidenced-based argument. The sequence of the formative tasks is as follows:

1. Write a summary of the plot of *Uncle Tom's Cabin* that includes main ideas and supporting details from Stowe's description of slavery in the book.

2. List four quotes in the sources that point to Stowe's motivation and write a paragraph explaining her motivation.

3. Make a T-chart comparing viewpoints expressed in newspaper reviews of *Uncle Tom's Cabin* and make a claim about the differences.

4. Participate in a structured discussion regarding the impact *Uncle Tom's Cabin* had on abolitionism.

Far more than busy work, formative performance tasks are designed as exercises to support student growth and success when approaching the summative task.

Building on the purpose and structure of the summative and formative performance tasks, extension exercises highlight the alternative ways in which students may express their arguments. Such activities are in keeping with the C3 Framework, which asks students to (a) present adaptations of their arguments; (b) do so with a range of audiences; and (c) do so in a variety of venues outside of the classroom. Unlike the summative argument, extension activities are *divergent* in that the products vary from inquiry to inquiry. For example, in the *Uncle Tom's Cabin* Inquiry, students have the opportunity to adapt their arguments into a digital documentary. In the other Toolkit inquiries, adaptations range from writing letters to the editor, engaging in a classroom debate, and participating in perspective-taking exercises.

Experiences in taking informed action are designed so that students can civically engage with the content of an inquiry. Informed action can take numerous forms (e.g., discussions, debates, presentations) and can occur in a variety of contexts both inside and outside of the classroom. The key to any action, however, is the idea that it is informed.

Eliza comes to tell Uncle Tom that he has been sold and that she is running away to save her child.

The IDM, therefore, stages the activities for taking informed action so that students build their knowledge and understanding of an issue before engaging in any social action. In the *understand* stage, students demonstrate that they can think about the issues behind the inquiry in a new setting or context. The *assess* stage asks students to consider alternative perspectives, scenarios, or options as they begin to define a possible set of actions. And the *act* stage is where students decide if and how they will put into effect the results of their planning.

In the *Uncle Tom's Cabin* inquiry, taking informed action is expressed as three steps at the conclusion of the inquiry:

- *Understanding*: Identify and describe a modern issue that needs reform (e.g., child labor, trafficking, poverty).
- *Assessing*: Create a list of possible actions that involve words, such as letters, editorials, social media, videos, and protests.
- *Acting*: Choose one of the options for taking informed action and implement it as an individual, small group, or class project.

Taking informed action is included within all 84 inquiries in the Toolkit, but we acknowledge that teachers may not be able to enact the sequence due to time constraints. In some cases, taking informed action is embedded into the formative and summative performance tasks to ease the time burden on teachers and to make civic opportunities more seamless within the inquiry.

Sources

With compelling and supporting questions in place, along with a series of formative and summative performance tasks, the use of sources completes the IDM model. Sources provide the substance and the content for an inquiry.

In the process of constructing an inquiry, teachers can use sources in three ways:

- To spark and sustain student curiosity in an inquiry;
- To build students' disciplinary (content and conceptual) knowledge and skills;
- To enable students to construct arguments with evidence.

These three uses of sources correspond with parts of the IDM blueprint: staging the compelling question, formative performance tasks, summative performance tasks, and additional tasks (i.e., extensions and taking informed action exercises).

Sparking curiosity is about engaging students as they initiate and sustain an inquiry. Just how to generate curiosity is, in large part, a pedagogical issue. The IDM suggests that sources can play an important role in helping students become curious about and interested in knowing more about an inquiry topic.

Each of the inquiries offers a 10 to 30-minute activity called *Staging the Compelling Question* to spark student curiosity activities. In the *Uncle Tom's Cabin* inquiry, students are asked to react to a quote by Nathaniel Hawthorne:

> Words—so innocent and powerless as they are, as standing in a dictionary, how potent for good and evil they become in the hands of one who knows how to combine them.[3]

After reading the quote, students discuss the following prompts: Does what you say matter? Does how you say something matter? How responsible should we be for the words we say and write? Next, teachers might ask students about a time when they spoke up for something they thought was unfair. This should appeal to a student's sense of fairness and introduce the idea that words can also create positive change. Using the ideas generated from the class discussion on the Hawthorne source, teachers can begin to stage the compelling question "Can words lead to war?" and set the historical stage for the inquiry.

Throughout an inquiry, students encounter sources to build their disciplinary knowledge (content and concepts) and skills (e.g., historical thinking, or geographic reasoning). The C3 Framework encourages shifting instructional practice to integrate disciplinary knowledge and disciplinary skills purposefully.[4] The inquiries in the Toolkit put this idea into practice through the formative and summative performance tasks.

The image (on page 60) is a source for the first formative performance task in the inquiry on *Uncle Tom's Cabin*. As such, it provides a powerful visual representation of an important episode in the book and key content in the inquiry. In this illustration, Eliza comes to tell Uncle Tom and his wife, Chloe, that Tom in addition to Eliza's son, Harry, have been sold to a slave trader. Eliza had just overheard the news from her master, Mr. Shelby, that the trader will arrive in the morning to take Tom and Harry away. In a panic, Eliza plans that night to run away. The illustration and other sources in the task (another illustration and four text passages) collectively give students an opportunity to build their understanding about how Harriet Beecher Stowe described slavery through the fictionalized experiences of the characters in the book.

The summative performance task in the IDM calls on students to construct and support arguments, and sources play a big role in that process. Throughout an inquiry, students examine sources through the sequence of formative performance tasks. Doing so allows students to develop the knowledge they need in order to build arguments through evidence-based claims.

Each of the sources in this inquiry holds the potential to contribute to the arguments students might make. For example, the source on "Sales of *Uncle Tom's Cabin*" is useful as evidence in establishing the popularity of *Uncle Tom's Cabin*. Using this source, students might make an inference that the popularity of this book reflected a larger abolitionist sentiment in the country. This information, combined with other information from sources, can be used as evidence to make claims about the impact of the book.

It is rare that a source, as created, will be perfectly suited for use in an inquiry. Instead, most of the sources in the inquiries serve as interpretative materials. Some sources, such as photographs, may be used as they are in an inquiry, but many sources require adaptation in one of three ways:

- *Excerpting*. This involves using a portion of the source for the inquiry. Care should be taken to preserve information in the source that students may need to know about the creator and context of the source.
- *Modifying*. This involves inserting definitions and/or changing the language of a text. Modifying texts increases the accessibility of sources.
- *Annotating*. This involves adding short descriptions or explanations. Annotations allow teachers to set a background context for sources.

Examples of each of these three approaches to adapting sources are evident in the seventh-grade inquiry on *Uncle Tom's Cabin*.

- *Excerpting*—Text passages from *Uncle Tom's Cabin* are all carefully selected passages from a larger text.
- *Modifying*—The summary of *Uncle Tom's Cabin* was slightly modified to add information about the story that was

missing from the original source.

- *Annotating*—The illustrations include annotations.

Some observers may object to making changes to sources, arguing that changing sources does more harm than good. When considering this point, teachers should keep in mind the purpose of the source in the inquiry and ask themselves whether they are using the source for the source's sake or to accomplish some other learning goal. It is probably rare to need to use sources just for the sake of using the original source.

Bringing it all together

The Inquiry Design Model takes inquiry as its general starting point. A compelling question serves to initiate an inquiry. A summative performance task, where students address that question, serves to pull the inquiry together. The beginning and end points are important, but no more so than the elements—supporting questions, formative performance tasks, and sources—that comprise the middle of the Inquiry Design Model.

Using inquiry as the descriptor for the curriculum topics portrayed, however, reflects a specific, conscious decision not to produce fully developed and comprehensive curriculum units or modules. Teachers should find considerable guidance within each inquiry around the key components of instructional design— questions, tasks, and sources. What they will not find is a complete set of prescriptive lesson plans. Experience suggests that teachers teach best the material that they mold around their particular students' needs and the contexts in which they teach. Rather than scripts reflecting generic teaching and learning situations, the IDM encourages teachers to draw on their own wealth of teaching experience as they add activities, lessons, sources, and tasks that transform the inquiries into their own, individual pedagogical plans.

Notes
1. Harriet B. Stowe, *Uncle Tom's Cabin*, 1st ed. Boston: John P. Jewett and Company, 1852. Public Domain.
2. J. Bruner, *The Process of Education* (Cambridge, Mass.: Harvard University Press, 1960): 33.
3. N. Hawthorne, "American Note-Books of Nathaniel Hawthorne," *The Atlantic Monthly* 18, no. 110, December 1866. Public Domain.
4. K. Swan, J.K. Lee, and S.G. Grant, *C3 Instructional Shifts*. C3teachers.org, 2014. Available online at www.c3teachers.org/c3shifts/.

Social Education **82, no. 3 (2018): 133–137**

Questions, Tasks, Sources:
Focusing on the Essence of Inquiry

Kathy Swan, John Lee, and S.G. Grant

How many times should I do inquiry in a year? This is the number one question educators ask us about inquiry, and we understand why. One of the inescapable challenges to inquiry is its lack of efficiency in "covering" content. Inquiry necessarily takes longer than direct instruction and this can be problematic for teachers struggling to find time to cover the breadth of content outlined in most social studies courses. As a result, we often suggested that teachers begin with two to four inquiries a year, believing that a couple of meaningful inquiry experiences a year is better than none.

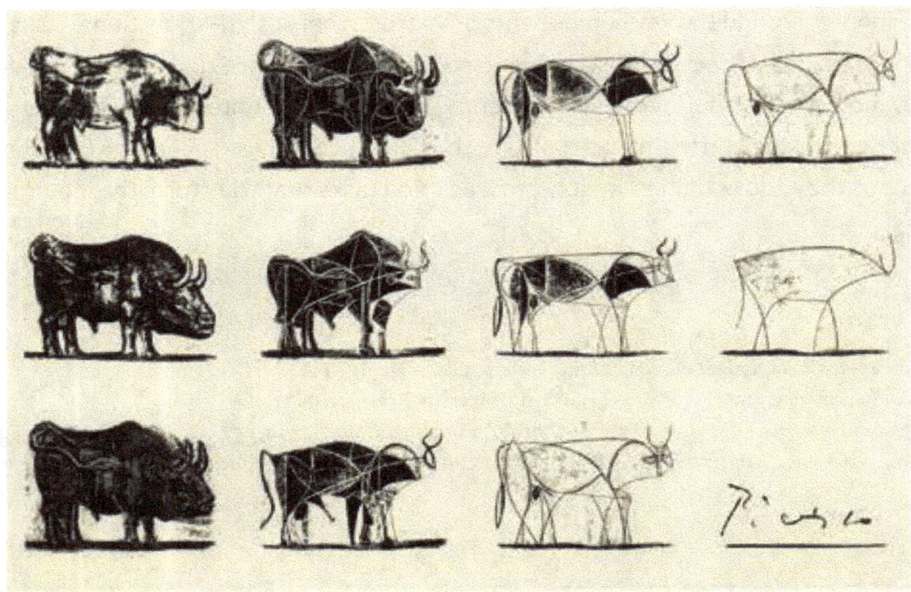

Figure 1: Picasso's representations of a bull (Picasso, 1945–1946)

Impressed by C3 teachers who have embraced and tinkered with the Inquiry Design Model (IDM) blueprint,[1] we are now rethinking our original response. These innovative IDM practitioners have reached out to show us how they have played with the elements of inquiry so that they can weave inquiry into the fabric of their courses not twice a year, but as part of their daily instruction. That is, when they look at *doing* inquiry, they have made a compelling question, an argumentative task, and a set of sources the centerpiece of every (or almost every) lesson or unit. As a result, we have developed a new answer to the persistent question: How many times should I do inquiry in a year?

To answer that question, we offer an analogy. We have been inspired recently by a set of 11 lithograph drawings by Pablo Picasso titled *Bull* (1945–1946).[2] In this series, Picasso visually dissects the figure of a bull by moving from a representative drawing to increasingly more abstract drawings until he whittles the bull down to its essence. (Figure 1 presents a composite of these drawings.) Even as the drawings shed details such as the fur and muscles and begin to morph with Cubist and minimalist technique, they retain the core elements of a bull and can be recognized as such.

Not unlike Picasso, who investigated the figure and form of a bull, teachers experimenting with inquiry have sought to get to the essence of inquiry through its central elements.[3] Those elements—questions-tasks-sources—represent the whittling down of a fully fleshed out IDM blueprint while retaining the essence of the original.

We have paid attention to these early adopters and started playing with an adaptation that we are calling a *focused* blueprint. In this article, we walk through the architecture of a focused blueprint on Pearl Harbor, demonstrating how the contraction of a blueprint can enable teachers to overcome the time constraints of protracted inquiry and to become increasingly artistic in their implementation of inquiry.

Focused Inquiry

The original IDM blueprint is structured so that students explore a compelling question through supporting questions, formative and summative performance tasks, and a range of disciplinary sources.[4] The inquiry crescendos into an evidence-based argument, which can be broadened through an expressive extension and/or a civic experience. Teachers play an important role in this process by engaging students in the compelling question, scaffolding their source work, and ensuring they are mastering the content and developing skills through the successive formative performance tasks. Ultimately, we suggest that teaching the IDM blueprint will take between 4–7 days of instruction.

But teachers do not always have 4–7 days of instruction for any one topic. Many IDM-inspired teachers want more flexibility in its implementation, so they can target particular content and skills. These teachers have mined IDM for its essence—questions, tasks, and sources—and have treated the blueprint as a pedagogical accordion expanding and contracting based on the needs of their students as well as their curricular scope and sequence. Some have expanded outward, developed longer inquiry units, while others have condensed in ways represented by the focused inquiry concept.

In these new focused inquiries, there is still a compelling question to be answered by an evidenced-based argument, but the question is narrower in scope and the argumentative task is condensed to a single claim and counterclaim. Instead of 3–4 supporting questions with the attendant formative tasks and disciplinary sources, there are only 1–2. Staging the compelling question has always been a limited exercise, so it remains as is in a focused inquiry. The end of the blueprint, which can stretch out if desired, features either an extension or an action opportunity, but not both. Overall, the focused inquiry shrinks the instructional demands to one class period.

It is important to note that focused inquiries are still grounded in the core elements of the original blueprint— questions, tasks, and sources. Teachers tell us that having flexibility allows them to stitch together different kinds of inquiry-based experiences, increase their frequency, and move their practice so that inquiry lives in—rather than simply visits—their classroom. When we asked C3 Teacher Ryan New how often he does inquiry, he promotes its everyday value:

> Since IDM, I have made questions, tasks, and sources the soul of my instructional practice. I have found that if you only visit inquiry now and again, then students will never develop proficiency with the skills the inquiry process teaches—that is, to become discerning and engaged citizens. If students experience inquiry every day, they develop the habits of mind that makes these larger, nobler civic goals possible.

We agree with Ryan and teachers like him. In the section that follows, we walk through a focused inquiry and highlight its key elements noting, where appropriate, the differences between the focused and the standard blueprint.

Anatomy of a *Focused* Inquiry: Did the Attack on Pearl Harbor Unify America?

The Inquiry Design Model is rooted in the *blueprint*, a one-page representation of the common elements of inquiry-based practice—questions, tasks, and sources. Whether you are looking at the original or a focused adaptation, the blueprint offers a visual snapshot of an entire inquiry such that the individual components *and* the relationship among the components can all be seen at once. As such, the two blueprint forms have a similar structure: (1) compelling and supporting *questions* that frame and organize this inquiry; (2) formative and summative performance tasks that provide opportunities for students to demonstrate and apply their understandings; and (3) the disciplinary *sources* that allow students access to the relevant content as they practice disciplinary thinking and reasoning (See Figure 2).

Questions

Questions are a foundational component of any form of inquiry. In the Inquiry Design Model, questions come in two forms—compelling and supporting. Compelling questions initiate an inquiry and supporting questions help to unpack important content and/or concepts embedded within the compelling question.

A good compelling question is both academically rigorous and personally relevant to students. For example, the compelling question "Did the attack on Pearl Harbor unify America?" is academically rigorous and calls on students to conduct an inquiry in the tradition of social history, where they examine the activities of people who are sometimes overlooked. The question of how everyday people responded to Pearl Harbor is not as simple as it may seem at first. Students quickly find that the men and women "on the street" were practically unanimous in support of a declaration of war. But other questions linger. How long did people expect the war to last? Why did people think Japan took such a risk in attacking the United States? Who was to blame for what was sure to be a bloody conflict? What was the larger meaning of the war? Why should Americans respond to injustice abroad when injustices at home linger on?

By examining the hidden voices in history through "man on the street" interviews, students are able to tap into unconventional or unexamined narratives from the past. Doing so satisfies the second criteria of a compelling question—the question must be interesting to students. Many students feel their voices often go unheard so examining similarly unrecognized voices helps them understand that everyday actors can still play important roles in history.

Focused inquiries retain the general substance of a compelling question, but tend to be narrower in the scope of content examined. Many IDM inquiries focus on broader topics or ideas (e.g., voting rights, the French Revolution, or westward migration). Compelling questions in a focused inquiry typically explore a particular event, person, or concept. By design, these blueprints abbreviate the investigation with only 1–2 supporting questions. In the Pearl Harbor inquiry, the supporting question "What did people say about American involvement at the beginning of the war?" helps students see the historic event through multiple perspectives and to determine if the voices were unified.

Figure 2: A focused inquiry on Pearl Harbor

Pearl Harbor *Focused* Inquiry

	Did the attack on Pearl Harbor unify America?
C3 Framework Indicator	D2.His.4.9-12. Analyze complex and interacting factors that influenced perspectives of people during different historical eras.
Staging the Question	Listen to FDR's "Day of Infamy" Speech and read the description of the Library of Congress collection, After the Day of Infamy: "Man-on-the-Street" Interviews Following the Attack on Pearl Harbor. Predict what people across the country said about going to war with Japan.

Supporting Question
What did people say about American involvement at the beginning of the war?

Formative Performance Task
Create a graphic organizer that categorizes the different reactions that everyday Americans had to the attack on Pearl Harbor.

Featured Sources
Source A: "Man-on-the-Street," New York, New York, December 8, 1941 Source B: "Dear Mr. President," New York, New York, January or February 1942 Source C: "Man-on-the-Street," Austin, Texas, December 9, 1941 Source D: "Man-on-the-Street," Nashville, Tennessee, December 1941 Source E: "Dear Mr. President," New York, New York, January or February 1942 Source F: "Dear Mr. President," Minneapolis, Minnesota, January or February 1942

Summative Performance Task	**ARGUMENT** Did the attack on Pearl Harbor unify America? Construct a claim and a counterclaim that address the compelling question using historical evidence.
	EXTENSION Examine the story of Pearl Harbor told by a history textbook and propose revisions based on the perspectives represented in the featured sources

Tasks

The heart of each inquiry, however, rests between two points—the compelling question and the summative argument. The formative work (i.e., supporting questions, formative performance tasks, and featured sources) is designed to prepare students to move constructively between those two points. In a focused inquiry, the argument includes a single claim and counter claim. Because the compelling question is narrower, the inquiry has only 1–2 formative performance tasks.

In the Pearl Harbor inquiry, the formative performance task calls on students to use a graphic organizer to categorize the reactions of six American citizens to the attack. This work, along with the background information gleaned in the Staging the Compelling question exercise, allows students to move quickly to the summative claim-making task. Ultimately, students do not construct a fully developed argument but make a single evidence-based claim like the ones below:

- Many Americans felt the attack on Pearl Harbor was a galvanizing event that unified Americans in entering the war.

- Evidence to support this claim can be found in an interview with a clerical worker named Frank Tatrey: *I think the time has come when we should all get behind our country. After all, we are all Americans and we should all be united against these dictator countries who are trying to invade our country and spoil our way of living.*
- Some Americans felt the war at home against anti-Semitism and Jim Crow laws was more significant than the war abroad.
  - Evidence to support this claim can be found in an interview with a college student named David Heldeld: *We feel that as long as we have fascism at home it is rather futile to fight it on the outside if we are not at the same time fighting it from within.*
- Some Americans wanted to join the war effort long before the attack on Pearl Harbor.
  - Evidence to support this claim can be found in an interview with a YMCA secretary in Nashville, Tennessee, named Fadie France: *This war situation had to reach a head soon. The United States was bound to enter this war. Just what the fuse was supposed to be was the only uncertain factor.*

Building on the summative claim-making task, students are able to extend their understanding creatively or civically through either an Extension or Taking Informed Action task. The Pearl Harbor inquiry asks students to examine the story of Pearl Harbor as written in their history textbook and propose revisions based on source work from the inquiry.

Sources

Sources complete the IDM model. Disciplinary sources require students to dig into the materials and to apply their analytical skills to move the inquiry forward.

The Pearl Harbor inquiry features a set of sources from a special collection of "Man on the Street Interviews" at the Library of Congress (www.loc.gov/collections/interviews-following-the-attack-on-pearl-harbor/about-this-collection/).The following excerpt from the collection describes their origin:

> On December 8, 1941 (the day after the Japanese attack on Pearl Harbor), Alan Lomax, then "assistant in charge" of the Archive of American Folk Song (now the American Folklife Center archive), sent a telegram to fieldworkers in ten different localities across the United States, asking them to collect "man-on-the-street" reactions of ordinary Americans to the bombing of Pearl Harbor and the subsequent declaration of war by the United States. A second series of interviews, called "Dear Mr. President," was recorded in January and February 1942.[5]

The Pearl Harbor inquiry heavily excerpts six of the interviews included in the collection. An example of two of the sources are included in the center column of this page.

Focused inquiries need to have sources that align closely with the outcomes planned for the inquiry. That's just good inquiry design. But it will require that teachers make good decisions about what to include. No fluff here. Through focused inquiry, teachers direct students to the heart of the matter, carefully selecting, excerpting, and adapting sources so students are able to efficiently access the content they will need to complete the inquiry tasks.

Carl Nimkov: My name is Carl Nimkov. I came to this country three years ago from Germany. Today, when I heard the president's speech and I saw the United States enter this war, I was fully in favor of this declaration and I think that the United States' entry in this war will bring to a sooner close this great tragedy and will have a very beneficial effect to the future state of the world.
Source: https://www.loc.gov/item/afc1941004_sr06/

Interviewer: The next person to speak is W.C. Curry, FSA Fellow from Newport News, Virginia.

W. C. Curry: The Japanese attack on the United States and the imminent threat of Italian and German aggression is a direct result of the appeasement policies towards these countries since 1934. The naval defeat Sunday and the unpreparedness of the United States is mainly due to the pro-fascist forces within this country. This is the gravest period in our country's history. One of the gravest dangers at this time is not from abroad, but lies in those fascist-minded forces within. Courage, vigilance, and dogged determination to win should be our slogan.

The Negro as in every other crisis in our country's history will laudably distinguish himself in the defense of these United States, his country. And will also equally share in the better world which the ultimate victory will bring.
Source: https://www.loc.gov/item/afc1941004_sr05/

In this inquiry, the sources were curated so that the individual voices contrasted with one another, providing multiple perspectives on the event. Additionally, each source sheds new light on the Japanese attack by providing contextual information about the individuals and the time they were written. In the first source, Carl Nimkov, a recent German immigrant, speaks about the "future state of the world." In the second source, W.C. Curry asks the interviewer to consider issues of appeasement, fascism, and race as we entered the war. As students move through the sources, they learn more about important content (e.g., German immigration, appeasement, and fascism) and see how individual voices were unified in some ways but often different in their reaction to the attack on Pearl Harbor.

Conclusion

Abbreviating inquiry into a 1- to 2-day lesson means some ideas are going to be left on the cutting room floor. But that is true for curriculum in general. Teachers must make decisions about what to teach within the allotted time for social studies. Although content breadth is an opportunity cost of inquiry, it is important to remember what students gain in the process of inquiry. When students work with the elements of inquiry, they wrestle with important questions, mine disciplinary sources for answers and insight, craft evidenced-based claims/counterclaims, and then communicate their conclusions expressively or civically. If given a chance to do this process repeatedly, students become more proficient at it, helping us achieve the goals set out in the C3 Framework.

In a recent article, Parker talks about inquiry experiences as the *spine* of the curriculum:

But here's the secret sauce: At the heart of deeper learning is curriculum, not instruction. Before implementing instructional strategies, teachers need to make strategic decisions about the content and skills to be learned—those that will be learned deeply, iteratively, rather than only "covered."[6]

The Inquiry Design Model aims in the same direction by organizing curriculum around the foundations of inquiry: questions, tasks, and sources. Spines provide structure but must be able to flex. By collapsing (or expanding) a standard blueprint, we are illustrating how the IDM can operate as a curricular framework that flexes to meet the contextual needs of teachers.

Several focused inquiries including the one above have recently been published on C3 Teachers (www.c3teachers.org/). Additionally, blank focused inquiry blueprints are available for download on the site. We invite you to begin playing around with the newest blueprint and help us populate the site with interesting focused inquiries.

Notes

1. S.G. Grant, Kathy Swan, and John Lee, *Inquiry-Based Practice in Social Studies Education: The Inquiry Design Model* (New York: Routledge, 2017); Kathy Swan, John Lee, and S.G. Grant, *The Inquiry Design Model: Building Inquiries in Social Studies* (Silver Spring, Md.: National Council for the Social Studies and C3 Teachers, 2018).
2. Pablo Picasso, *The Bull* (*Le Taureau*) [Painting]. (1945–1946). Estate of Pablo Picasso, Museum of Fine Arts, Boston.
3. Grant, Swan, and Lee, *Inquiry-Based Practice in Social Studies Education*.
4. Ibid; Swan, Lee, and Grant, *The Inquiry Design Model: Building Inquiries in Social Studies*.
5. "Dear Mr. President" collection (AFC 1942/003), American Folklife Center, Library of Congress, www.loc.gov/collections/interviews-following-the-attack-on-pearl-harbor/about-this-collection/;"Man-on-the-Street" interviews collection (AFC 1941/004), American Folklife Center, Library of Congress, www.loc.gov/collections/interviews-following-the-attack-on-pearl-harbor/
6. Walter Parker, "Projects as the Spine of the Course: Design for Deeper Learning," *Social Education* 82, no. 1 (2018), 48.

References

National Council for the Social Studies. *College, Career, and Civic Life (C3) Framework for Social Studies State Standards*. Silver Spring, Md., 2013.

Social Education **82**, no. 1 (2018): 14–17

Making Inquiry Critical: Examining Power and Inequity in the Classroom

Ryan M. Crowley and LaGarrett J. King

What does it mean to approach inquiry from a critical perspective? It is not quite as simple as it may sound. We use the term *critical* in a way that is distinct from the broader educational goal of encouraging critical thinking. Although critical thinking is a crucial skill, our use of "critical" refers specifically to the use of critical theory.

Critical theory is one of the predominant schools of thought in the social sciences. Like all theory, it is a framework used for explaining—and examining—something about the world. Critical theory pays special attention to the social world, focusing on the hierarchical nature of social relations and examining how these unequal power relationships lead to privilege for some and oppression for others.[1]

Researching, teaching, learning, thinking, and taking action within critical theory call for engaging in ongoing "social critique [that is] tied … to raised consciousness of the possibility of … liberating social change."[2] In other words, critical theory is about identifying and confronting social injustices with the goal of transforming those unjust social relations. Current research and activism undertaken from a critical perspective often focuses on racism, sexism, ableism, class bias, cultural bias, religious intolerance, heterosexism, and other forms of structural and individual discrimination.

Roots of Critical Theory

Although current ideas about critical theory are quite broad, most observers trace its roots to a group of intellectuals who founded the Institute for Social Research (known as the Frankfurt School) in Germany in the 1920s.[3] These thinkers sought to extend Marxist theory into the changing social, political, and economic landscape of the twentieth century by talking about how culture and ideology encourage and sustain social inequality. Although their work was diverse, a primary thrust focused on how modern capitalist societies acted as new, and subtler, forms of social control. These societies manufactured consent by creating a level of affluence and consumption that obscured ongoing inequality. Critical theorists argued that this consumer culture helped to create an illusion of freedom that prevented individuals from seeing that they were not the autonomous actors they seemed to be.[4]

Although their specific societal critiques still resonate today, the Frankfurt School's extension of Karl Marx's call to produce knowledge and to take action from the standpoint of the oppressed may be its greatest impact. This movement inspired subsequent scholars and activists to engage in work as a "'transformative endeavor' unembarrassed by the label 'political' and unafraid to consummate a relationship with emancipatory consciousness."[5] Action taken from a critical perspective eschews neutrality, actively siding with the oppressed and promoting their liberation.

Critical Pedagogy

Critical theory's emphasis on emancipation is most visible in educational practice through critical pedagogy. This approach to teaching and learning centers an analysis of oppression and builds knowledge from the lived experiences of the participants.[6] Drawing inspiration from the writings of Brazilian educator Paulo Freire, critical pedagogues suggest that "the school curriculum should, in part, be shaped by problems that face teachers and students in their effort to live just and ethical lives."[7]

Freire critiqued traditional education for employing a "banking method" in which teachers deposited information into passive student recipients. In place of this model, he called for problem-posing education in which students generate questions, concerns, or themes crucial to their lives that then become the object of shared inquiry. Although the teacher does not relinquish all authority in this model, it places a greater emphasis on dialogue with and among students and on students as active creators of knowledge. Ultimately, critical pedagogy aims to help students become more conscious of their place in the world and consider how they can take action to create a more just, egalitarian society.[8]

Critical Social Studies Pedagogy

With citizenship education as its central mission and with content that allows for examination of past and current injustices, social studies should be a natural home for critical theory and critical pedagogy.[9] The adoption of the C3

Kenny Stancil teaching at Lafayette High School in Lexington, Kentucky.

Framework[10] and the development of the Inquiry Design Model[11] offer a useful template for implementing a critical social studies pedagogy. Inquiry-based practices position students as creators of knowledge and, when appropriate, allow students to pursue questions that are important to their lives and that touch upon important disciplinary knowledge.

However, as we outline in the next section, there are certain criteria that teachers should consider when attempting to make inquiry critical. When these standards are met, inquiry offers students the chance to identify social injustices, to build knowledge from the perspective of the oppressed, and to conceptualize action that disrupts the status quo.

Making Inquiry Critical

Constructing a critical inquiry requires a conceptualization process that may be foreign or uncomfortable to many social studies educators. Critical inquiries rely on teachers who question the commonsensical ways the world works and how social studies knowledge is presented. Teachers building critical social studies inquiries should begin with the premise that there is no such thing as neutral or objective knowledge. In contrast to traditional views of teaching as value-free, critical theory helps teachers see that knowledge is socially constructed and is beholden to how people see (or want to see) the world around them. People often construct their individual worldviews based on their personal experiences, so even when teachers believe they are being objective, they often do not account for their own biases and partial ways of knowing.[12]

Critical inquiries should be designed to identify and to challenge master narratives that legitimate systems of oppression and power. We define master narratives as overarching ideas, stories, and approaches within school curriculum that promote the worldviews of those in power in society. Master narratives shape belief systems and act to marginalize those in society who do not come from white, male, middle class, heterosexual, able-bodied, Christian, and other dominant identity group backgrounds. Critical inquiries should highlight what these master narratives ignore and provide counter-narratives that complicate and expand students' understanding of the world.[13]

Crafting a Critical Inquiry with the Inquiry Design Model

To help teachers construct a critical inquiry using the Inquiry Design Model (IDM) template,[14] we offer three important guidelines:

1. Ask compelling and supporting **questions** that explicitly critique systems of oppression and power;
2. Expose students to **sources** that include the perspectives of marginalized and oppressed groups;
3. Develop **tasks** and a Taking Informed Action activity that push students to take tangible steps toward alleviating the injustice explored in the inquiry.

To provide an example of these three components in action, we examine an IDM published on the Kentucky hub of the C3 Teachers site (https://c3teachers.org/kentucky-c3-hub/) focused on economic inequality: *Can we afford the super rich?*[15] The inquiry was designed by Kenny Stancil, a geography teacher at Lafayette High School in Lexington, Kentucky. We highlight and explain its critical dimensions as well as offer a few suggestions that could better align the inquiry with the goals of critical theory. *Asking critical questions.* First, drawing from the previous list, critical inquiries must ask questions that critique systems of oppression. One way to do this is to stay away from inquiries that ask limiting, exploratory *"what"* questions. Critical inquiries do more than merely explore a certain social studies event or phenomenon. For example, an inquiry that focuses on a topic like apartheid in South Africa, but only examines the reasons the system ended would not be considered a critical inquiry. Without an examination of the motivations behind apartheid and a discussion of the people who benefitted from it, students would not receive a critical perspective on the topic.

Critical inquiries should be concerned with the *why*, the *how*, and the *who* of a topic. For example, in Kenny's inquiry, *Can we afford the super rich?*, the compelling question is concerned with the *who* of economic inequality and considers *how* this inequality produces negative consequences. This inquiry questions whether extreme economic inequality is commensurate with democracy. Capitalism is rarely questioned within mainstream economics curricula in the United States. The master narrative within our economics courses implies that capitalism is the best (and, perhaps, only) economic system suitable for democratic nations. What is rarely exposed within the official curriculum is *who* benefits and *who* suffers from capitalism. Doing so is important to consider because a capitalist economy depends upon winners and losers to make it function. This IDM questions the viability of an unfettered free market and, in doing so, questions the value system of the United States.

Including the voices of the oppressed. The second criterion of a critical inquiry presumes that the viewpoints of oppressed groups should be central. Within the IDM framework, a critical inquiry should explore these voices through appropriate source selections. Economics education generally assumes that the free market has the ability to help everyone achieve their own piece of the American dream. Discussion of class stratification or the difficulties of upward class mobility rarely occurs, which largely silences poor and working class experiences.[16] By contrast, the IDM *Can we afford the super rich?* analyzes class dynamics directly and its sources highlight the plight of the unfortunate or the working class individual.

Sources such as "Only Little People Pay Taxes," "Congress Ignores the Poor Yet Again," and "The Ones We've Lost: The Student Loan Debt Suicides" center the effects of economic inequality by examining how government action (and inaction) benefits the wealthy at the expense of the poor.[17] Although these perspectives are a refreshing change from mainstream economic discourses, all of the sources are secondary in nature. Secondary sources are valuable, but we suggest that this critical inquiry would benefit from including accounts of individuals who are on the wrong end of the wealth divide. This addition would enhance its authenticity by putting faces and voices to the people victimized by economic policy.

Moving toward action in a critical inquiry. Finally, critical inquiries must provide students with opportunities to address the injustices identified in the inquiry. Within the IDM framework, Taking Informed Action (TIA)[18] creates this opportunity by encouraging students to extend the inquiry outside of the classroom. Of course, we understand that societal change is not going to occur through one inquiry. What TIA does, however, is aid in the development of a critical consciousness and create a disposition toward working for change. These are important steps in helping students imagine critical civic engagement within a democratic society.

Within *Can we afford the super rich?*, the TIA portion asks the students to invite members of the community, within and outside the school, to attend a townhall event to discuss the consequences of economic inequality. This civic action asks students to do something that can influence their community and invites collaboration. The action is also something that could reasonably be accomplished as a project outside of classroom time. For this activity to be effective, however, it would be important to pay attention to the participant list. In order to promote social change, the students and teacher should invite change makers and people from various walks of life. Participants should not only be the traditional "experts," but also parents, community organizers, union representatives, local store owners, and others who could help represent the views of the focal groups, the poor and working classes. The key for TIA within a critical inquiry is to help students understand where power resides in the topic of study and to devise actions that challenge those power mechanisms.

Concluding Thoughts

In this article, we hoped to make it clear that one must be purposeful when designing a critical inquiry. It is not quite as simple as examining a topic (e.g., Jim Crow, Indian Removal, same-sex marriage, the gender wage gap, Islamophobia) that could connect to social justice issues. To truly stay within the bounds of critical theory, there must be a focus on identifying unequal power relationships in society coupled with the goal of transforming those unjust social relations. To remain true to critical pedagogy, teachers should work to identify questions that are important to students' lives and that encourage them to reflect on the ways that they are either privileged or oppressed by social dynamics. And, finally, to enact these concepts in the context of the IDM, the inquiry must ask critical questions, analyze sources from the viewpoint of the oppressed, and encourage action that can make a tangible contribution toward justice.

Notes

1. When we use the term "oppression," we are referring to unjust treatment of subordinate social groups (e.g., women, racial/ethnic minorities, LGBTQ individuals) by dominant social groups (e.g., men, white people, heterosexuals) and not individual instantiations of suffering. In other words, prejudice + power = oppression.
2. Yvonne S. Lincoln, Susan Lynham, and Egon G. Guba, "Paradigmatic Controversies, Contradictions, and Emerging Confluences, Revisited," in *Handbook of Qualitative Research*, N.K. Denzin and Y.S. Lincoln, eds. (Thousand Oaks, Calif.: Sage Publications, 2011): 119.
3. M. Crotty, *The Foundations of Social Research* (London: Sage, 2003).
4. D. Strinati, *An Introduction to Theories of Popular Culture* (New York: Routledge, 2004).
5. Joe L. Kincheloe, Peter McLaren, and Shirley R. Steinberg, "Critical Pedagogy and Qualitative Research: Moving to the Bricolage," in *Handbook of Qualitative Research*, 164.
6. Joe L. Kincheloe, *Critical Pedagogy Primer* (New York: Peter Lang, 2008).
7. Kincheloe, McLaren, and Steinberg, "Critical Pedagogy," 165.
8. Paulo Freire, *Pedagogy of the Oppressed* (New York: Continuum, 2000).
9. Gloria Ladson-Billings, ed., *Critical Race Theory Perspectives on Social Studies: The Profession, Policies, and Curriculum* (Greenwich, Conn.: Information Age Publishing, 2003); Abraham P. DeLeon and E. Wayne Ross, eds., *Critical Theories, Radical Pedagogies, and Social Education: New Perspectives for Social Studies Education* (Rotterdam: Sense Publishers, 2010).
10. Read about and download the C3 Framework here: www.socialstudies.org/standards/c3.
11. The Inquiry Design Model (IDM) is a framework for creating inquiries that include the main elements of the Inquiry Arc of the C3 Framework. An IDM consists of three components: questions, tasks, and sources. To learn more about IDM, see S.G. Grant, Kathy Swan, and John Lee, *Inquiry-Based Practice in Social Studies Education: Understanding the Inquiry Design Model* (New York, N.Y.: Routledge and C3 Teachers, 2017).
12. For more information on critical social studies, see: Avner Segall, "Revitalizing Critical Discourses in Social Education: Opportunities for a More Complexified (Un) Knowing," *Theory & Research in Social Education* 41, no. 4 (2013): 476–493.
13. For more information on master narratives, see Derrick P. Aldridge, "The Limits of Master Narratives in History Textbooks: An Analysis of Representations of Martin Luther King, Jr." *Teachers College Record* 108, no. 4 (2006): 662; Bruce VanSledright, "Narratives of Nation-State, Historical Knowledge, and School History Education," *Review of Research in Education* 32, no. 1 (2008): 109–146.
14. Kathy Swan, John Lee, and S.G. Grant, *The Inquiry Design Model: Building Inquiries in Social Studies* (Washington, D.C.: National Council for the Social Studies and C3 Teachers, 2017).
15. The full inquiry available for download here: www.c3teachers.org/wp-content/uploads/2015/10/EconomicInequalityIDM_KYHub.pdf
16. See LaGarrett J. King and Shakealia Y. Finley, "Race is a Highway: Towards a Critical Race Economics Approach in Social Studies Classrooms," in *Doing Race in Social Studies: Critical Perspectives*, ed. P. Chandler (Greenwich, Conn.: Information Age Publishing. 2015): 195–228.
17. See Featured Sources at www.c3teachers.org/wp-content/uploads/2015/10/EconomicInequalityIDM_KYHub.pdf
18. To learn more about Taking Informed Action as a component of the IDM framework, read Meira Levinson and Peter Levine, "Taking Informed Action to Engage Students in Civic Life," *Social Education* 77, no. 6 (2013): 339–341.

Social Education **84, no. 6 (2020): 377–383**

Blueprinting an Inquiry-Based Curriculum: Planning with the Inquiry Design Model

Kathy Swan, S. G. Grant, and John Lee

Teachers introduced to the Inquiry Design Model (IDM) are often relieved to learn that inquiry isn't a fuzzy ideal, but rather is a curricular approach with a defined vernacular—questions, tasks, and sources. The inquiry blueprint is a one-page visual representation of the questions, tasks, and sources that define an inquiry.[1] In the blueprint, there are compelling and supporting questions, formative and summative performance tasks, and disciplinary sources that aid students in answering the inquiry's questions.

It is not uncommon to hear teachers say, "Ah, now I know what inquiry looks like!" after working through their own blueprints. That contentment, however, does not usually last long. The questions that teachers ask us include: How many times should they do inquiry in a year? When do students get to investigate their own questions? How can inquiry change over a year or course of study? Can I play with, change or alter the blueprint?

These questions and more surface as teachers move from an inquiry-based experience within a year (one blueprint) to inquiry-based experiences across a curriculum (multiple blueprints). But they worry that there won't be enough time, that students' interest will flag if teachers use a single blueprint model that doesn't appear to vary, or that students never get to ask and answer their own questions.

In this column, we feature answers to some of these questions and concerns. To do so, we draw on our recent book, *Blueprinting an Inquiry Curriculum: Planning with the Inquiry Design Model* to describe five different types of Inquiry

Ryan Lewis, a teacher at Woodford County High School in Versailles, Kentucky, works with students to build evidentiary claims.

Design Model blueprints that promote the kind of curriculum flexibility teachers need.[2]

Why another book on the Inquiry Design Model? We blame teachers! Every time our weekly conference calls turn to checkins about our kids and colleagues, up pops an email from a teacher who has done something so cool, so ambitious with the blueprint that we cannot help but expand our original IDM thinking. It turns out that the C3 Framework, the Inquiry Arc, and our original blueprint model featuring questions, tasks, and sources was just the beginning. Teachers have taught us that those three elements of inquiry provide a foundation for all kinds of blueprint configurations and ways to think about building an entire curriculum around IDM.

In our most recent book, we introduced the idea of moving from blueprinting a single inquiry to blueprinting an entire, inquiry-based curriculum. Structured Inquiry was our first blueprint design. We call it the "Coke Classic" because it presents all of the ideas that initially grounded our thinking about inquiry; questions, tasks, and sources have endured as central to IDM, regardless of blueprint type. Whether we design a one-calorie blueprint or add some cherry flavor to it, we always return to the structured blueprint as our starting place to teach about inquiry.

Over the last few years, we have developed four additional inquiry types for a total of five different kinds of blueprints: structured, focused, embedded action, guided, and student-directed. We use this array of blueprint types to think about the inquiry experience across a course of study. And we now talk about a curricular inquiry "loop" as a way to help teachers reinforce the content knowledge and skills essential to a rigorous and meaningful social studies education.[3]

Once teachers in a department or school collectively begin to loop inquiry, it opens up all sorts of possibilities to improve the perception of social studies by students, parents, administrators, and teacher colleagues in ways that make it more coherent, engaging, and ambitious.

Building a Curricular House of Inquiry

We argue that an inquiry-based curriculum allows students to explore the foundational elements of an inquiry—questions, tasks, and sources—through five different types of blueprints: structured, embedded action, focused, guided, and student-directed. Taken together, these configurations help teachers build out a variety of inquiry experiences for students that move from an isolated experience to a full school year. To envision that move and in keeping with our construction metaphor, we represent the relationship between these inquiry elements and inquiry types through the image of a house. (See Figure 1)

Foundation

The foundation of the House of Inquiry consists of inquiry's essential elements—questions, tasks, and sources. All inquiry blueprints have a compelling question as a starting place and supporting questions to scaffold the content of the inquiry. All inquiry blueprints have formative and summative tasks, which enable students to practice and demonstrate disciplinary and civic skills. And all inquiries ask students to use disciplinary sources as the building blocks of knowledge within an inquiry. These three components—questions, tasks, and sources—are both elemental and interdependent and, as such, are always present in an inquiry.[4]

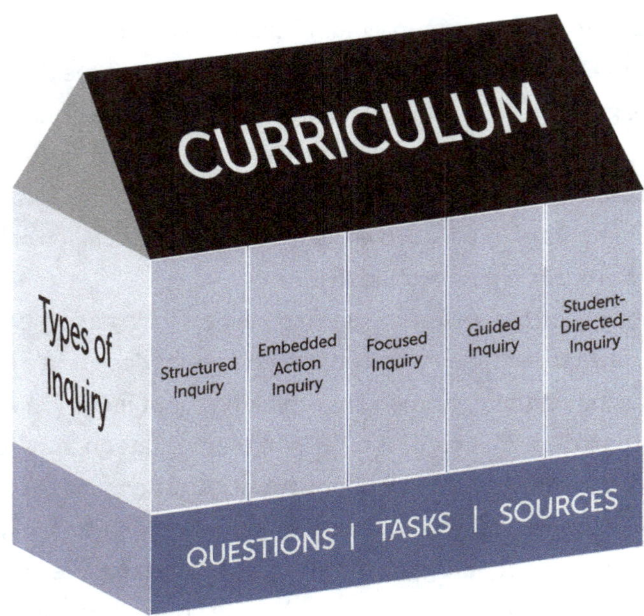

Figure 1: Building a Curricular House of Inquiry

Rooms

With questions, tasks, and sources as the foundation for the House of Inquiry, we offer five different rooms or types of inquiry in the IDM Curriculum House. (For a summary of the elements of these types of inquiry, see Table 1)

Structured Inquiry is the original blueprint type, about which we have written extensively.[5] In this inquiry approach, teachers develop a compelling question along with three to four supporting questions to guide the investigation. Students work through corresponding formative performance tasks and a summative argument task, an extension, and/or an informed action opportunity. Teachers select a series of disciplinary sources (typically 3–4 per supporting question) that enable students to explore the supporting question and complete the formative and summative tasks. This type of inquiry typically takes three to ten instructional periods and is developed by the teacher.

> **Example of a Structured Inquiry:** An example of a middle-level inquiry is one on the Great Compromise of 1787, which leads students through an investigation of the compelling question "Is compromise always fair?" The inquiry examines the Great Compromise that was reached during the Constitutional Convention and established the bicameral legislative structure of the United States and the representation that each state would have. Students work through four supporting questions, four corresponding formative performance tasks, and an array of featured sources in order to construct an evidence-based argument that answers the compelling question. Students examine the structure of government under the Articles of Confederation, investigate two proposals (Virginia and New Jersey plans) for a new arrangement, and analyze the role of the Connecticut Plan and the Great Compromise in the development of the United States Constitution. By completing this inquiry, students begin to understand the importance of compromise in democracies and to apply that knowledge in a mock Constitutional debate (the Extension) or in a Taking Informed Action exercise where students seek compromise around an issue related to representation in their school or community. See: www.c3teachers.org/inquiries/great-compromise

Embedded Action Inquiry allows students to practice taking informed action as an integrated part of the academic inquiry. Here, the compelling question is crafted around a social problem. The formative work (i.e., supporting questions, featured sources, and formative performance tasks) provides the instructional space whereby students examine the problem. Then, the summative argument task enables students to demonstrate what they know and how they might address the problem in a contemporary fashion. This type of inquiry generally takes five to ten instructional sessions and is developed primarily by the teacher, although the students determine the social issue they research and the action they take.

> **Example of an Embedded Action Inquiry:** A high school-level Public Policy inquiry leads students through an investigation of the debate over the Affordable Care Act (ACA). The compelling question—"Why is the Affordable Care Act so controversial?"—calls out the persistent arguments around this legislation and asks students to grapple with the roots of disagreements through the examination of the origins, opportunities, shortcomings, and constitutionality of the ACA. Throughout the inquiry, students work with a variety of data (e.g., polling numbers, graphical representations, and economic costs) and try to interpret, create, and analyze data and consider the reliability and trustworthiness of the sources. Students work through four supporting questions, four corresponding formative performance tasks, and an array of featured sources in order to construct an argument that answers the compelling question. However, in an embedded action inquiry, the Taking Informed Action exercise is built into the formative work. The first two supporting questions help students *understand* the problem, the last two supporting questions enable students to assess possible solutions to the problem, and then students *act* directly on their chosen solution(s) after completing the summative argument. See: www.c3teachers.org/inquiries/affordable-care-act

Focused Inquiry collapses the inquiry experience into a one-to-two-day lesson. In this blueprint, teachers develop a compelling question, but one that is narrow in scope. Doing so saves instructional time by necessitating only one to two supporting questions. The corresponding formative performance tasks are fewer, the summative argument task collapses to a single claim and/or counterclaim, and the end of the blueprint features either an extension or informed action opportunity, but not both. Lastly, teachers typically select fewer sources for students to explore, which further reduces the instructional time.

> **Example of a Focused Inquiry:** A high school-level inquiry on the Federal Debt leads students through an investigation of increasing federal deficits and the overall federal debt. The compelling question— "Does Debt Matter?"—focuses on a persistent source of political polarization; the debt is a current topic that sheds light on several national economic concepts such as taxation, federal government spending, government budgets, deficits, and the federal debt itself. Students work through two supporting questions, two corresponding formative performance tasks, and a small collection of featured sources in order to construct an argument that answers the compelling question. There is an Extension exercise included within this blueprint that asks students to create a proposal for the upcoming federal budget. See: www.c3teachers.org/wp-content/uploads/2020/03/2_DoesDebtMatter.pdf

Guided Inquiry provides students with an opportunity to become more independent within a teacher-developed inquiry. In this blueprint, teachers construct the compelling and supporting questions along with the corresponding formative and summative tasks. But they craft at least one independent research opportunity within the formative work in which students find the sources that help them answer the supporting question. Because of this additional research time, this type of inquiry may take a bit longer than a structured inquiry—up to 10 instructional sessions.

Example of a Guided Inquiry: A secondary-level inquiry on Civil Rights leads students through an investigation of the U.S. civil rights movement using the lens of nonviolent direct-action protest. The compelling question—"What made nonviolent protest effective during the civil rights movement?"—asks students to grapple with the means of achieving the various objectives of the movement for civil rights, including an end to segregation as well as the achievement of voting rights and true equality as citizens.

In this inquiry, students work as a whole group through the first supporting question, which focuses their study of non-violent protest on the individuals who participated in the Greensboro Sit-In. The next two supporting questions and corresponding tasks provide opportunities for students to hone their research skills. In the second supporting question, students work in collaborative groups focusing on the actors and actions in the Montgomery Bus Boycott, the Birmingham Bus Boycott, or the Selma to Montgomery marches. This work sets the stage for the third supporting question, which asks students to engage in an independent research experience investigating other actors who impacted the movement through non-violent means. As in all of the IDM inquiry types, students construct an argument in response to the compelling question and apply their knowledge in an Extension and/or Taking Informed Action exercise. See: www.c3teachers.org/inquiries/civil-rights

Student-Directed Inquiry occurs when students take on the development of the blueprint by defining the compelling and supporting questions, the formative and summative performance tasks, and the disciplinary sources for their inquiry. Teachers act in an advisory capacity nudging students' thinking about a topic, offering guidance about their investigative paths, and providing assistance in locating sources. Because students are working more independently around their own questions, tasks, and sources, this type of inquiry may take as many as two weeks of instructional time.

Example of a Student-Directed Inquiry: A high school-level Social Change inquiry leads students through an investigation of the LGBTQ+ movement, primarily driven by the history of the movement through various accounts and perspectives. What makes this inquiry unique is that it was developed by Wesley Wei, a student at Boyle County High School in Kentucky. Like other inquiry types, student-directed inquiry begins with a topic that is fashioned into a compelling question that is both interesting to the student crafting it and is academically worthwhile. Wesley argued that his question—"What makes a movement successful?"—examined a topic he was passionate about but was typically avoided in most classes. In order to answer the compelling question, Wesley understood that he needed to know about the origins of the movement, how the public has reacted to it, the public policies that have shaped it, and personal accounts of those influenced by it. As a result, he created four supporting questions that would serve as a useful structure for exploring these main ideas. Using the compelling and supporting question architecture, Wesley built out the formative and summative tasks and located disciplinary sources to help complete his investigation. See: www.c3teachers.org/inquiries/lgbtq-movement

Table 1: Summary of the Elements of the House of Inquiry

Types of Inquiry

	Focused Inquiry	Structured Inquiry	Embedded Action	Guided Inquiry	Student-Directed Inquiry
Description	The teacher develops the inquiry but focuses on a particular disciplinary skill and piece of content (e.g., causation, map work, research).	The teacher develops the blueprint to scaffold the disciplinary and civic outcomes of the inquiry.	The teacher develops the inquiry, but focuses on structuring the Taking Informed Action (understand-assess-act) sequence into the core of the blueprint.	The teacher develops the inquiry but there are dedicated spaces in the formative work for students to conduct independent research.	The student develops the blueprint on a question that he or she is interested in and plans the inquiry using the blueprint.
Example	Is compromise always fair? *Middle School Constitution Blueprint*	Does Debt Matter? *High School Fiscal Policy Blueprint*	Why is the Affordable Care Act so controversial? *High School Public Policy Blueprint*	What made nonviolent protest effective during the civil rights movement? *High School Civil Rights Blueprint*	What makes a movement successful? *High School Social Change Blueprint*
Blueprint	Is Compromise Always Fair?	Does Debt Matter?	Why Is the Affordable Care Act So Controversial?	What Made Nonviolent Protest Effective during the Civil Rights Movement?	What Makes a Movement Successful?
	www.c3teachers.org/inquiries/great-compromise/	www.c3teachers.org/wp-content/uploads/2020/03/2_DoesDebtMatter.pdf	www.c3teachers.org/inquiries/affordable-care-act	www.c3teachers.org/inquiries/civil-rights	www.c3teachers.org/inquiries/lgbtq-movement
Teacher to Student Driven	Teacher-developed	Teacher-developed	Teacher-developed	Teacher- and Student-developed	Student-developed
Questions	The teacher develops the Compelling and Supporting Questions	The teacher develops the Compelling and Supporting Questions	The teacher develops both the Compelling and Supporting Questions. The Compelling Question typically is created so that it explores a social problem.	The teacher develops the Compelling Question, but 1-2 Supporting Questions are deliberately structured so students are investigating a broad question.	The student develops the Compelling and Supporting Questions with guidance from the teacher.
Tasks	The teacher develops the Summative and Formative Tasks.	The teacher develops the Summative and Formative Tasks.	The teacher develops the Summative and Formative Tasks, but some of the Formative Tasks might be structured so that students are researching a supporting question.	The teacher develops the Summative and Formative Tasks, but 1–2 Formative Tasks are structured so that students are researching a supporting question.	The student develops Summative and Formative Tasks with guidance from the teacher.
Sources	The teacher selects a small collection of sources.	The teacher selects sources	The teacher selects most of the sources, but students might select some sources as they relate to the research opportunity.	The teacher selects some sources and students select some sources as they relate to the research opportunity.	The student selects sources with guidance from the teacher.
Time	1–2 days	3–10 days	5–10 days	5–10 days	2 weeks

We offer these brief blueprint descriptions as an introduction to and a demonstration of the options teachers have for designing their own houses of inquiry.

Roof

As teachers plan for these different types of blueprints over a course, a curricular roof emerges on our inquiry house. In the *College, Career, and Civic Life (C3) Framework for Social Studies State Standards,* of which we were the lead writers, we defined an Inquiry Arc that helps students "ask good questions and develop robust investigations into them; consider possible solutions and consequences; separate evidence-based claims from parochial ones; and communicate and act upon what they learn."[6] But we did not stop there. We asserted that students must be given opportunities to take on the inquiry reins:

> And most importantly, students must possess the capability and commitment to repeat that process as long as is necessary … in order to traverse successfully the worlds of college, career, and civic life.[7]

As questions, tasks, and sources form the foundation of the curricular house and the different inquiry types provide optional room arrangements, we become more intentional about the larger social studies curriculum. Instead of a shed outside the house where students infrequently gather tools, inquiry becomes essential for holding up the curriculum.

This house metaphor has helped us break out of the initial blueprint box to include other types of inquiry, all of which animate the aims of the C3 Framework. In Table 1, we distinguish the five types of inquiry as they relate to the foundational elements of inquiry (questions, tasks, sources) and two curriculum variables, agency and time.

A Note about Inquiry Types

As we have in our previous work around the Inquiry Design Model, we add a disclaimer: We are sure that there are more than five types of inquiry out there and, as such, we know that there are exponential ways to alter a blueprint. We trust teachers' intuitions, knowledge, and experiences and offer these five pathways as a starting place for them to think about using a blueprint to differentiate the inquiry experiences of their students.

An additional question raised by teachers is whether we intend for the curriculum house diagram to suggest a pecking order with student-directed inquiry representing the highest form of inquiry. We hedge a bit on that question as we see the unique value of each type of inquiry. However, all types of blueprints from structured to embedded action to focused to guided to student-directed are curricular scaffolds for students learning through inquiry.

The nature of scaffolds is that they are ultimately removed so that a structure can stand independently. The pedagogical nature of curricular scaffolds follows that same aim. As the scaffolds for questions, tasks, and sources are removed and students work more independently to create their own questions, to find their own sources, and to create their own meaning and answers to questions, we see a dynamic and meaningful inquiry arc take shape in social studies classrooms.

The move from scaffolded to unscaffolded inquiry demands instructional savvy; it also demands an inquiry mindset. An inquiry mindset is one where teachers work to lift up the experiences of their students by offering them opportunities to embrace knowledge, skills, and dispositions that define a fully developed life. With questions, tasks, and sources expressed across a range of inquiry types, we enable our students to construct inquiry mindsets of their own.

Conclusion

In a recent article, Walter Parker talks about inquiry experiences as the spine of the curriculum.[8] Parker posits that when inquiry-based projects are the spine of a course, they are systematically sequenced so that they provide the substance of the course and thereby drive deeper learning. But then he zeroes in on the core role of curriculum:

> But here's the secret sauce: At the heart of deeper learning is curriculum, not instruction. Before implementing instructional strategies, teachers need to make strategic decisions about the content and skills to be learned— those that will be learned deeply, iteratively, rather than only "covered."

The Inquiry Design Model aims in the same direction by organizing curriculum around the foundational elements of inquiry—questions, tasks, and sources. By collapsing or expanding and, in some cases, shifting the authorship of a blueprint, we illustrate how the IDM can operate as a curricular framework that flexes to meet the contextual needs of teachers.

Note: This article is based on a chapter from our recent book, *Blueprinting an Inquiry Curriculum: Planning with the Inquiry Design Model.*

Notes

1. S.G. Grant, Kathy Swan, and John Lee, *Inquiry-Based Practice in Social Studies Education: The Inquiry Design Model* (New York: Routledge and C3Teachers, 2017)
2. Kathy Swan, S.G. Grant, and John Lee, *Blueprinting an Inquiry Based Curriculum: Planning with the Inquiry Design Model* (Silver Spring, Md.: National Council for the Social Studies and C3Teachers, 2019).
3. Walter Parker, "Projects as the Spine of the Course: Design for Deeper Learning," *Social Education* 82, no. 1 (January-February 2017), 45–48.
4. S.G. Grant, Kathy Swan, and John Lee, *Inquiry-Based Practice in Social Studies Education.*
5. S.G. Grant, Kathy Swan, and John Lee, *Inquiry-Based Practice in Social Studies Education*; Kathy Swan, John Lee, and S.G. Grant, *Inquiry Design Model: Building Inquiries in Social Studies* (Silver Spring, Md.: National Council for the Social Studies and C3Teachers, 2018);
6. For the C3 Framework, see www.socialstudies.org/standards/c3 or National Council for the Social Studies (NCSS), *Social Studies for the Next Generation: Purposes, Practices, and Implications of the College, Career, and Civic Life (C3) Framework for Social Studies State Standards* (Silver Spring, Md.: NCSS, 2013). The quoted excerpt is on page 3 of the C3 Framework.
7. C3 Framework, p. 3.
8. Walter Parker, "Projects as the Spine of the Course: Design for Deeper Learning," op. cit.

Social Education **85, no. 3 (2021): 167–172**

Power, Injustice, Costs and Benefits: Looping Curricular Concepts with the Inquiry Design Model

Kathy Swan, S. G. Grant, John Lee, Andrew Danner, Christy Cartner, and Grant Stringer

Ideally, inquiry is not a once in a while experience. After all, inquiry is the essence of social studies and we know students need lots and lots of practice to get better at it.[1] In other words, we want inquiry to loop throughout the social studies curricula. What do we mean by the term "looping"? At its simplest, we mean offering students opportunities to engage in inquiry in regular intervals and in a coherent fashion within and across grade levels.[2]

Almost 60 years ago, Jerome Bruner wrote, "we begin with the hypothesis that any subject can be taught in some intellectually honest form to any child at any stage of development."[3] In other words, even the most complex social studies ideas, if properly structured and presented, can be understood by very young children. Looping or spiraling curriculum is an outgrowth of this foundational belief. Like Bruner, we believe novices can engage with really complex ideas (e.g., human rights, spatial reasoning, economic decision making) and use powerful inquiry skills (e.g., questioning, source work, argumentation). They can do this work if the ideas and processes are thoughtfully sequenced so that students encounter them first in their simplest forms and then move to more sophisticated forms. Each time students revisit an inquiry-based idea and/or process, it is reinforced and solidified until they begin to demonstrate some degree of facility with the ideas and with the skills.

In the following sections, we examine three examples of inquiry-based curricular loops, each of which focuses on a particular social studies concept. We begin with a civics teacher (Andrew Danner) who uses a series of structured inquiries highlighting the concept of power as it relates to the three branches of government and the role of citizens in a representative democracy. Next, we feature a teacher (Christy Cartner) who uses a critical lens to examine U.S. history and racial injustice. Finally, we profile an economics teacher (Grant Stringer) who asks students to practice cost-benefit analysis at various economic scales. We end this article with a discussion of curricular coherence and how concepts like power, injustice, and cost and benefits can serve as a meaningful focus for inquiry specifically, and social studies more broadly.

Looping the Concept of Power in an Inquiry-Based U.S. Government Curriculum

Students' first substantive experiences learning about the role of government in their lives often comes in a middle or high school civics class. In these classes, students typically learn about the powers of the three branches of government, the system of checks and balances, and how the roles of these branches have evolved as the United States has grown and expanded. Foundational knowledge of our democracy is important, but students' ears often perk up when teachers linger on the word, "power." The word itself is one that often operates as the default answer to any number of questions posed in social studies classrooms. Why do countries build empires? "Power." Why do nations go to war? "To get more power." Why do people run for public office? "To have power." Students have likely encountered the concept of power personally (e.g., parent-to-child, teacher-to-student, bully to bullied). Pulling that thread of power into a study of government and the role it plays in a student's political life can be … powerful.

Andrew's inquiry loop above features a question stem that asks, "How powerful should the _______ be?" to examine the concept of power as it relates to each branch of government (legislative, judicial, and executive) and the extent to which this power should rest with the people in a representative democracy (See Figure 1). By revisiting this question of power multiple times throughout the year, Andrew is enabling his students to question and reflect upon the scope of government in their own lives while also providing conceptual coherence to the curriculum. In the sections that follow, we break down four inquiries that define this curricular loop and may frame a U.S. Government class.

A curricular loop allows students opportunities to engage with important concepts and to practice inquiry skills with regularity and in a coherent fashion across a course of study.[4] The first three inquiries of this curricular loop ask students to examine the powers of each branch of government: Executive, Legislative, and Judicial. The supporting questions stay fairly constant across these three inquiries as students explore the powers granted to each branch by the U.S. Constitution, how power within each branch has changed over time, how the system of checks and

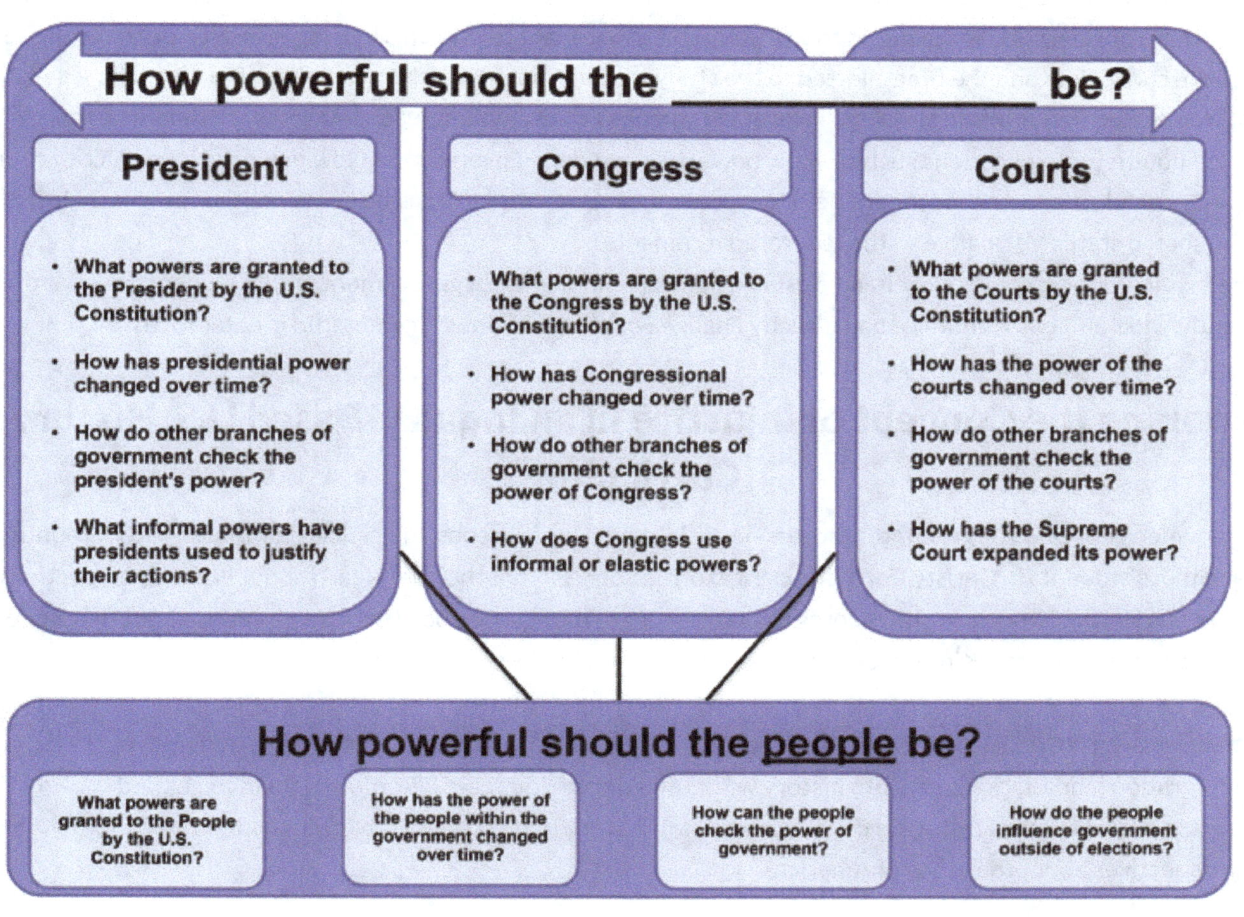

Figure 1: The Separation of Powers Curricular Loop

balances keeps each branch from having too much power, and how each branch has exerted power in unique ways. At the completion of each inquiry, students consider the unique role that that branch plays in a representative democracy with their arguments centering on how powerful that branch should be. In doing so, they may revisit their understanding of governmental power as their knowledge of the scope and scale of the federal government grows and becomes more complex.

The curricular loop closes with a fourth inquiry featuring the compelling question: "How powerful should the people be?" Inherent within the power of any elected or appointed official is the power of the people who helped get them where they are, as well as those who oppose them. But more importantly, "the people" are those who directly feel the impact of the decisions made by those in power. A series of supporting questions in this fourth inquiry involve the historical role of the people in government and the powers granted in the U.S. Constitution, how the people check the power of government officials, and how the people have been able to influence government outside of merely getting involved in the electoral process. Together, these supporting questions examine how citizens exert power in a representative democracy.

When encouraging students to become informed and engaged citizens, this fourth inquiry could also serve as a gateway to any number of informed actions within their communities. Whether teachers move quickly between inquiries or take their time, the ultimate goal is for students to practice and hone their argumentative skills as they revisit and refine their knowledge about the concept of power. As Parker (2018) states, this approach "allows the core concepts and skills to be applied in different scenarios. This adds complexity, thanks to the novelty of each context."[5]

One further consideration is the depth to which teachers may want to take this looping effort. Depending on the scope of the curriculum and the time allotted to the study of government, teachers could use the compelling question stem to frame other inquiries on state and local governments. For example, a teacher might ask students to do additional inquiries into questions such as: How powerful should the governor be? How powerful should a city council be? How powerful should a school board be? How powerful should corporations be in the political process? How powerful should states be relative to the federal government?

As the inquiry looping comes closer and closer to home, the influence of government within students' lives and, more importantly, their ability to influence and directly engage with those in power, comes into greater focus.

Looping the Concept of Injustice in an Inquiry-Based U.S. History Curriculum

Each year when February rolls around, teachers fill social media with lessons and articles for Black History Month. More and more students in Christy Cartner's class express concern that they only learn about limited perspectives when studying Black history, and they express a desire to learn more about positive contributions about Black people, *from* Black people. LaGarrett King echoes these sentiments and implores educators to:

> move away from policies that promote historical uniformity (all histories are the same) and historical integration (add Black people into history without taking serious consideration of their voices and perspectives) to more historical contentiousness (a history that is comfortable with competing perspectives about the ethos of America).[6]

These concerns led to the development of an inquiry loop intended to detrivialize Black history by treating Black voices as an integral thread to understanding U.S. history.

The particular topics of this loop exist within most U.S. history courses but are designed for teachers to slow down and dig into key moments in Black history from Reconstruction to the modern era. Given the age-old choices between depth and breadth in history classes, this curriculum loop is intended to allow historical turning points in Black history to be the points of depth. The value of this particular inquiry loop is the flexibility of the conceptual thread that holds it together—quest for racial justice. The compelling question, "What does it take to counter racial injustice?" shifts the curricular focus to the actors who have worked to dismantle oppression across time. There is the opportunity for students to see how the efforts of individuals and groups from one era pave the way for the actions of the next and how racial injustice persists.

As students move through a sequence of inquiries in this loop, they use the same supporting questions to build their understanding of continuity and change over time. For the first three inquiries, the supporting questions are "What racial injustice existed during this period?" "Who worked to counter racial injustice?" and "How successful were these efforts?" For the fourth inquiry, the questions move from past tense to present. Although these supporting questions are relevant to any era of U.S. history, this particular loop focuses on the eras of Reconstruction, early twentieth century, the Great Depression, the mid-twentieth century, and modern times.

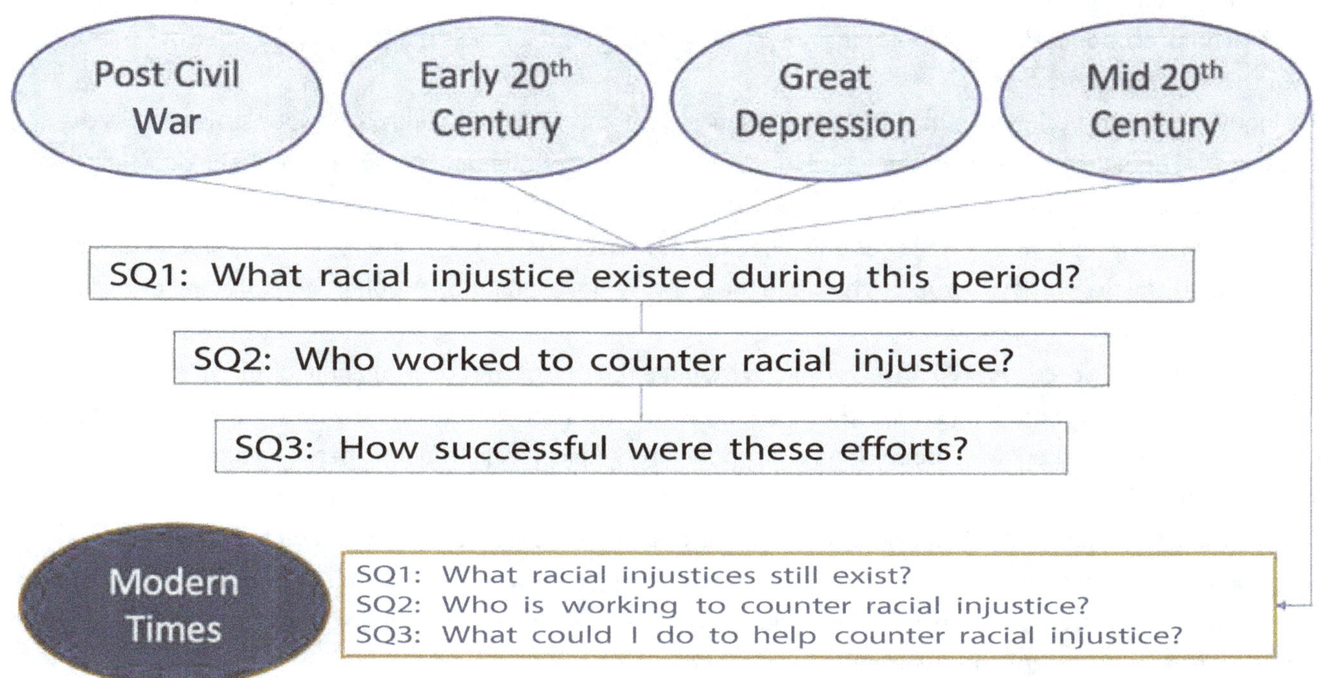

Figure 2: U.S. History Injustice Curricular Loop

This inquiry loop provides opportunities for teachers to support their students as they explore the intertwined threads of justice and activism over time. For example, students might learn about the experiences of Henry Adams who was born into slavery and testified to a Senate Committee in 1880 on the migration of Blacks out of the Jim Crow South. Years later, Adams's experiences bolstered the establishment of the NAACP and the expressions of the Harlem Renaissance. Students may then learn about James Bevel, a Depression-era activist who led marches for justice in the 1950s and 1960s. Later, children of the 1950s and 1960s like Bryan Stevenson became modern-day advocates for racial justice. This cycle continues, as cycles in history often do. Such is the beauty of looping students' learning experience, building inquiry upon inquiry, and revisiting and exploring the overlapping nuance of themes over time.

The final inquiry in this loop offers students the chance to examine the racial reckoning facing the United States today. Students grapple with systemic racism through testimonies and research polls on modern racial issues; they meet young people working to make a difference through a "Who's Who" of "Activists to Know Now" blogs; and they collaborate to determine what taking informed action looks like in various situations. The end of the inquiry provides a space for students to design a plan of action to combat one element of racial injustice in the modern world and to work together to make a difference.

Looping the Concepts of Costs and Benefits in an Inquiry-Based Economics Curriculum

Economics is grounded in the concept of scarcity, which ultimately means there is not enough stuff (e.g., food, movie theaters, healthcare) to go around. As a result, economic reasoning emphasizes making informed decisions about how to distribute goods and services efficiently and in ways that yield the best outcomes. It seems like a straightforward process. But determining what should be produced and how goods and services are made available is a tricky problem that involves predicting human behavior, understanding unintended consequences, and calculating worth. Teaching students to think economically means learning how to do a cost-benefit analysis that weighs the value of something and whether it is worth the cost.

This inquiry loop was designed to have students practice economic decision making at various scales across the major economic domains, including at the foundational, macro, micro, global, and personal levels. The question stem for this loop asks, "Is _Worth It?" To address the question, students examine the costs and benefits of (1) economic freedom within a market system; (2) the national debt and its impact on the U.S. economy; (3) federal subsidies for the corn market; (4) plastics within the supply chain and the growing global pollution problem; and (5) college degrees and their impact on an individual's earning potential.

In the first inquiry, "Is Freedom Worth It?", students examine the role of the government in different economic systems (e.g., command, market) and weigh the costs and benefits of each system. To answer the question, students must grapple with the concept of scarcity along with opportunity costs or the tradeoffs between alternative options. In economics, there is never a perfect solution— rather, there is a relatively better decision measured by the opportunity lost, or the thing one chooses not to do. In order to do this cost-benefit analysis, students need to consider human behavior and whether economic freedom can, in fact, be the "rising tide that lifts all boats." This inquiry sets the stage for understanding why freedom is an important value in a market system and the ongoing tension that exists between political parties around the role of government in an economy.

One of the most common, and perennial, economic problems that confronts policymakers is a macroeconomic concern—the national debt. Currently, America's national debt is approximately $28 trillion. Economists and politicians debate the significance of this debt and the impact it has on our economy and the future of our country. There is no shortage of perspectives on the debt; open any newspaper and one is likely to find an article, op-ed, or political cartoon that makes mention of our recurring budget deficit, the growing debt, and whether we can afford one more government program. This inquiry, "Is [National] Debt Worth It?" asks students to examine the history and magnitude of the national debt and to look at the potential impact of the debt on Americans and how different economists view the problem.

In the third inquiry, "Is Corn Worth It?", students shift from a macro-economic lens to a micro-economic one by examining a single commodity (corn) and the ways that federal subsidies can affect a market. Within the investigation, students learn about the pervasiveness of corn and corn products from ketchup to Gatorade to Windex. The United States has long been a leader in corn production, but output has exploded over the past few decades. Although many factors have influenced corn production, U.S. government subsidies have played a huge role. This inquiry asks students to examine corn subsidies and the intended and unintended consequences of government intervention into a market economy.

Is It Worth It?

Foundations	Macro	Micro	Global

Is Freedom Worth It?

SQI: What is the difference between a command and market economy?

SQ2: What are the benefits of a market economy?

SQ3: What are the costs of a market economy?

Is Debt Worth It?

SQI: What is the National debt?

SQ2: What are the costs of having such a large National debt?

SQ3: Are there any benefits of having such a large National debt?

Is Corn Worth It?

SQI: What role does corn play in the economy?

SQ2: Why does the federal government subsidize corn?

SQ3: How do corn subsidies help and hurt the economy?

Is Plastic Worth It?

SQI: How extensive is the use of plastic in the supply chain?

SQ2: How does plastic hurt us?

SQ3: What, if anything, can be done about plastics?

Personal Finance	Is College Worth It?

SQI: How much does it cost to go to college?

SQ2: How much do you make with a college degree?

SQ3: How do people afford college?

Figure 3: Economic Costs and Benefits Curricular Loop

The fourth compelling question in the inquiry loop asks students to consider the global economic issue of plastics. Within the inquiry, "Is Plastic Worth It?", students explore the growing use of plastics in the international supply chain and the negative impacts the use of plastics has on the environment. Upon seeing the impact and scope of plastic usage, students are presented with alternatives to our current plastic consumption. Students must then construct their own responses to "Is Plastic Worth It?" by stacking up the global costs and benefits of investing in plastic alternatives versus the cost efficiencies of continuing plastic usage.

The inquiry loop culminates with the question, "Is College Worth It?" Here, students investigate the rising cost of college tuition and the burden of student loan debt. While most parents want their children to attend college, many students and their families face challenging decisions on how to manage the costs. As college tuition has skyrocketed in the past few decades, families are digging deep to meet these rising costs despite stagnating wages. In this inquiry, students look at the costs and benefits of various colleges and at projected wages from various occupations or the long-term financial return that a college degree can yield. This inquiry loop shows students that economic thinking is not a trivial exercise, but a deeply personal one as these students will have to answer that question upon graduation from high school.

Blueprinting towards Curricular Coherence

In a recent article, Walter Parker wrote about inquiry experiences as the spine of the curriculum. Parker posited that when inquiry-based projects are the spine of a course, they are systematically sequenced so that they provide the substance of the course and thereby drive deeper learning:

> But here's the secret sauce: At the heart of deeper learning is curriculum, not instruction. Before implementing instructional strategies, teachers need to make strategic decisions about the content and skills to be learned—those that will be learned deeply, iteratively, rather than only "covered."[7]

The Inquiry Design Model aims in the same direction by organizing curriculum around the foundational elements of inquiry—questions, tasks, and sources. Across a loop of inquiries, designed to help students engage with content, concepts, and skills in a coherent manner, students are able to learn more deeply and find connections among what might otherwise seem to students to be just, "one damn thing after another." Ultimately, there must be a logic for how the inquiries in a curriculum loop hang together. In the government inquiry loop, the logic flows through iterative examinations of the concept of power in a democracy toward developing the deep knowledge needed for civic life. The curriculum loop on racial justice focuses on the pervasiveness of racism in this country and what changes and stays firmly rooted in each era. The economics loop allows students to work through a cost-benefit analysis at various scales in the economy including personal, micro, macro, and global.

Regardless of how teachers decide to loop their inquiries, one major advantage is the opportunity to help students build their content knowledge and skills over time. We know that inquiry is not a one-and-done kind of idea. Students need to wrestle with sources, develop and support claims and counter-claims, and construct and support arguments. Mastery of these skills take time. Teachers who invest their curricular energies in inquiry should expect to see maturation in students' use of concepts and skills, comfort in asking their own questions, and reassurance that their arguments can result in more than one valid answer.

Notes

1. C3 Framework, www.socialstudies.org/standards/c3.
2. Walter Parker, "Projects as the Spine of the Course: Design for Deeper Learning," *Social Education* 82, no. 1 (2017), 45–48.
3. Jerome Bruner, *The Process of Education* (New York: Vintage, 1960).
4. Parker, "Projects as the Spine of the Course"; Kathy Swan, S.G. Grant, and John Lee, *Blueprinting an Inquiry Based Curriculum: Planning with the Inquiry Design Model* (Silver Spring, Md.: National Council for the Social Studies and C3Teachers, 2019).
5. Parker, "Projects as the Spine of the Course."
6. LaGarrett J. King, "Black History is Not American History: Toward a Framework of Black Historical Consciousness," *Social Education* 84, no. 6 (2020), 335–341.
7. Parker, "Projects as the Spine of the Course."

Section 2: Conclusion

Standards documents and the curricula that align with them are exercises in hope. That is, when done right, they represent our greatest hope for student engagement and achievement. The C3 Framework provided a focal point for that hope in social studies—that students would engage in disciplinary inquiry so that they would be prepared for any college they chose to attend, for the myriad of careers that they might find themselves in, and, most importantly, for their lives as citizens in our pluralistic democracy. The Inquiry Design Model helped build on that hope with teachers constructing curricular maps to point the way.

But hope is hope, and reality is reality. In the next section, we tackle the next big leap forward in the C3 revolution of ideas: inquiry-based instruction in *real* classrooms with teachers and students pushing forward unto the breach.

Section 3: Instruction

Section 3: Instruction

Inquiry is not for the faint of heart and requires grit to move through the growing and sustaining pains of inquiry-based teaching. In other words, hope faces reality. Teachers need space to tinker with their practice and to confront the challenges that inevitably come with ambitious teaching. Students also need room to adjust their expectations of social studies coursework as they move toward asking and answering their own compelling questions and summoning evidence to back up their thinking. We know changing practice is not easy and teachers will often face resistance and doubt in many forms—from students, parents, colleagues, administration, and sometimes, from themselves.

In a brief we published a year after the C3 Framework,[1] we noted five instructional shifts that would need to take place if teachers were to align their teaching with the ambitions of the inquiry arc. Those shifts include:

1. Craft questions that spark and sustain inquiry,
2. Cultivate and nurture collaborative civic spaces,
3. Integrate content and skills purposefully,
4. Promote literacy practices and outcomes, and
5. Provide tangible opportunities for taking informed action.

While we would not dispute any of these points, the last ten years have taught us that those original five shifts could be multiplied by ten with an exponent of fifty for good measure. What we have learned from *real* inquiry teachers is that you are never done with inquiry. Once teachers commit to an inquiry-based approach, they sign on to a teaching life that requires constant change, reflection, change, and then, more reflection and some more change.

Real inquiry teachers tell us about classroom victories that propel them through the next instructional hurdle. Critics might compare it to a game of whack-a-mole; another, more optimistic view, suggests that inquiry teachers and their students are in a perpetual state of becoming. They are becoming more curious. They are becoming more pedagogically precise. They are becoming more open to change. They are becoming more unsatisfied with the status quo. Inquiry-based teaching is about democratizing the classroom—it is about embracing inevitable fears, fiery hopes, and perpetual shifts and being present for all of it alongside students who are also moving along the same, sometimes scary, intellectual journey.

Our role has been to listen and encourage these journeys through a variety of channels. Those channels include the blogs and professional learning seminars sponsored by C3 Teachers. Along with our colleagues, Emma Thacker and MaryBeth Yerdon, we have established the C3 Framework columns in *Social Education*, *Middle Level Learning*, and *Social Studies and the Young Learner* to give voice to inquiry teachers willing to share their journeys with others. As university faculty, we have worked alongside pre-service and in-service teachers both in classrooms and in the field as they hone their inquiry-based pedagogy, and we have tried to chronicle their growth in research pieces and documentaries about teaching with the Inquiry Design Model (IDM).

In the following section, we present four articles from the "Teaching the C3 Framework" archive in *Social Education* and one from our latest "C3 Teachers Talk Inquiry" archive in *Middle Level Learning*. Each highlights the kinds of conversations that have been had and the insights that have been gleaned over the last decade.

* * * * *

In the first article in this section, "C3 Teachers: The Heart of the Inquiry," John Lee, Alicia McCollum, and MaryBeth

Yerdon tell the origin story of C3 Teachers, a network launched in 2015. Lee and team share the purpose of the platform, which is to connect teachers and to iteratively innovate around the C3 Framework using open source and Creative Commons licenses. Today, C3 Teachers has over 15,000 members and has partnered with schools and districts from around the world, with state departments of education across the U.S., and with regional and national organizations who want to engage with inquiry. All told, the C3 Teachers team has trained over 20,000 teachers who have participated directly in professional learning experiences related to the C3 Framework and the IDM. Using blogs, hubs, briefs, webinars, and film, C3 Teachers is a place where teachers can openly and honestly grapple with the instructional challenges and triumphs of inquiry-based instruction.

Classroom research around the C3 Framework and the IDM is growing. The second piece in this section is by Emma Thacker and Josephine Valentine, who detail findings from an empirical study about the use of the IDM in Valentine's second-grade classroom. The team provides background on an elementary inquiry that sought to "engage in inquiry-based social studies instruction with students in a low-income, majority-minority elementary school with attention to both her challenges and successes" (p. 103). Using a critical lens, the teacher constructed the compelling question, "How can I give back to Indigenous People today?" along with three supporting questions and formative performance tasks, and two summative tasks to deepen students' understanding. The inquiry was intentionally constructed to "represent Indigenous people more authentically and holistically" and to "emphasize that Indigenous communities not only existed in the past, but are living and active in our nation today" (p. 104). The authors discuss the challenges they faced and the lessons learned about revising a compelling question for more deliberation, making the formative tasks more interactive, and scaffolding challenging sourcework. They also share classroom victories, including how the experience "empowered the vision" Valentine had as a teacher wanting "to give [students] more opportunities to discover ideas independently using truthful sources" (p. 108). This study represents a prime example of *real* inquiry teachers who have started on the journey and committed to a fearless, searching process of inquiry. And, who never looked back.

The next article in this section comes from our latest NCSS series "C3 Teachers Talk Inquiry" in *Middle Level Learning*. Led by MaryBeth Yerdon, the team interviews inquiry teachers from around the world about their insights, motivations, challenges, and innovations with inquiry-based teaching. In this article, we feature an interview with Ckristina Bennett, an eighth-grade teacher from Syracuse City Schools in New York about teaching an IDM curriculum loop created by Kathy Swan and team.[2] This loop features the conceptual question, "How do we make peace with the past?" and asks students to grapple with this timely question across six "hard history" inquiries each using a different historical context (e.g., segregation, internment, redlining). Bennett shares how the IDM has changed her practice, how it allowed her to "let the reins go, you've got to turn it over to the students," and how that makes it "so much better than when we were in middle school" (p. 113). She goes on to connect these instructional shifts with skill-building that is essential for a healthy democracy. Ultimately, she is "creating a space for hope through inquiry" (p. 114). And, *that* just makes us smile.

In the fourth piece of this section, we share our most collaborative article to date. "Art of the Blueprint: Inquiry in the Classroom" was featured in the special issue of *Social Education* that celebrated the 10th anniversary of the C3 Framework. Kathy Swan, John Lee, and S. G. Grant, along with 13 fellow inquiry "travelers," tell the story of teaching the blueprint through nine "Portraits of Inquiry." These short but powerful vignettes demonstrate how the IDM blueprint has taken on different hues and tones as educators bring them to life in classrooms, districts, and professional learning spaces. Starting with compelling questions and staging questions, moving to formative and summative tasks, and then highlighting innovations (e.g., the jigsaw blueprint and assessment) and issues (i.e., teaching teachers to teach with inquiry), we organized these stories so that readers could take a gallery walk of our most accomplished pedagogical artists. The article demonstrates the collaborative nature of inquiry-based teaching, not just from a classroom perspective but also from the perspective of a professional learning community that spans districts, grade levels, and content areas.

We conclude this section with a piece on trust, a teaser on what is to come from the C3 Teachers studio. In "Trusting Inquiry: Teaching with the Inquiry Design Model," Kathy Swan, S. G. Grant, and John Lee return to an idea that Grant declared in one of the first articles about the C3 Inquiry Arc (also featured in Section 2 of this book). He wrote then, and we still believe now, that:

> Trust matters. The Inquiry Arc reflects a level of trust between teachers and students that is not part of the traditional pattern of schooling. Good teachers know that students will blunder sometimes as they embrace the greater responsibilities an inquiry approach demands, but they also know that students will not become the kinds of life-long learners that we desire if they are not trusted to take an active role in their own education.[3]

Returning to the idea of trust has been a *Eureka!* moment for us, further deepening our curiosity about its relationship to inquiry. We have landed on three key inquiry processes that build a culture of trust in the classroom: deliberation, collaboration, and production. We write that, "by allowing students space to think (**deliberate** ideas), talk (**collaborate** around ideas), and do (**produce** ideas)" (p. 132), teachers become trustworthy to their students. This trust begets a willingness to take intellectual risks and a space where students can develop empathy, interdependence, and agency that accelerates inquiry-based learning in the classroom. While we know these processes and attributes are not exclusive to social studies, they do connect deeply to the mission of preparing students for democratic life.

We end this article on trust with an invitation to engage in additional conversations with our network of C3 teachers who want to collaborate on this framework for inquiry instruction. And, thus starts our next chapter in the C3 inquiry revolution.

* * * * *

1. John Lee, Alicia McCollum, and MaryBeth Yerdon, "C3 Teachers: The Heart of the Inquiry," *Social Education* 87, no. 6 (2023): 388–394.
2. Emma S. Thacker and Josephine L. Valentine, "Designing and Teaching a Critical Inquiry: Lessons Learned," *Social Education* 87, no. 4 (2023): 233–240.
3. MaryBeth Yerdon, Kathy Swan, John Lee, and S. G. Grant, eds., "Creating a Space for Hope through Inquiry: An Interview with Ckristina Bennett from Syracuse, New York," *Middle Level Learning* 76 (January/February 2023): 10–13.
4. Kathy Swan, John Lee, S. G. Grant, and Fellow Inquiry Travelers, "Art of the Blueprint: Inquiry in the Classroom," *Social Education* 87, no. 6 (2023): 367–387.
5. Kathy Swan, S. G. Grant, and John Lee, "Trusting Inquiry: Teaching with the Inquiry Design Model," *Social Education* 87, no. 5 (2023): 328–331.

Notes

1. Kathy Swan, John Lee, and S. G. Grant, "C3 Instructional Shifts," *C3 Teachers Briefs*, September 2014, https://c3teachers.org/c3shifts.
2. Kathy Swan, K., Ryan Crowley, Nick Stamoulacatos, Bonnie Lewis, and Grant Stringer, "Countering the Past of Least Resistance: A Hard History Inquiry-Based Curriculum," *Social Education* 86, no. 1 (2022): 34–39.
3. S. G. Grant, "Inquiry, Instruction, and the Potential of the College, Career, and Civic Life (C3) Framework," *Social Education* 77, no. 6 (2013): 351

Social Education 87, no. 6 (2023): 388–394

C3 Teachers: The Heart of the Inquiry

John Lee, Alicia McCollum, and MaryBeth Yerdon
with testimonials from C3 Teachers

The publication of the *College, Career, and Civic Life (C3) Framework for Social Studies State Standards* in 2013 opened a door for inquiry practice in social studies.[1] After a century of fits and starts with inquiry in social studies, the C3 Framework sought to put inquiry firmly at the forefront of social studies teaching and learning.[2] However, we knew that the C3 Framework was unlikely to gain traction as a standards innovation without the engagement and commitment of the teachers who would be asked to implement the inquiry innovations within. In the early years of the C3 Framework's publication, we learned that while the Framework resonated with teachers, they struggled with key aspects within—such as taking informed action in the classroom and using questions to initiate an inquiry.[3] Research and theory on teacher professional growth tells us that teacher networks focused on content, self-reflection, enthusiasm, and the application of innovative instructional approaches can enhance teaching and learning.[4] With this in mind, our collaborative launched the C3 Teachers network (https://c3teachers.org) in 2013 to support teachers' implementation of the C3 Framework.

Building a C3 Teachers Network

The C3 Teachers network aims to empower teachers as they wrestle with the big ideas and instructional implications of the C3 Framework and the embedded Inquiry Arc. The vision of C3 Teachers is for the regular practice of social studies teaching and learning to be driven by questions that frame students' exploration of content, the expression of arguments in response to questions, and a realization for how student learning connects to their lives inside and outside of school.

C3 Teachers began as a small group of 15 teachers who joined together just after the publication of the C3 Framework in 2013 to reflect on the Framework and how the ideas within could activate students in their classrooms. We asked these teachers to see themselves in the C3 and kick the tires of the Inquiry Arc. That was 2013, and the voices of those 15 teachers struck a cord that still resonates today. Their stories launched a movement that has sustained and advanced the inquiry revolution in social studies.

With its simple start, the C3 Teachers network has grown into a platform for launching ideas and innovations aimed at bringing the C3 Framework to life. C3 Teachers provides access to hundreds of open-source inquiries designed by and for teachers using the Inquiry Design Model (IDM).[5] Today, C3 Teachers is over 16,000 strong and enables teachers to experience the innovations launched by the C3 Framework.

Stories from the Heart of Inquiry

Teachers inspired by the C3 Framework are moving social studies forward and giving us visions of the possible. We've been watching and listening to C3 teachers and continue to be amazed by their energy and creativity. Their experiences run the gamut from personal introspection to institutional change. We have been sharing the perspectives of teachers on our C3 Teachers blog.[6] Here, we offer some of those stories from C3 teachers and their experience with the C3 Framework.

While the story of C3 Teachers began with those first 15 teachers reflecting on the C3 Framework back in 2013, it was the New York K-12 Social Studies Toolkit (https://c3teachers.org/new-york-hub) that pumped life into the heart of inquiry, enlivening the C3 Framework, and inspiring inquiry design.[7] The Toolkit project in 2014-2015 was the work of an inspired group of talented New York teachers. Joe Karb, the 2012 National Council for the Social Studies Outstanding Middle School Teacher, was part of a team who wrote what became the first major collection of C3 inspired inquiries. Joe brought his skills as a teacher to some of the earliest work on inquiry curriculum development. His reflection of those earlier years sets the stage for how the C3 Teachers network would bring new life to social studies:

> *I was first introduced to the C3 Framework in 2013 at a social studies meeting hosted by the American Federation of Teachers. At that point, the C3 was in draft form and the Inquiry Design Model (IDM) was still being developed. Needless to say, the Framework and IDM piqued my interest as a teacher. For many years prior there was an emphasis in New York on primary and secondary sources and DBQ writing. While DBQs have value, it seemed like they had become formulaic with the emphasis being on earning the most points on an exam as opposed to thoughtful claim-making using evidence. The C3 approach provided a different way to engage students using compelling questions, sources, and having students dig deeper by interacting with a curated collection of sources.*
>
> *I was sold on the C3 approach and eventually had the opportunity to be an inquiry writer on the New York Toolkit project. As one of the middle school writers, I collaborated with the toolkit team to create 6 of the 84 inquiries that were eventually released in New York and nationally through C3 Teachers. In my seventh grade classroom, I taught these inquiries, and the differences in student learning were clear. Students were engaged and interested in doing challenging work with sources and claims. Instead of using sources as a supplement to lecture, our Toolkit inquiries put sources at the center of my teaching and encouraged my students to think for themselves and do a deep dive in the content they are learning. The New York Toolkit project has inspired so many educators. I've been fortunate to take what we learned in the project and apply it to many other contexts including my work with the Korean War Legacy Project where we developed a collection of inquiries using IDM (https:// koreanwarlegacy.org/teaching-tools/korean-war-legacy). I'm proud of what we were able to do in New York and how we put the C3 Framework into motion.*

Amber Makaiau was another early C3 teacher leader. Amber is an educator at the University of Hawaii, Manoa and director of the Hanahau'oli School Professional Development Center. Amber was part of a team who enabled a group of teachers in 2015-2016 to develop C3-inspired inquiries in the early years after the publication of the C3 Framework. The work led to the development of the Hawaii' C3 Hub (https://c3teachers.org/hawaii-c3-hub). Since then, C3 Teachers has supported educators in developing over 30 C3 Hubs (https://c3teachers.org/c3-hubs). Here, Amber reflects on how C3 teachers inspire their students:

> *C3 teachers have a progressive philosophy of education, centered around the idea that schools can help to better society. They know that teaching is an "art," which requires balancing well-laid plans with the willingness to respond to the emergent and diverse needs of individuals, communities, and places. C3 teachers use the innovative structure of the C3 Inquiry Arc as a pathway for cultivating and nurturing student citizens who think for themselves, collaborate with others, and are committed to caring for the planet. C3 teachers are committed to*

making school meaningful. They provide opportunities and experiences for students to become, in the words of the C3 Framework, "aware of their changing cultural and physical environments; know the past; read, write, and think deeply; and act in ways that promote the common good."[8]

While inquiries designed by C3 teachers have core elements, which can be recognized across time and place, no one inquiry is alike because individual learners are diverse and all school communities are unique. C3 teachers are dedicated to designing learning experiences grounded in what students need to thrive in today's rapidly changing world, and inspiring students to imagine and enact new realities and possible futures.

Kēhau Glassco, another Hawaiian C3 teacher, is a school leader at Kapālama Campus of Kamehameha Schools, Hawaii. Here, Kēhau Glassco and two of her teacher colleagues, Ray Parker and Ehā Hiu, both social studies teachers at Kamehameha Middle School, describe what it means to be a C3 Teacher:

Kēhau Glassco: A C3 teacher is not your traditional social studies teacher. Facts and timelines are not the focus. The C3 Framework allows students to be curious about history and how they can contribute to their communities given what they learned. The C3 shifts the student experience from being told about history to a personalized journey. My favorite thing about being a social studies educator is teaching the students to give back and participate in their communities. The C3 Framework empowers social studies teachers to have their students apply their knowledge and engage in civic activities that create positive change in their communities. In my 25 years as an educator, I've learned that students don't remember the facts, events or people, but they remember the inquiry projects we did that ended with civic engagement.

Ray Parker: Implementing the C3 standards has led to a noticeable change in how we educate our students. Instead of having them just learn facts, we now focus on helping them become active and engaged members of their community. This means they learn not only what's in the textbooks but also how to think critically, make informed decisions, and get involved in important community issues.

Ehā Hiu: For me, being a C3 Teacher means helping students learn content using a curriculum that allows them to learn about topics that are relevant to their lives and to make positive contributions to the world. It means providing students with a relevant, meaningful, and engaging curriculum that connects and ties them back to their families, their communities, and to their identities as kanaka oiwi [i.e., Native Hawaiian].

Janae Bell is a C3 teacher at Silverado High School in Las Vegas, Nevada. She also mentors both practicing and student teachers in Clark County, Nevada. Janae has been working for almost a decade to support the transition away from memorization-based teaching to instruction based on the C3 Framework. Since 2015, Janae has been an exemplar of pairing culturally relevant and responsive pedagogy with the implementation of inquiry in the classroom. Janae understands that it's one thing to know the C3 Framework and quite another to move to the beat of inquiry. Here's her story:

There is no simple answer to the question "What does it mean to be a C3 teacher?" I learned about the C3 Framework in 2015 and fell into fully employing the model in the airport on my way home from the NCSS Conference that year! Since then, the influence of the C3 Framework is found throughout my classroom and in my pedagogy. It is reflected in the art that I choose to adorn my classroom. It is reflected in the topics that my students and I choose to deeply explore. It is most certainly reflected in the questions that we use to stimulate conversation surrounding historical situations.

For me, truly being a C3 teacher means that I continuously make space for inquiry. My classroom has become a safe space for questioning, where students are both challenged and encouraged to question the world around them. Students are motivated to find and explore the varying perspectives in relation to their questions. Taking this approach, I've learned to release the fear of challenging the dominant perspective and to actually make space for the future changemakers in the world. Being a C3 teacher provides me with a framework in which I can guide my students to become those changemakers.

The C3 movement has reached thousands of teachers like Joe, Amber, Kēhau, Ray, Ehā, and Janae. But, it's not just individual teachers and schools that have been activated by the C3 Framework and Inquiry Arc. We've seen entire school districts take on the challenge of implementing C3 Framework-inspired inquiry in the classroom. Dessie Olson is a Teacher Specialist for the Salt Lake City School District. Moved by the possibilities of the C3 Framework, Dessie recently led a group of teachers in her district to build a collection of inquiries. Their work is available on a Utah C3 Hub at https://c3teachers.org/utah-c3-hub. Dessie's comments reflect what we've heard from so many district leaders about how C3 Teachers enable curriculum reform:

C3 Teachers believe in creating the ideal learning environment for students, where students are excited to engage in rigorous thinking and learning and where students feel safe and valued. A C3 Teacher is reflective, yet forward thinking. They strive to meet students where they are and find ways to engage students in active learning. C3 Teachers seek out collaboration and expertise from others, constantly looking for ways to improve their knowledge, skills, and abilities. A C3 Teacher is student focused and dedicated to helping students find relevance and meaning in what they learn. They continuously ponder ways to frame their instruction around inquiries that matter to students, while delving into the complex issues and unsettled arguments that define our world, regardless of space or time. A C3 Teacher strives to make learning authentic, nurturing students to develop the knowledge, skills, and dispositions necessary for their own success as well as for the success of our democracy.

Institutions have also been instrumental in bringing the C3 Framework to life. Colleen Smith was an early leader in the C3 Teachers network. She is a C3 teacher with both classroom teaching and content development experience who has developed a body of curriculum work alongside both museums and K-12 schools. In her previous work, with colleagues at the Smithsonian Institute, Colleen collaborated with Native communities and cultural experts to create Native Knowledge (NK) 360° (https://americanindian.si.edu/nk360). Today, the NK 360° project features one of the premier inquiry collections in our field. Currently, Colleen is an Educational Resources Specialist at the Library of Congress. Here, Colleen describes her vision for being a C3 teacher:

Being a C3 teacher means being purpose driven. The purpose being, to support students in developing evidence-based arguments about meaningful topics, issues, and questions that are relevant to their lives. When I first discovered the C3 Framework and the Inquiry Design Model, I knew it would be important to be engaged with other teachers. Early on, I participated in an IDM Institute sponsored by NCSS and C3 Teachers. I was reminded that as a curriculum developer, I needed reality checks from innovative and engaged teachers. I've stayed plugged in and have learned much over the years as a C3 teacher. One of the best reality checks came in the form of learning about argument stems and creative ways to start inquiry design. My colleagues can attest to my obsession with drafting and always coming back to these argument stems.

I put what I learned from other C3 teachers into action in my work to support the Native Knowledge 360 project and the collection of inquiries that are a part of that work. One thing I know is that C3 teachers will push you to always know your purpose in building inquiry and help reveal where things might fall apart.

Amy Bottomley is the director of Educational Initiatives at the National Underground Railroad Freedom Center and is another institutional leader/innovator in the C3 movement. Amy and her team developed a collection of inquiries aimed at pursuing inclusive freedom by promoting social justice for all, available in a C3 Hub (https://c3teachers.org/national-underground-railroad-freedom-center).[9] Here, Amy describes her perspective on C3 teachers:

> *C3 Teachers ask, "What will my students need when they are 30?" Thus, we teach the information, understandings, and skills necessary to become a productive member of civic society. The United States is a representative democracy, so we need citizens who value inquiry and will question our leaders and the status quo. In the age of the internet and social media, we need citizens who value facts and evidence and can distinguish credible from non-credible information. Because we are a vast and diverse country, we need citizens who value diversity and seek out multiple perspectives.*
>
> *Since democracy is of the people, by the people, for the people, we need citizens who value communication and who discuss, debate, and deliberate with one another and then advocate for issues they believe in. Finally, because we are products of our history, we need citizens who understand the lessons of the past and will apply them in creating a better tomorrow for all Americans. The C3 framework and C3 teachers help accomplish this by maintaining emphasis on big concepts and skills that will aid students in adulthood, as opposed to the minutia they are likely to forget.*

We are also learning from teacher educators and researchers about how teachers activate the C3 Framework. Nada Wafa is an assistant teaching professor at North Carolina State University. She has investigated how teachers' personal perspectives and global context impact their inquiry planning and teaching. Nada also developed the *C3 Teachers Global C3 Hub* (https://c3teachers.org/global-hub) as a place for educators to access global inquiries and connect with others who share their passion for inquiry in global contexts. Here, she touches on her vision for expanding the work of C3 teachers:

> *At the core of my work as an educator is inquiry, but not just any type of inquiry—it's how inquiry comes to life in global contexts through the C3 Framework. For me, the power of the C3 Framework is how it bridges theory to practice and opens doors to exploring global perspectives. As a scholar, I recently investigated how a novice global education teacher developed a C3 Framework-infused global education curriculum. This inquiry-based curriculum focused on students developing global literacy skills, building their knowledge of global content, and acting on what they were learning. In my research, I found that the teacher's conceptual knowledge about inquiry related to how her students engage in the inquiry process. In other words, understanding the theory of the C3 Framework and the Inquiry Arc helped the teacher I worked with to better engage her students with inquiry.*
>
> *While researching the connections between theory and practice, I also had the opportunity to take action on what I was learning. The Global C3 Hub provided a platform for another project that examined how C3 teachers from all around the world created, used, and implemented the C3 Framework using a global education lens. This project connected six C3 teachers from various parts of the world—Malaysia, South Korea, Austria, Lebanon, [and in the United States] Maine, and Wyoming—as they designed inquiries. Through this project, I found that when*

teachers infuse global content and perspectives into their inquiry design, students are able to follow their interests in ways that connect content to personal experiences.

C3 Teachers Moving Forward

The intuitions of C3 teachers and their passions for teaching and learning with inquiry are moving social studies in exciting directions. Rather than having students sit, listen, and parrot what they've heard, C3 teachers know students should learn how to think for themselves. Inquiry is a means to that end. From the earliest days, C3 Teachers has focused on building innovative inquiry resources to support teachers in their journey to actively engage students. As such, at the core of every C3 teacher's work is the Inquiry Design Model and the IDM Blueprint. These teachers have used IDM to produce hundreds of inquiries. Today, C3 Teachers has become a dynamic network for innovation about inquiry. We believe that our work at C3 Teachers can help teachers to realize this vision, but in order to reach our goals teachers must be activated to apply their best instincts to inquiry instruction. If teachers trust the Inquiry Arc in the C3 Framework and their views are honored, the C3 Framework has a chance to continue bringing about real change. That's the power of the C3 Teachers network. It represents an opportunity to move teachers to the forefront of reform in social studies education. With teachers in the lead, we know that the heartbeat of inquiry will be strong for years to come.

Notes

1. *The College, Career, and Civic Life (C3) Framework for Social Studies State Standards* (Silver Spring, MD: NCSS, 2013).
2. Kathy Swan,"The Importance of the C3 Framework," *Social Education* 77, no. 4, (2013): 222–224.
3. Emma S. Thacker, John K. Lee, and Adam M. Friedman, "Teaching with the C3 Framework: Surveying Teachers' Beliefs and Practices," *The Journal of Social Studies Research* 41, no. 2 (2017): 89-100.
4. Roelande H. Hofman and Bernadette J. Dijkstra, "Effective Teacher Professionalization in Networks?" *Teaching and Teacher Education* 26, no. 4 (2010): 1031-1040.
5. S. G. Grant, Kathy Swan, and John Lee, "Bringing the C3 Framework to Life," *Social Education* 79, no. 6 (2015): 310-315.
6. Carly Muetterties, "C3 Teachers Blogging: Grappling with the Realities of Inquiry," *Social Education* 82, no. 5 (2018): 287-290.
7. S. G. Grant, Kathy Swan, and John Lee, *Inquiry-based Practice in Social Studies Education: Understanding the Inquiry Design Model* (Taylor & Francis, 2022).
8. John Lee, Kathy Swan, and S. G. Grant, "By Teachers, for Teachers: The NYS Toolkit and C3 Teachers," *Social Education* 79, no. 6 (2015): 325-328.
9. *The C3 Framework*, 5.

Social Education **87**, no. 4 (2023): 233–240.

Designing and Teaching a Critical Inquiry: Lessons Learned

Emma S. Thacker and Josephine L. Valentine

Since the publication of the *College, Career, and Civic Life (C3) Framework for Social Studies State Standards*, social studies teachers, school leaders, and teacher educators have explored ways to implement it in the classroom, with various results. Much of the published work around the implementation of the *C3 Framework* in classrooms highlights its use in middle and high school classrooms; however, particularly in the context of limited instructional time for social studies in elementary classrooms, the possibilities of using the *C3 Framework* to bring more inquiry-based elementary social studies instruction needs more attention. In this article, we explore how a second-grade teacher used the Inquiry Design Model (IDM) as a way to engage in inquiry-based social studies instruction with students in a low-income, majority-minority elementary school with attention to both her challenges and successes.[1]

Background

We know that elementary social studies instruction is minimized across educational contexts and that the quality of social studies instruction that students receive in low-income schools is substandard compared to their peers in affluent contexts.[2] Solomon and colleagues argued that the deficit-driven perspective with which policymakers—as well as some educators—view diverse schools, students, and families, can mean narrow and less relevant curricula, and increased emphasis on test preparation at the expense of curricula that represent students' lived experiences.[3] The inquiry arc of the *C3 Framework* speaks to the preparation of youth for a more inclusive and critical citizenship, by helping students to ask questions (Dimension 1), to use disciplinary knowledge and skills (Dimension 2), to evaluate sources (Dimension 3), and to communicate conclusions and take informed action (Dimension 4) on social issues that are relevant to their lives.[4]

Swan and colleagues developed the Inquiry Design Model (IDM) to provide guidance for social studies teachers and teacher educators as they create relevant and rigorous social studies inquiries. They defined questions, tasks, and sources as the foundational elements of inquiries—components that are familiar to social studies teachers.[5] By culminating in taking informed action, such inquiries have the potential to prepare students for informed, engaged, and critical citizenship. Building off this work, Crowley and King described three components of critical social studies inquiries: (a) asking "compelling and supporting questions that explicitly critique systems of oppression and power," (b) selecting "sources that include the perspectives of marginalized and oppressed groups," and (c) designing "formative and summative tasks and a Taking Informed Action activity that push students to take tangible steps toward alleviating the injustice explored in the inquiry."[6] In this article, we share the lessons we learned as Josephine Valentine designed and implemented a second-grade inquiry and consider the extent to which the inquiry worked towards the goals of critical inquiry.

Context

Spotswood Elementary School has among the highest percentages of economically disadvantaged and racially or linguistically marginalized students of any elementary school in Harrisonburg, Virginia, a diverse school district that boasts over 50 languages spoken and serves students who hail from over 50 countries. Not surprisingly, given what we know about educational policies and standardized assessments, Spotswood is the only local elementary school that was accredited with conditions (i.e., conditionally accredited) by the state at the time of this work. Those conditions were due to more pronounced "achievement gaps" for students with disabilities and African American students on state standardized test scores— meaning the school was identified as one that needed to improve students' test scores. What may be more surprising is the progressive approach Spotswood administrators and teachers take to addressing these "gaps." Rather than focusing narrowly on preparing for standardized tests, the school puts resources into creating relevant curriculum and meeting students' learning needs in innovative ways.

As part of the school's goal of providing a social justice-oriented curriculum, I (Emma) led a professional learning project guiding the second- and fourth-grade teams in learning about and developing critical inquiry-based units for their social studies classes in the 2020-2021 school year. We began this project and partnership in fall 2019, when I wrote a grant proposal to support the work in partnership with Spotswood's principal. We were awarded the funding in July 2020, after COVID-19 had shut down in-person learning in our area. Grant funding supported stipends for teachers for their curriculum design work.

After an all-day virtual workshop introducing teachers to the IDM, the teams worked throughout fall 2020 and into early winter 2020/2021 to design critical inquiries and prepare to implement them in their virtual classrooms in spring 2021. In this article, we highlight Josie's experience with the design and implementation of the second-grade inquiry with the compelling question, "How can I give back to Indigenous People today?" (see Figure 1).

Lessons Learned

In the following sections, we organize our lessons learned around the central inquiry components—questions, tasks, and sources—and reflect on the ways the inquiry aligned with goals of critical IDMs. Josie has so far taught the second-grade inquiry twice, in the spring of 2021 and then again in the spring of 2022, so we share ways she has adjusted the IDM blueprint since its design as well as ideas for going forward.[7]

Questions to Critique Systems of Power and Oppression

The compelling question served to center the inquiry in critical ways. Our second-grade team asked, "How can I give back to Indigenous People today?" and specifically included historical and current events in which Indigenous people were/are treated inequitably. We made the decision to focus our content around a compelling question that would represent Indigenous people more authentically and holistically and emphasize that Indigenous communities not only existed in the past, but are living and active in our nation today. Though some Virginia standards mention teaching about Native American lives today, that part of the standard typically provides an incomplete history and does not receive as much focus in instruction. We did not want to reproduce common flaws in teaching this content, such as perpetuating the false narrative that Native Americans are people of the past, or utilizing crafts that minimize Native American traditions and contribute to cultural appropriation. In emphasizing the modern *presence* of Native Americans in Virginia and throughout the United States, our inquiry pushes back on one of the failings of traditional curriculum.[8]

Figure 1: IDM Blueprint of a Second-Grade Inquiry

Inquiry Design Model (IDM) Blueprint™	
Compelling Question	How can I give back to indigenous people today?
Standards and Practices	VA SOL 2.3: The student will compare the lives and contributions of three American Indian cultures of the past and present.
Staging the Question	Facilitate class discussion on what it means to give back and how giving back can create change. Read *Malala's Magic Pencil* and discuss how she took action to create change.

Supporting Question 1	Supporting Question 2	Supporting Question 3
What did Native Americans do/create in the past that shaped the way we live today?	What past events influence the need to give back to indigenous people?	How can we join in the work that's being done?
Formative Performance Task	**Formative Performance Task**	**Formative Performance Task**
Graphic organizer to identify and describe Native American contributions and their connections to today.	Discuss observations of mistreatment against Native Americans. What trends are prevalent? Students complete "thought bubbles" on images of mistreatment.	Create a list of opportunities to be involved in supporting indigenous-led activism. Choose one to support.
Featured Sources	**Featured Sources**	**Featured Sources**
Source A: Teacher-created slideshow featuring contributions such as language medicine, and government **Source B:** guest speaker about Powhatan Nation	**Source A:** Teacher-created slideshow featuring quotes and images of injustices around land rights, featuring sources from Native Knowledge 360° highlighting Native resistance, Cherokee perspectives on forced removal, and "invasion of America" map **Source B:** Teacher-created slides focused on environmental abuse, featuring quotes and photographs by Ponca Tribe and of the Torres Martinez reservation **Source C:** Teacher-created slides featuring images and secondary text highlighting Boarding Schools and cultural abuses.	**Source A:** TRUST Arizona video featuring Jaime Lynn Butler, Navajo youth climate activist **Source B:** *We are water protectors* (Lindstrom & Goade, 2020) **Source C:** Earthguardians website featuring indigenous leadership from over 20 nations

Summative Performance Task	**Argument**	Construct an argument using evidence that addresses the compelling question about how you can give back to indigenous people today.
	Extension	Create an action plan to support your chosen action from Formative Performance Task 3.
Taking Informed Action		Brainstorm a variety of action items from Formative Performance Task 3. From these action items students will choose one to put into action (e.g., school audit, fundraiser to donate to Native-led activism, tracking and lowering carbon footprint, creating protest signs, writing thank you letters to indigenous activists, write a letter to cancel Keystone XL pipeline).

Further, we wanted to ensure that we did not only focus on oppression of Native Americans, but rather centered Native resistance and resilience. We accomplished this goal in the third supporting question, "How can we join in with the work that's being done [led by Indigenous people today]?" We wanted students to understand how Indigenous people have been mistreated, but we also wanted to highlight that they are people who have always resisted and are still resisting, and there are ways that students can support that resistance.

In looking back on our compelling question, we notice that we could have designed it to be more open-ended. By asking "how can I give back," we presume students will conclude that some kind of reparation is appropriate. Trying to apply the traits of a strong compelling question while at the same time crafting questions that critique systems of power and oppression was a challenge and our compelling question in the end was more critical and less open-ended. Going forward, we need to learn how to better balance both expectations. We did not change any of the questions in the second implementation, but are working to make some revisions in the future. A question such as "How can I demonstrate citizenship as I learn about the way Indigenous people have shaped today's world through their contributions and resistance?" would allow students to investigate the same information included in the inquiry, but without first concluding that it is necessary for them to give back to Indigenous communities. There would also be more standards-based activities to use when staging the compelling question because there are state standards centered around citizenship.

Tasks to Alleviate Injustice

In the first implementation, my (Josie's) students were engaged in mostly discussion-oriented tasks throughout supporting questions two and three, particularly about justice, though I included some scaffolds to support their discussions. For example, in students' second formative performance task, they used "thought bubbles" to respond empathetically to images showing modern and historical systemic mistreatment of a variety of Native American groups. They began to recognize the impact of removal, and environmental mistreatment by sharing words such as "sad, angry," and "disgust" to describe feelings they might have had if they were treated the same way. The thought bubbles exercise was one that I added to support students' engagement with the sources. I recognized that students needed varied ways to engage and interact with each other and the sources, particularly since we designed the inquiry to be implemented virtually and ended up teaching it in-person. Going forward in designing IDM blueprints, I will infuse more interactive and active formative tasks throughout from the outset.

As a first-year teacher planning an inquiry with the additional constraints of navigating a school year disrupted by COVID-19, I had to give myself grace for running out of time before implementing the taking informed action piece of the inquiry. Still, I was proud of the space we created for students to engage in meaningful dialogue. The conversations students had throughout the inquiry showed that they were increasing their understanding of the need to alleviate injustice against Indigenous people and learning about meaningful ways to do so. Students were able to critique the *power* dynamics and Indigenous agency, and learn about and move towards supporting Indigenous activism and *partnerships*, but we needed more time to carry out the summative argument task and for taking informed action.[9]

In the second implementation, we took a multi-disciplinary approach and focused on deepening students' interactions with the content of the inquiry and on the integration of language arts and social studies through tasks that asked students to read, write, and speak about their understanding of the sources provided. Integrating social studies inquiry with English Language Arts can allow for more instructional time. I also continued to focus on creating opportunities for students to interact with the material in a way that supported them in processing topics that highlighted some of the injustices in U.S. history, since that had been an effective addition in our first implementation.

In formative performance task 2, for instance, in addition to the "thought bubble" task, I asked students to respond in real time using Pear Deck (a Google Slides Add-On that can collect and display student thinking during a lesson) as they analyzed sources about environmental mistreatment. Students typed responses to questions such as "What do you notice about the picture?" "What is something you wonder about what you have learned so far?" and "Type a feeling word in response to the information from the article." This activity prompted students to grasp what was being expressed through pictures and words in the slides and articulate their ideas in a way that made their thinking visible and embedded more student writing in the inquiry. The culminating formative performance task for supporting question 2 asked students to participate in a whole group discussion to summarize their observations from the three sources describing mistreatment and to search for trends they noticed. We constructed a class anchor chart (Figure 2), which shows that students understood multiple injustices experienced by Native Americans and recognized that this treatment was systemic.

The trends students identified from their learning throughout supporting question 2 are powerful in that they express the motivation behind the mistreatment inflicted upon Native Americans "by the [U.S.] government," the understanding that these actions "changed the way Native Americans lived," as well as the perception of justice and empathy they expressed when saying "it wasn't fair." The addition of more structured written tasks supported students as they interpreted sources and provided stronger assessment evidence for me that students were able to achieve deeper levels of historical understanding.

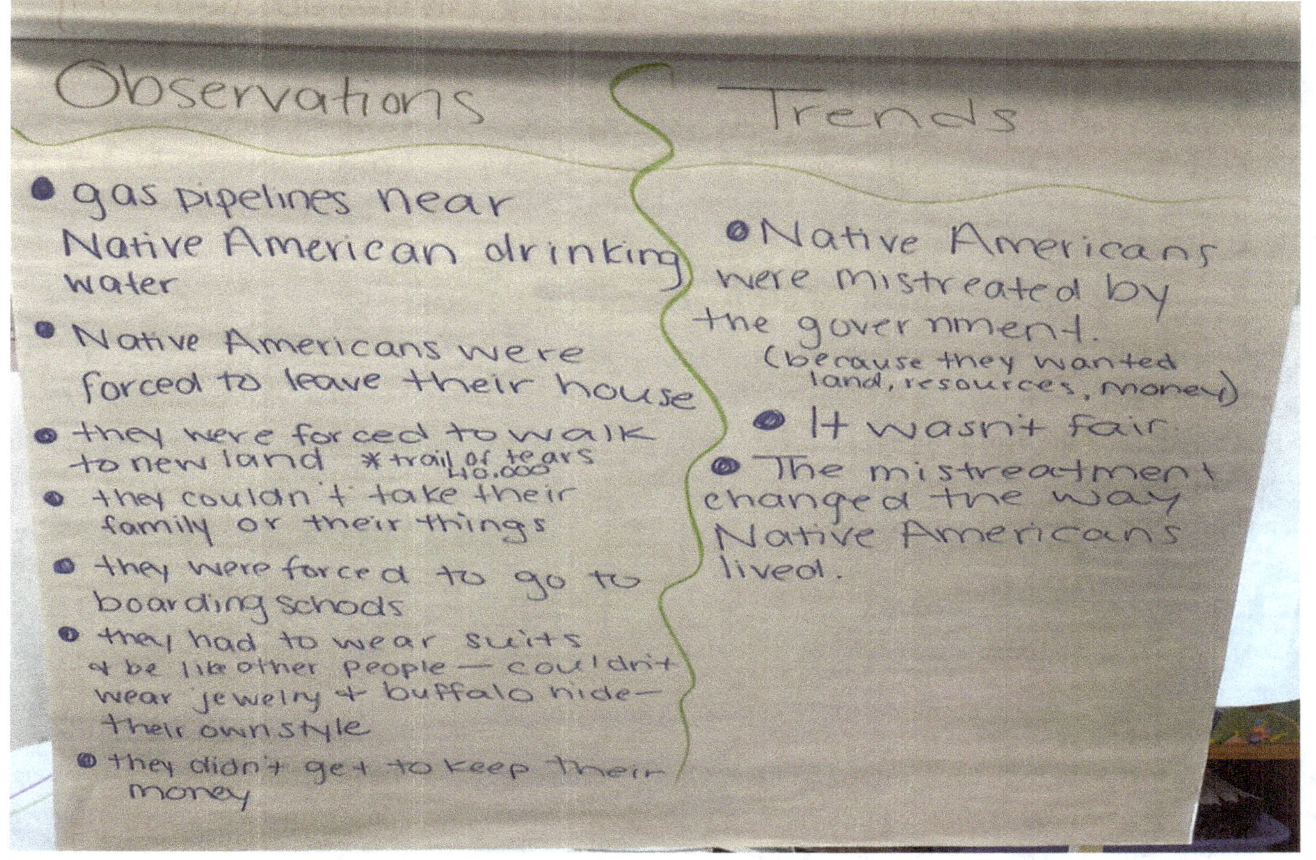

Figure 2. Formative Task 2 Anchor Chart.

Sources to Center the Perspectives of Marginalized Groups

In our efforts to make instruction authentic, we chose sources for our inquiry that included Indigenous voices. For example, we included multiple sources drawn from Native Knowledge 360°, part of the educational resources at the National Museum of the American Indian as well as the Anishinabe/Métis-authored and Kiks.ádi-illustrated children's book *We Are Water Protectors*.[10] The Indigenous voices in our sources supported students in developing and expressing empathy toward their perspectives in their eagerness to make sense of the harm being done to Indigenous communities. The sources for supporting question 3 intentionally amplify Indigenous activism so that students are serving as allies to Indigenous-led projects, rather than assuming they know what is best for Indigenous communities when they begin to take informed action. After reflection, we noticed that the featured sources in supporting question 1 presented *about* rather than *through* Native American voices and perspectives, and it was in supporting question 1 that students were expected to access all of the content required by the state standard, focusing on Native Americans' contributions to ways of life in the United States today. We needed to identify more sources authored by Native Americans for supporting question 1, rather than relying on sources teachers had used in the past.

Recognizing the limited Indigenous voices in the first supporting question, we added the Standing Rock Sioux-authored children's book *Greet the Dawn: The Lakota Way* to the sources for supporting question 1 in the second implementation of this inquiry. We also added Cherokee Nation-authored children's book *We Are Still Here* to the sources for supporting question 2.[11] *Greet the Dawn: The Lakota Way* provided background knowledge for students to understand the importance of the relationship between the environment and Indigenous cultures. *We Are Still Here* summarized 12 aspects of Native Nations' lived experiences in a way that shares inclusive history and is comprehensible for young people. It was used as an interactive read aloud to clarify and review information students engaged with throughout the other resources in supporting question 2 and act as a bridge for moving into supporting question 3. Sorell wrote in the Author's Note, "I hope this book's text, art, and timeline make it clear that Native people have always been actively engaged in protecting our sovereignty and culture."[12] The focus on Indigenous resistance made this a powerful read aloud for bridging to supporting question 3.

Ms. Valentine's Reflection

I am extremely grateful I had the opportunity to participate in the inquiry design work and the ways it empowered the vision I have as a teacher—to educate students in a way that fosters agency, empathy, knowledge and collaboration through equitable and accurate pedagogy. As a first-year teacher, I feared becoming employed in the current education system and losing my passion for social justice teaching, but this project provided me the opportunity to strengthen it. Planning an IDM-based inquiry is a challenging task because of the time-consuming efforts to deepen my own understanding of content as well as find sources that are both accurate and that highlight the voices and perspectives of marginalized groups. Particularly as a teacher in the K–2 grade band, I spent a lot of time adapting sources that I found to make them interactive and developmentally appropriate for younger students without detracting from the content.

After implementing this inquiry twice and presenting the inquiry to other staff members for use in their instruction, I've learned how important it is to continue learning and growing when teaching with the IDM. Each time I have taught the inquiry, I have changed it to make it more meaningful to students and to give them more opportunities to discover ideas independently using truthful sources. I see the teacher's responsibility as providing scaffolds for students to draw conclusions and acting as a facilitator in student conversations. It's important especially in today's climate to protect the use of pedagogy like the Inquiry Design Model by making it student-centered and factual and eliminating as much teacher bias as possible. Doing so helps create space for rigor and critical thinking in the learning process and I believe that analyzing sources is a powerful skill that will serve students and the world well if they are able to learn it. The next time I teach this inquiry, I expect to focus on strengthening and adapting the summative performance task and taking informed action pieces so that students can not only share their understandings but also use them to inform their decisions about how they react to the information they consume about their country's history, past, and present. This approach should give the inquiry and the students a greater sense of purpose.

Despite the countless hours it took to design the inquiry, I found it to be a huge growth opportunity for me and my students. I was able to learn (and unlearn) so much about Indigenous people and increase my awareness of the need to continue educating myself about ways to be an ally to marginalized groups in society. It was rewarding to hear the conversations students were having because they were deeply engaging with the material and it gave me great hope for how students might advocate for social justice in their futures, or at least have less biased understandings of U.S. history as they grow older. As teachers, we want our students to grow up to be agents of change and that starts with us being change-makers in our classrooms with the content we teach. IDM excites me as a teacher because it enables us to present accurate information to students in a way that is centered around making student thinking visible. I am eager to see how I might use inquiries in my future to continue pushing my students to dig deeper into social studies and the meaning of equity.

Conclusion

Previous research on the implementation of the *C3 Framework* in K–12 schools has been encouraging, with findings indicating that teachers believe using inquiry is effective and worth the effort to design and implement instruction in this way, even in elementary settings.[13] Our students should be prepared to question social issues and to take informed civic action to disrupt and dismantle racist and unjust systems. While recognizing the importance of this work, teachers also need support to do it. In particular, Josie points to the time needed to increase her own content knowledge, find appropriate sources, and modify sources for her students. Depending on the school and local context, teachers may also worry about administrative support for implementing critical inquiries such as the one described here; Josie was confident in the support of her administration, which helped her feel confident to teach ambitiously.

Notes

1. National Council for the Social Studies, *College, Career, and Civic Life (C3) Framework for Social Studies State Standards* (Silver Spring, MD: NCSS, 2013); S.G. Grant, Kathy Swan, and John Lee, *Inquiry-based Practice in Social Studies Education: Understanding the Inquiry Design Model* (New York, NY: Routledge, 2017).

2. Tina L. Heafner and Paul G. Fitchett, "Principals' and Teachers' Reports of Instructional Time Allocations in Third Grade," *Journal of International Social Studies* 5, no. 1 (2015): 81–100; Meira Levinson, *No Citizen Left Behind* (Cambridge, MA: Harvard University Press, 2012); Bettina L. Love, "What is Hip-Hop-based Education Doing in Nice Fields Such as Early Childhood and Elementary Education?" *Urban Education* 50, no. 1 (2015): 106–131; Judith Pace, "The Complex and Unequal Impact of High Stakes Accountability on Untested Social Studies," *Theory and Research in Social Education*, 39 no. 1 (2011): 32–60.

3. R. Patrick Solomon, Andrew M. A. Allen, and Arlene Campbell, "The Politics of Advocacy, Strategies for Change: Diversity and Social Justice Pedagogy in Urban Schools," in *Urban Teacher Education and Teaching: Innovative Practices for Diversity and Social Justice*, ed. R. P. Solomon and Dia N. R. Sekayi (Mahwah, NJ: Lawrence Erlbaum Associates, 2007), 207–225.

4. NCSS, *College, Career, and Civic Life (C3) Framework for Social Studies State Standards*; Kathy Swan, John Lee, and S. G. Grant, *Inquiry Design Model: Building Inquiries in Social Studies* (Silver Spring, MD: NCSS and C3 Teachers, 2018).

5. Swan, Lee, and Grant, *Inquiry Design Model*; Kathy Swan, S. G. Grant, and John Lee, *Blueprinting an Inquiry-Based Curriculum: Planning with the Inquiry Design Model* (Silver Spring, MD: NCSS, 2019); Grant, Swan, and Lee, *Inquiry Design Model*.

6. Ryan Crowley and LaGarrett King, "Making Inquiry Critical: Examining Power and Inequity in the Classroom," *Social Education* 82, no. 1 (2018): 16.

7. Josephine Valentine was a first-year teacher in the 2020-2021 academic year.

8. Leilani Sabzalian, "The Tensions Between Indigenous Sovereignty and Multicultural Citizenship Education: Toward an Anticolonial Approach to Civic Education," *Theory & Research in Social Education* 47, no. 3 (2019): 311–346.

9. Sabzalian.

10. Carole Lindstrom and Michaela Goade (illustrator), *We are Water Protectors* (New York, NY: Roaring Book Press, 2020).

11. S.D. Nelson, *Greet the Dawn: The Lakota Way* (Rapid City, SD: South Dakota Historical Society Press, 2012); Traci Sorell and Frane Lessac (ill.), *We Are Still Here: Native American Truths Everyone Should Know* (Watertown, MA: Charlesbridge, 2021).

12. Sorell, 39

13. Emma S. Thacker, Adam M. Friedman, Paul G. Fitchett, Wayne Journell, and John K. Lee, "Exploring How an Elementary Teacher Plans and Implements Social Studies Inquiry," *The Social Studies* 109 no. 2 (2018): 85-100; Erin Casey, Cynthia F. DiCarlo, and Kerry L. Sheldon, "Growing Democratic Citizenship Competencies: Fostering Social Studies Understandings Through Inquiry Learning in the Preschool Garden," *Journal of Social Studies Research* 43, no. 4 (2019): 361–73.

This work was supported by the Lara Parker ('92) and Eric D. ('91) Major Faculty Fellowship Endowment through the College of Education at James Madison University.

Middle Level Learning 76 (January/February 2023): 10–13.

Creating a Space for Hope Through Inquiry: An Interview with Ckristina Bennett from Syracuse, New York

Edited by MaryBeth Yerdon, Kathy Swan, John Lee, and S.G. Grant

This might be Ckristina Bennett's first full year in a social studies classroom, but she cut her teeth as a substitute teacher in the Syracuse City School District. This past fall, Ckristina brought her experience to one of Syracuse Latin School's eighth-grade social studies classrooms. In her new classroom, Ckristina uses inquiry to support her culturally relevant and sustaining teaching. Despite the past year's uptick in curricular oversight and controversy surrounding social studies content, Ckristina is not deflated. In fact, she says she sees hope in inquiry's ability to facilitate relevant and sustaining content and for teaching the democratic discourse missing in our current social and political landscape. C3 Teachers sat down with Ckristina Bennett to discuss her first full year of teaching, using inquiry in the class- room, and teaching hard history by using an Inquiry Design Model (IDM) curricular loop.[1]

C3 Teachers: How did you come to inquiry and the IDM for the first time?

CB: I fell in love with teaching during my practicum placement at Nottingham High School. I know that is not always the case with student teaching; however, I had a great mentor teacher and he routinely used inquiry and the IDM in his

Revolution of Ideas: A Decade of C3 Inquiry | 111

psychology class. At first, I didn't realize that he was using a specific type of model, but he would always start off with a question and guide students through a topic, ending with some kind of argument- based project. When I watched him, I immediately noticed the intentional backward design. So, I asked him if he could show me how he planned these lessons, and he showed me the IDM Blueprint. Then, at the beginning of this year, before students came back, I attended a professional development where we talked about teaching hard history using an IDM curricular loop focused on teaching hard history and how people are making peace with the past.[2]

C3 T: Was there a particular aspect of the IDM or the curricular loop that sparked your interest?

CB: Yes, first during that professional development, we learned about how to thread six inquiries together to make a curricular loop around the question "How do we make peace with the past?"[3] The focused inquiry that really hooked me was "Did the return of Bruce's Beach bring justice?" [about the California bill that enabled Black families like Charles and Willa Bruce to reclaim land seized decades ago.[4]] Now, I find myself defaulting to the language and methods embedded in the IDM. For example, like my mentor teacher, everything starts with a question, and instead of thinking about a Do Now or some other version of an anticipatory set, I think about how to stage questions, even when I'm not necessarily doing a full-scale inquiry.

C3 T: It seems like you came into inquiry first by observing inquiry in the classroom, then by taking a deep dive into inquiry during a professional development. Were there any particular "aha" moments during that professional development?

The 8th Grade Curricular Loop: How Do We Make Peace with the Past?
Kathy Swan et al., "Countering the Past of Least Resistance: A Hard History Inquiry-Based Curriculum," *Social Education* 86, no.1 (2022): 34–39.

CB: Absolutely. In the inquiry loop that was featured at our professional development in Syracuse, students are expected to confront challenging events of the past, and one of the ways they do this is by engaging in Harkness discussions. In these discussions, the teacher sits on the outside, and students lead the discussion.[5] We spent time talking about all the parts of an inquiry and I saw how those parts come together during the Harkness discussion. Plus, I got to facilitate the discussion around Bruce's Beach with the other teachers at the professional development. At times the Harkness discussion got really intense, and I could see the importance of having kids grapple with these hard questions. It was at this moment that I saw how inquiry works and how the IDM comes together to empower students to wrestle with a big idea and find their own way out.

C3 T: You said that you often default to the language and methods embedded in the IDM. Would you say that the language of inquiry has become a classroom vernacular?

CB: Yes. I started talking inquiry and at first, I didn't even notice that I was doing it. It just makes sense to talk about teaching in terms of inquiry. Visualizing the Blueprint makes sense in my brain. Once you get it, inquiry makes its way into all aspects of your planning. But most importantly, inquiry forces you to let the reins go, you've got to turn it over to the students. Once you get used to being the facilitator, it just makes the classroom so much better than when we were in middle school.

C3 T: Finally, in our current moment, social studies education is being heavily critiqued. What are some of the challenges you are facing in your state as a social studies teacher? And, do you see inquiry and the IDM as a means to mediate or interrupt some of these concerns?

CB: I don't think that we can teach social studies or American History without analyzing and examining the intersections of race, class, gender, sexual identity, ability, and other identity categories. We are a bit protected here in New York State from restrictive curricular mandates. But, even though New York comes off as "liberal,"

these curricular debates infiltrate lots of communities here, and I've heard it all. I've experienced some of the more inflammatory rhetoric and even intimidation tactics from people who want an uncritical version of social studies. I see inquiry and IDM mediating restrictive curricular oversight; through inquiry, we are giving students credible resources and asking questions about important and sometimes controversial topics. We are asking questions and facilitating the discussions, but the kids are doing the work, they are analyzing sources and making arguments. These skills and discussions that come out of them are essential for a healthy democracy and that gives me hope. In my classroom, I'm creating a space for hope through inquiry.

Notes

1. Kathy Swan et al., "Countering the Past of Least Resistance: A Hard History Inquiry-Based Curriculum," *Social Education* 86, no.1 (2022): 34–39.
2. Swan et al., "Hard History," 35.
3. Swan et al.
4. In "Did the return of Bruce's Beach bring justice?", students learn about the landmark California bill enabling Black families to reclaim lands seized decades ago. The inquiry focuses on the case of Charles and Willa Bruce, who owned a once-flourishing seaside resort called Bruce's Beach Lodge in Manhattan Beach, California.
5. Swan et al., 36.

This interview, conducted over two sessions, has been edited and condensed.

Teachers from around the world are using inquiry and the IDM in the classroom. Creating community through connecting teachers is one of C3 Teachers' primary goals. Through inquiry development, hubs, blogging, the C3 Teachers Institute, and the Making Inquiry Possible Project, C3 Teachers strive to support teachers as they implement inquiry in the classroom. Join us! We want to hear from you.

This interview is the second in a series of interviews with practicing C3 Teachers from around the country. Visit us at www.c3teachers.org or contact us at info@c3teachers.org.

The C3 Teachers initiative is guided by **MaryBeth Yerdon** (State University of New York, Cortland), **Kathy Swan** (University of Kentucky), **John Lee** (North Carolina State University), and **S. G. Grant** (Binghamton University). Kathy, John, and SG have worked as leaders and writers in the C3 Framework project and know first-hand the critical role teachers play in the implementation and realization of the C3 goals and aspirations. Their work extends beyond the C3 into teacher education and preparing new teachers to tackle the challenges of teaching social studies in the 21st century. They look forward to learning from C3 Teachers and the ways in which they lead the effort!

Social Education 87, no. 6 (2023): 367–387

The Art of the Blueprint:
Inquiry in the Classroom

Kathy Swan, John Lee, S.G. Grant, and fellow inquiry travelers

Over the past 10 years, we have asked and reasked our own compelling question, "What is inquiry?" Our first answer to that question came in the form of a standards document, the *College, Career, and Civic Life (C3) Framework for Social Studies State Standards.*[1] We defined inquiry as a set of interlocking and reinforcing dimensions that move from developing questions and planning inquiries to communicating conclusions and taking informed action. Content and skills matter in the C3 Framework, but they do not matter in isolation. Instead, they are integrated into the Inquiry Arc in such a way that they become part of a curriculum and instructional whole. The Inquiry Arc is composed of four distinct but inter-related dimensions: (1) developing questions and planning inquiries, (2) applying disciplinary concepts and tools, (3) evaluating sources and using evidence, and (4) communicating conclusions and taking informed action. Some 38 states have adopted elements or whole sections of the Framework into their state standards such that approximately 35 million students now have opportunities to experience inquiry-based teaching and learning.[2]

After the publication of the C3 Framework, we again asked, "What is inquiry?" but this time focused on the curricular elements that would enable teachers to model inquiry and to shift classroom instruction to meet the demands/vision of the C3 Framework. Our answer was the Inquiry Design Model (IDM), a theory of inquiry-based instruction centered on a one-page blueprint that defines three essential elements of inquiry-based instruction: questions, tasks, and sources (See the example that follows).[3] Here is a quick rundown of those elements:

- *Questions* are the starting place for inquiry. Compelling questions frame an inquiry by asking a rigorous and relevant question (e.g., What symbol best represents the United States?). Supporting questions sustain the line of inquiry by helping students build necessary background knowledge that help them answer the larger compelling question (e.g., What is a symbol? How do words, actions, and objects represent different ideals that symbolize the United States?).
- *Sources* are the building blocks of inquiry. Students use a variety of disciplinary sources (e.g., objects, photographs, film, etc.) to investigate compelling and supporting questions and to complete formative and summative performance tasks.
- *Tasks* are the assessment spaces of an inquiry. Formative performance tasks allow students to answer supporting questions by developing key understandings using the sources analyzed in the inquiry process. Summative performance tasks allow students to answer compelling questions through an evidenced-based argument, creative project, or civic action.

We see these elements as mutually reinforcing. In other words, you cannot have one without the other. Let's illustrate this interdependence by zooming in on the role of sources and their relationship to questions and tasks. Why are students reading and analyzing sources? They are in search of answers to supporting and compelling questions, ques-

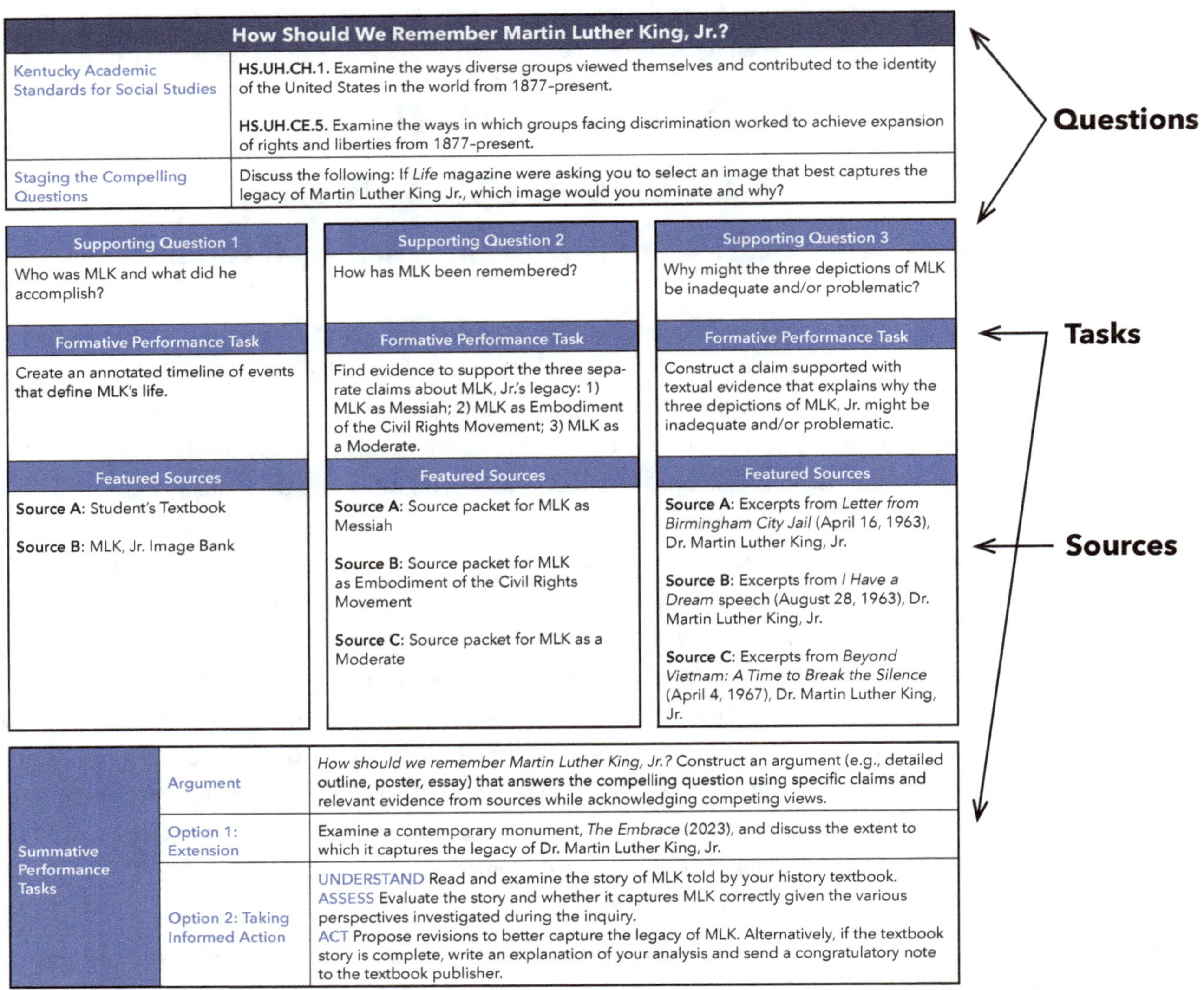

How Should We Remember Martin Luther King, Jr.?	
Kentucky Academic Standards for Social Studies	**HS.UH.CH.1.** Examine the ways diverse groups viewed themselves and contributed to the identity of the United States in the world from 1877–present. **HS.UH.CE.5.** Examine the ways in which groups facing discrimination worked to achieve expansion of rights and liberties from 1877–present.
Staging the Compelling Questions	Discuss the following: If *Life* magazine were asking you to select an image that best captures the legacy of Martin Luther King Jr., which image would you nominate and why?

Supporting Question 1	Supporting Question 2	Supporting Question 3
Who was MLK and what did he accomplish?	How has MLK been remembered?	Why might the three depictions of MLK be inadequate and/or problematic?
Formative Performance Task	**Formative Performance Task**	**Formative Performance Task**
Create an annotated timeline of events that define MLK's life.	Find evidence to support the three separate claims about MLK, Jr.'s legacy: 1) MLK as Messiah; 2) MLK as Embodiment of the Civil Rights Movement; 3) MLK as a Moderate.	Construct a claim supported with textual evidence that explains why the three depictions of MLK, Jr. might be inadequate and/or problematic.
Featured Sources	**Featured Sources**	**Featured Sources**
Source A: Student's Textbook **Source B:** MLK, Jr. Image Bank	**Source A:** Source packet for MLK as Messiah **Source B:** Source packet for MLK as Embodiment of the Civil Rights Movement **Source C:** Source packet for MLK as a Moderate	**Source A:** Excerpts from *Letter from Birmingham City Jail* (April 16, 1963), Dr. Martin Luther King, Jr. **Source B:** Excerpts from *I Have a Dream* speech (August 28, 1963), Dr. Martin Luther King, Jr. **Source C:** Excerpts from *Beyond Vietnam: A Time to Break the Silence* (April 4, 1967), Dr. Martin Luther King, Jr.

Summative Performance Tasks	Argument	*How should we remember Martin Luther King, Jr.?* Construct an argument (e.g., detailed outline, poster, essay) that answers the compelling question using specific claims and relevant evidence from sources while acknowledging competing views.
	Option 1: Extension	Examine a contemporary monument, *The Embrace* (2023), and discuss the extent to which it captures the legacy of Dr. Martin Luther King, Jr.
	Option 2: Taking Informed Action	UNDERSTAND Read and examine the story of MLK told by your history textbook. ASSESS Evaluate the story and whether it captures MLK correctly given the various perspectives investigated during the inquiry. ACT Propose revisions to better capture the legacy of MLK. Alternatively, if the textbook story is complete, write an explanation of your analysis and send a congratulatory note to the textbook publisher.

tions help frame the "why" of reading and interpreting sources. Students then use those sources to complete formative and summative performance tasks. Sources become the "how" of performance assessments within an inquiry. Students demonstrate their knowledge of *compelling and supporting questions* using information and evidence from *disciplinary sources* in their *formative and summative performance tasks.* It is impossible to remove either questions *or* tasks *or* sources from an inquiry—we argue that they are the "essence" of inquiry.[4]

We have used the IDM blueprint as a tool for making inquiry visible to teachers. In our second book on IDM,[5] we broke down inquiry development into a three-phase, 10-step process where teachers develop blueprints around inquiry topics that are central to social studies. In the first phase, teachers frame an inquiry using a backward design planning process of selecting a topic that is ripe for inquiry,[6] mining that topic for a rich compelling question, and ensuring that the question allows students to construct divergent arguments. Then, teachers fill an IDM blueprint by focusing on the formative work that students will do to build their background knowledge and capacity for evidence-based summative performance tasks that address the inquiry's compelling question. Lastly, teachers finish their blueprint by putting the finishing touches on their inquiry. In this phase, teachers plan the first and last days of an inquiry experience and provide instructional spaces for students to become curious and invested in the compelling question, to employ a range of old and new technologies to express their arguments, and to use those arguments to make a difference in the world. Together, this process of developing an inquiry helps teachers see the elements of inquiry (questions, tasks, and sources) within the content context of their courses (U.S. history, economics, government, etc.).

Once teachers are able to see these inquiry elements play out on a single blueprint, they are able to begin planning out a series of inquiry experiences for their students. We call this *looping*. At its simplest, looping means offering students opportunities to engage in inquiry in regular intervals and in a coherent fashion within and across grade levels.[7] In our book *Blueprinting an Inquiry Based Curriculum: Planning with the Inquiry Design Model*,[8] we outline five different kinds of blueprints that shrink inquiry down to 1–2 days of instruction (a "focused" blueprint) and give students more instructional agency in forming questions, selecting sources, and defining tasks (a "guided" or "self-directed" blueprint). We use this array of five blueprint types to think about the inquiry experience across a course of study or a curricular inquiry "loop" that features skills and/or concepts that repeat within or across grade levels. Once teachers begin looping inquiry, we start to see real shifts in instructional approaches but also investments in assessment, including standards-based grading approaches calibrated around inquiry. And, Kaboom! Inquiry really takes off when assessment practices change.

Issuing Creative Licenses for the IDM Blueprint

We intentionally created the IDM blueprint to be malleable,[9] enabling teachers to construct questions, tasks, and sources that uniquely animate their course content and instructional practice so it feels like their own. We underscore that flexibility with a creative commons license. Teachers are encouraged to openly share their ideas and for other teachers to adapt those ideas for their own context. In other words, teachers should do what they do best and our field should thrive in the marketplace of inquiry ideas. If you are thinking of the ethos surrounding the common good, you are on the right track!

In the remainder of this article, we introduce you to a group of innovative colleagues who continue to push our thinking about teaching with inquiry through the IDM Blueprint. The following nine *Portraits of Inquiry* are short but powerful vignettes written to demonstrate how the blueprint has taken on different hues and styles and organically come to life in classrooms, districts, and professional learning spaces. We organized these stories so that readers could take a gallery walk approach peering into the classroom studios of some of our most accomplished pedagogical artists. We start with questions and staging questions, move to formative and summative tasks, and then further outward highlighting both innovations (the jigsaw blueprint and assessment) and issues (teaching teachers to teach with inquiry). We conclude with a piece on trust, a teaser on what's to come from the C3 Teachers studio.

Portraits of Inquiry

Teaching for Questions

Ryan Lewis

Questions matter. As science educator Margaret Wertheim remarks, "The problem with most [text]books is that … they focus on the answers. But they don't explain the questions and *why the questions matter*" (emphasis added).[10] In a world of quick and Googl-able facts, the classroom is dangerously close to losing the art of the question. This is a problem. Questions are not just the means to an answer. Questions are also the window into the mind. Question asking reveals levels of understanding and curiosities. As teachers, how we use questions also exposes our teaching philosophies, our view of knowledge, and our own pedagogical dispositions.

Compelling questions surface these dispositions. However, as we get used to seeing units framed by compelling questions, I wonder if this familiarity will breed inertia? Become rote? A task list? If so, my call to teachers is for us to re-evaluate how we ask our questions, and to challenge ourselves not to lose the magic of questioning.

Walter Parker and Diana Hess posit a subtle but powerful distinction in the way teachers use classroom discussion: teaching *with* discussion and teaching *for* discussion.[11] Each reflects the mindset of the teacher: discussion as a vehicle to gather information (teaching *with*), and discussion as a goal worthy of its own end (teaching *for*). I think this simple distinction can apply to questions. Within the IDM, compelling questions are centered as the prime movers of learning. But not all of us approach inquiry this way. Just as teachers might use discussion in their classrooms but not make it the focal point, teachers might teach with questions without ever truly centering them. Here, I offer two dispositions for inquiry: teaching *with* questions and teaching *for* questions. This distinction, I believe, is key to harnessing the power of compelling questions in our classrooms.

What does it look like to teach *with* questions? The goal of questions is to gather information rather than explore it, to focus on the breadth of a topic versus its depth, writing that emphasizes recall over interpretation, and envisions the teacher as a "gatekeeper" that sifts out conflicting information. Most crucially, compelling questions become rigid and ornamental.

On the other hand, teaching *for* questions means compelling questions initiate transformation rather than frame facts. There is a focus on exploring the depth of a topic rather than its breadth. Writing focuses on interpretation rather than recall. The teacher becomes a "facilitator" and fellow questioner. Finally, compelling questions are dynamic, flexible, and full of possibilities. Compelling questions evolve, eliciting different ideas, prompting new directions, and challenging perspectives.

Why does this distinction matter? Because, questions matter.[12] Consider the evolution of a series of compelling questions from my own classroom addressing the Civil Rights Movement:

> *Was the Civil Rights Movement Successful?*
> *Is the Civil Rights Movement Finished?*
> *What is the Legacy of the Civil Rights Movement?*

With each new iteration of the question, the scope of what is possible changes. For each question, there is a change in what my students are prompted to consider. By the third question, the Civil Rights Movement is no longer time-bound and fixed. It is a true movement, crossing borders and creating new interpretations and ways of historical remembrance.

Perhaps why we teach *with* questions rather than *for* questions is that as teachers, we already know a lot about the answers. Questions become ornamental and fixed because they frankly do frame the answer. They become a pedagogical "paint by numbers." However, if I have learned anything, teaching *for* questions isn't a destination. It is a roadmap for teachers who want their students, and themselves, excited about questions. Teaching *for* questions is about engaging the question so that we are in it. The transformation keeps us on our toes as we think differently about the answers, allowing us to paint a new canvas alongside students.

Engaging with Staging
Christy Cartner

Covid changed inquiry. Researchers are trying to get to the bottom of the post-Covid student, but in the classroom, there has been a seismic shift on what I know for sure about my students. Where points of student interest and engagement were once fairly predictable, many students now struggle to pay attention or to even care about social studies.

One way I have learned to mitigate this challenge is through Staging the Compelling Question. When I first started teaching with the IDM blueprint, my focus was on the summative performance tasks—what were students going to ultimately *do* in the inquiry. I now focus much of my efforts on a good staging exercise as the pedagogical tipping point that might motivate students to linger in the complexity of a well-formed compelling question.

This past school year, I expanded the staging component into a more elaborate "social studies lab" in an effort to center students' own lives and soften students' entry point of wrestling with big ideas and deliberating tough, but relevant concepts.[13] Each social studies lab offers more than an introduction to the inquiry that follows. The lab is created so that students draw on their own stories, engage in a shared experience, and/or take on the role of a historian, photographer, or interviewer. For example, one staging lab asks students to photograph examples of how gender is portrayed in everyday settings such as their homes, the grocery, the mall, or online, prior to an inquiry on the feminist movement before tackling the compelling question, "x." Another lab asks students to conduct street-style interviews of friends and family, asking "what is a radical?" as a precursor to an inquiry on the Cold War, "Who's to Blame for the Cold War?"[14]

These labs can also create conceptual bookends with the Extension or Informed Action elements of an IDM. Here, I have created examples that range in scope and scale using an inquiry published on C3 Teachers about the development and legacy of Reconstruction.

Compelling Question: What does it take to secure equality?			
Original Staging - Introduce Topic and Build Curiosity (10-20 minutes)	Option 1 **Social Studies Lab -** Identify Patterns and Make Connections (20-30 minutes)	Option 2 **Social Studies Lab -** Make Connections and Curate Questions (45-90 minutes)	Option 3 **Social Studies Lab -** Research from the start of inquiry (Homework + Class)
Examine the picture *The Fifteenth Amendment. Celebrated May 19th 1870* and predict what could have prevented African Americans from experiencing the freedoms shown in the picture.	Use the news filter on a search engine to collect headlines and images published within the past six months using search terms "civil rights," "racial justice," "racial equality," etc. Work in groups to sort and group the articles based on topic, theme, and proximity to students' community.	Where do we see individuals and groups working to advocate for their rights in our community? Collaborate to create a class directory of organizations that includes who they represent and what they want. Develop a list of questions you'd ask their members about how/why they do what they do.	Interview a friend or family member using any of the questions below. Use followup questions to get as much detail from their responses as possible. What does political, social, or economic equality look like? What does it take to secure political, social, or economic equality? Work in small groups to look for patterns in responses.

What I know for sure about inquiry is that Staging the Compelling Question has become an essential gateway for the inquiry. The old adage about students knowing we care before they care what we know is amplified when students are centered in the inquiry from the very first moments of it.

When a T-Chart Isn't Just a T-Chart
Meghan Hawkins

When I was first introduced to IDM inquiry, the blueprint was clearly innovative, but I was confused by formative tasks. They seemed to be exactly what I was *already* doing in my classroom. I *already* assigned students T-charts. My students would read a source, write down some phrases on each side of the chart, share out, and then the class moved on. Simply put, students were learning, and yet my classroom did not feel particularly innovative or effective.

What I did not understand in these early attempts at inquiry, was that the IDM infuses a clear purpose into formative tasks. They aren't just formative tasks—they are formative *performance* tasks. Students *perform* a series of exercises so that they practice critical inquiry skills, acquire important content, and show me that they are ready for the summative argument task. Now, paired with a thoughtfully curated source set, a T-chart becomes so much more than a graphic organizer when guided by a robust compelling question and in service of a summative argumentative task. No longer an activity to dutifully complete (or stubbornly ignore), the T-chart becomes an exercise in critical thinking that students return to when crafting a claim. When I started using the formative tasks in this way, students stopped asking the pervasive "*Why* do I have to do this?" and I started really understanding the inquiry process.

Formative performance tasks may not be glamorous. They may appear simple. Yet this seeming simplicity belies the integral role of formative performance tasks in getting students to really grapple with the questions, wrestle with sources, and find their voice in summative performance tasks.

Formative performance tasks are most powerful when the task logic develops the skills students need to complete the summative task.[15] For example, the C3 Teachers' inquiry "Why Was the US on the Winning Side of World War II?"[16] was designed for students with inquiry experience—the formative performance tasks did not work for my inquiry novices. Based on the needs of my students, I built an identifying evidentiary task logic[17] to develop an initial skill in the inquiry process—reading a source and finding evidence. By the end of the series, students had accumulated key pieces of evidence that would help them build their claims about why the United States was on the winning side of World War II.

Formative Performance Task 1	Formative Performance Task 2	Formative Performance Task 3
Create a T-chart documenting the homefront and its impact on the war front.	Create a timeline highlighting American contributions to Allied victory in Europe.	Create a fishbone diagram of the causes that led to Allied victory in the Pacific.

After practicing how to identify evidence, the next inquiry's task logic focuses on identifying an author's argument. As students grapple with the C3 Teachers' inquiry "Who is to Blame for the Cold War?,"[18] the task logic allows students to discover that where agency is ascribed, whose behavior is described, and the choice of descriptors can help identify an author's claim.

Formative Performance Task 1	Formative Performance Task 2	Formative Performance Task 3
Create a T-chart of actions taken by the US and USSR that heightened tensions.	Make a list of the examples of problematic behavior by the USSR that each author provides.	Use a T-chart to record the adjectives and verbs the author uses to describe the US and the USSR.

And so it goes in my classroom, one task logic begets the next, begets the next. Sourcing skills stack upon claim-making skills, stack upon increasingly complex argumentation skills.

So, when you enter my classroom, you will likely see students with T-charts, Venn diagrams, concept webs, or timelines. You will see them reading sources and writing things down, as you would have in my first year of teaching. But, if you stop to listen, you will also hear students engaging in conversations about the sources, linking the sources back to their lives, and frequently repeating the compelling question somewhat quizzically as they grapple with what kind of claim they might make later in the summative task. And, if you come back a few days later, you will see students with the same T-charts, spread out on their desks with their other formative tasks, as they search for evidence to build an effective argument in support of a claim. The T-charts are no longer just T-charts.

The Jigsaw Blueprint: Learning to Flex with the IDM

James Carlson and Joel Hinrichs

Last year, the social studies department of Branford Public Schools in Connecticut began the process of "refreshing" our curriculum, a cycle that happens every 5–10 years in our district. This time around, we engaged in professional development around the Inquiry Design Model (IDM).[19] We started with a high school Current Issues course, which acts as our eleventh-grade core social studies course as well as our state-mandated course in Civics and American Government.

Our first challenge in writing an inquiry-driven curriculum was understanding how inquiries relate to larger units. Could an inquiry be an entire unit? Or, does an inquiry exist within a unit? Or, does an inquiry serve as the end product of a unit? The good news was the answer turned out to be "all of the above." An inquiry can serve as a standalone unit, a focused case study within a unit, or a culminating activity at the conclusion of a unit.[20] Furthermore, we went on to learn that the IDM blueprint template could be just as adaptable as the idea of inquiry itself. We took these insights about inquiry as a license to further flex the blueprint.

We started with an inquiry focused on Sino-American relations and the U.S. role in the Middle East. We wanted students to look at the region from a broad perspective so that they evaluated the complexity of economic, national security, and human concerns and their role in formulating U.S. policy. As we began to consider what ideas students needed to grapple with to formulate a more holistic U.S. policy, the list became daunting. How could we get students to fully consider a variety of issues and perspectives within the constraints of a high school schedule? The perennial challenge of breadth versus depth confronted us as we tried to do right by the IDM.

That's when we began to flex the blueprint. We played with a cooperative learning jigsaw approach for the formative work that would allow us to cover more content ground.[21] And then, inquiry magic! We adapted the IDM blueprint to accommodate a jigsaw. Below, we walk through elements of our blueprint innovation.

The compelling question, "How should the U.S. respond to China?" anchored the inquiry along with a Staging the Compelling Question exercise that asked students to read a story on growing concerns about TikTok and have a discussion about how the United States should respond.

From there, we developed a foundational supporting question and formative performance task that establishes a baseline for all students' understanding of the challenges of Sino-American relations with the supporting question, "What makes China so formidable?" Students are then placed into five expert groups to examine a particular aspect of China, including trade, security, human rights, geo-political, and environmental. Each group is assigned a supporting question for the expert group:

- Group 1 (Trade): How should the U.S. deal with China on **trade**?
- Group 2 (Security): How should the U.S. respond to China regarding **espionage**?
- Group 3 (Human Rights): Why should the U.S. respond to China's **human rights** record?
- Group 4 (Geo-Political): Why should the U.S. respond to China's aggression towards **Taiwan**?
- Group 5 (Environmental): How should the U.S. respond to China's **environmental** record?

The expert groups use a variety of featured sources to complete a formative performance task which includes constructing a claim with evidence answering their unique supporting question. (See formative work from the blueprint that follows).

Foundational Supporting Question	Group 1 Supporting Question	Group 2 Supporting Question	Group 3 Supporting Question	Group 4 Supporting Question	Group 5 Supporting Question
	Trade	Security	Human Rights	Geo-Political	Environmental
What makes China so formidable?	How should the US deal with China on **trade**?	How should the US respond to China regarding **espionage**?	Why should the US respond to China's **human rights** record?	Why should the US respond to China's aggression towards **Taiwan**?	How should the US respond to China's **environmental record**?
Formative Performance Task	**Formative Performance Task**	**Formative Performance Task**	**Formative Performance Task**	**Formative Performance Task**	**Formative Performance Task**
Create a 1-page infographic that shows how China is formidable geographically, economically, militarily.	Construct a claim with evidence on why the US should worry about trade with Chinese.	Construct a claim with evidence on why the US should worry about Chinese espionage.	Construct a claim with evidence on why the US should worry about China's human rights record.	Construct a claim with evidence on why the US should worry about China's aggression towards Taiwan.	Construct a claim with evidence on why the US should worry about China's environmental record.
Featured Sources	**Featured Sources**	**Featured Sources**	**Featured Sources**	**Featured Sources**	**Featured Sources**
Source A: CIA World Factbook: statistics, images, and map of China **Source B**: China on the World Stage, *Choices*, Background Essay **Source C**: Rise of China, Newsela.	**Source A**: People's Republic of Capitalism, Discovery Channel, Ted Koppel.	**Source A**: What the balloon saga tells us about China's espionage program, *Washington Post*, 2023. **Source B**: The China Threat, FBI, video and article	**Source A**: "Who are the Uyghurs and why is China being accused of genocide?", BBC News, 2022. **Source B**: "China Facial recognition and state control", The Economist, 2018 video.	**Source A**: China and Taiwan: A Simple Guide, BBC, 2022 **Source B**: "Why China-Taiwan relations are so tense." Council on Foreign Relations, 2022.	**Source A**: China's Environmental abuses, United States Department of State, 2021 **Source B**: Why China's climate policy matters to us all, BBC, 2021

We thought of these expert groups as small committees that could then "brief" the entire group in the summative argument task, almost like a classroom Model United Nations. Instead of constructing an argument, students are asked to answer the compelling question, "How should the U.S. respond to China?" with the following:

Prepare a brief for the Classroom Council that summarizes the issues that should worry the U.S. Report to the council any evidence that substantiates your claim about why the U.S. should worry about China.

After the Classroom Council, students engage with an extension and action. See the excerpted blueprint that follows.

Summative Performance Task	**ARGUMENT** *Why should the US worry about China?* Prepare a brief for the Classroom Council that summarizes the issues that should worry the US. Report to the council any evidence that substantiates your claim about why the US should worry about China.
	EXTENSION Analyze a series of political cartoons on the relationship between China and the US. Write a caption for the cartoon using what you have learned in the inquiry and detailing the artistic techniques used to convey a message.
	TAKING INFORMED ACTION: *How should the US respond to China?* **Understand:** Conduct additional research on a worrisome issue that faces the US because of worsening Chinese relations (trade, espionage, human rights). **Assess:** Examine options for how the US might address the issue noting the controversy and complexity of the possible responses. See handout for getting started. (Trade example) **Act:** Write a letter to your U.S. Representative or Senator advising them on how to handle the future relationship between the US and China. Supporting posters can also be made.

We are proud of our "jigsaw" IDM blueprint and the way it supports and structures a unit-based approach allowing us to overcome the breadth-depth dilemma. We have gone on to create additional jigsaw inquiries as we continue to flex our inquiry muscles in all of our social studies courses.

When Questions Have No Right Answer
Bonnie Lewis

The presence of search engines on the internet can make us think that every question has an answer. Worse, our reliance on soundbites and social media posts can make it seem like every question has a *right* answer. But most questions worth asking don't have a clear answer, which is usually why we ask—and keep asking—them. *What defines a people? How do we make peace with the past? How do we make our voices heard?* The C3 Framework and the IDM blueprint are about the journey *and* the destination when asking and answering compelling questions.[22] During an inquiry, students engage in deliberation before constructing arguments so that they can wrestle with the evidence before taking a stance. This process is an essential practice of democratic citizenship that gets lost when we only engage in debating and arguing. Argumentation within the C3 Framework and IDM blueprint is so much more than writing claims backed with evidence. It is about students learning how to think for themselves within the classroom so that, one day, they can do so in their communities.

Today, social studies is in the hot seat. It is not the first—or presumably the last—time this will happen. However, it does mean that what is foundational to inquiry-based social studies, asking and answering questions, can create contention within communities and classrooms. Social studies speaks to our humanity: who we are, who we have been, and who we hope to be. Each year, as we march through our curriculum maps, we implicitly ask and try to answer these questions. Social studies is controversial today because it feels personal. It is personal. Yet, the controversy does not stop us from engaging in the act of teaching good social studies but instead requires us to thoughtfully design our inquiries around compelling questions that have multiple correct answers.

In my roles as a pre-service teacher, in-service teacher, and now teacher educator, I have observed countless teachers teach using IDM blueprints. The compelling question makes or breaks the inquiry, especially when the topic is contentious. In 2021, I was a part of a team that wrote inquiries around *hard histories* for Syracuse City schools.[23] We used inquiry to engage in the hard parts of our past during a national moment of reckoning and political pushback. We knew that the compelling questions we crafted needed to be able to hold their own as rigorous, intellectually stimulating, and, above all else, *deliberative*. Each compelling question had to be designed in such a way as to have multiple ways it could be answered using evidence so that the inquiry encourages independent thinking. Designing compelling questions this way did two things. First, it guarded against accusations of indoctrination by allowing space for different perspectives. Second, it protected teachers and students from tangential arguments by grounding student responses in curated sources.

For our inquiry on American Reconstruction, we used the compelling question, *What does Reconstruction say about the U.S.?* This compelling question provides the opportunity for multiple evidentiary arguments. For example, by using voting records from the 1870s and images of Black congressmen as evidence, students could argue the Reconstruction period shows that the U.S. cares about equal representation in government. On the other hand, students could argue that Reconstruction shows that the U.S. did not follow through on its promises to extend freedoms to Black citizens, citing evidence from voting records from the 1880s and the emergence of the Ku Klux Klan. Both would be right, despite arguing different stances.

We need inquiries that reflect the complexity inherent in questions that matter. In the years that I have engaged with the C3 Framework and IDM inquiries, I have come to see the argument stems from compelling questions as the most important and innovative piece of designing an inquiry. Compelling questions open classrooms to civic deliberation by helping students understand that there is more than one way to construct an evidentiary claim addressing a compelling question. These types of questions teach us that *both can be true.*

Seeing Democracy
Ryan New

When you walk into a music room, you expect to hear music. When you walk into an art room, you expect to see and experience art. When you walk into a social studies classroom, you should expect to see and hear democracy. Taking Informed Action (TIA) provides an instructional opportunity for seeing democracy.[24] Yet, taking *informed* action can be seen as the most overwhelming part of the inquiry. There is no textbook, no teacher's edition, and often no right answers. In the following sections, I suggest several ways that teachers can overcome some of the hurdles of making TIA more visible in social studies.

1. **Start small, start with the familiar.**

   An accessible first Taking Informed Action is to invite a guest speaker. Recently, a fifth grade social studies classroom investigated the compelling question, "How Can Power Lead to Oppression?" and students invited their principal to discuss power and oppression in their school. Students worked in small groups to develop, refine, and prioritize questions to ask. The first question the principal was asked was, "Have you ever accidentally oppressed a student and how did you use your power to fix it?" The principal, moved by the students' thoughtfulness, answered with candor, regret, and hope. Students listened to their principal's honest reflection, transformed by their own agency. A seemingly small action became a profound moment. The lesson for us was don't be afraid to go small!

2. **Use the IDM to ensure Taking Informed Action is authentic problem solving.**

    TIA exercises make connections beyond the classroom, helping students learn the real world power of making a difference in their own communities. The following two examples show how we have used the Inquiry Design Model to animate action in our work with two different communities, the Kentucky's Frazier History Museum and the U.S. Census Bureau.

Example 1: In a high school inquiry, "How Does Where You Live Affect How You Live?" students explore redlining and connect it to Kentucky's Frazier History Museum West of 9th Exhibit.

Taking Informed Action	UNDERSTAND After learning about the impact that history has on the way people live today, consider which aspect of your neighborhood you would like to know more about. ASSESS Interview 1-2 members of your community to understand how they experience the neighborhood they live in. ACT Compose a classroom blog of compiled interviews conducted in your school.

Example 2: In the middle school inquiry, "What Story Does the Census Tell Us?" students address barriers by partnering with the U.S. Census Bureau to complete the 2010 decennial census.

Taking Informed Action	UNDERSTAND Investigate barriers that might result in undercounting residents of Kentucky (e.g., language barriers, perceptions of Census's use of data, etc.). ASSESS Examine potential ways to overcome those barriers and make the Census more accessible to Kentucky residents. ACT Create an information campaign that will make the community aware of the Census's importance to ensure an accurate count for the 2020 Census.

These two TIAs show the power of moving from a compelling question to an authentic issue in the community. True, students can construct wonderful arguments, but by concluding the investigation with a real-world experience, students connect to the community and can leave a lasting legacy about the real power of social studies.

3. **Don't go it alone: Partner with civic organizations that specialize in civic action.**

    The MIKVA Challenge is an action civics program we adopted as a cornerstone for Taking Informed Action in Jefferson County, Kentucky. It often serves as the Taking Informed Action part of our blueprinted curriculum. For example, *Project Soapbox* provides opportunities for students to write and deliver a speech about an issue that is important to them. Students from third grade to seniors in our district have called us to action around diverse topics such as mental illness, gun control, microplastics, need for school nurses, the eviction crisis, political polarization and sexual assault. Student speeches are a reminder that our classrooms are porous places, and we have a responsibility to help students address issues facing them.

One of the greatest threats to democracy is apathy, disillusionment, and inertia. Taking *Informed* Action is our music, our art, and our pedagogical tool for helping students see democracy.

Knuffle Bunny in the Blueprint?
How Social Studies and ELA Connect
in the Elementary Classroom

Laura Darolia

In November of 2022, my kindergartener came home with a paper grocery bag cut into the shape of a vest and scribbled with various designs he'd created. When I asked what (in the actual heck) this craft was, he responded, "my Indian outfit." In January 2023, my second grader wrote a piece about if he "had a dream," a common elementary social studies lesson on Martin Luther King Jr.'s legacy. My son wrote that his dream is "to win the World Cup."

It is a common assumption that young children cannot think critically and should not engage with complicated topics.[25] However, elementary teachers who use inquiry in their classrooms know this is not true. The examples I provided represent missed pedagogical opportunities. Using the same lessons year after year and offering the same superficial content to children robs them of the chance to think deeply and to develop and sharpen their skills of analysis and argumentation.

In what other ways could elementary teachers teach about Thanksgiving and Martin Luther King Jr.? What happens when *questions* are posed that ignite curiosity in a room of five and six year olds, who are already inherently curious? What light bulbs turn on when young children dive into *sources* (photographs, maps, videos, artifacts) to help them make sense of content? In what ways is thinking challenged and expanded when our youngest learners complete *tasks* that show how they grapple with content?

The IDM Blueprint offers teachers a starting point by outlining questions, tasks, and sources for an inquiry rooted in academic standards.[26] In an elementary school classroom, sources—the meat of the inquiry—can take a variety of forms. Visual sources like photographs, artifacts, or artwork remove reliance on decoding words, which provides pre and emergent readers access to analysis. Teachers can modify text-heavy sources in a variety of ways (annotating, excerpting, simplifying vocabulary) to make them more accessible to young students. Additionally, trade books—a staple of elementary school classrooms—can be used as meaningful sources in inquiries.

One significant challenge is that time dedicated to social studies is limited in elementary classrooms. English Language Arts (ELA) and mathematics are prioritized, for the sake of standardized test scores. It is true, however, that social studies lessons include intentional opportunities for students to read, write, listen, speak, and create, and to do so like historians, economists, political scientists, and geographers. Notably, social studies instruction has a positive impact on reading improvement in young children, while increasing minutes of ELA instruction does not.[27]

Consider a first-grade inquiry guided by the compelling question, "How can two people see the same event differently?" This is an introduction to multiple perspectives, which is an important foundational concept to studying history (and life in general). Instruction is organized around supporting questions, tasks, and sources that create space for children to grapple with the idea of perspective.

Note that the sources included in this inquiry are all trade books. First graders, who are likely used to sitting on the carpet listening to their teacher read a story aloud, do so with intent through this inquiry. While listening to the classic tale of *Knuffle Bunny*, they think about why people get upset and then connect the idea of disagreements to their own lives. *The Terrible Thing That Happened at Our House* focuses students on life changes and the ensuing emotions. Considering how to communicate feelings is the pulse of *The Day the Crayons Quit*. While students may be familiar with these books, posing supporting questions and assigning meaningful tasks adds an extra dimension to the stories, allowing students to engage with them through a different lens.

The IDM Blueprint provides a structure to design lessons rooted in social studies content that incorporate ELA skills. This is effective and efficient teaching and elementary students are ready for it.

<table>
<tr><td colspan="2">Can two people see the same event differently?</td></tr>
<tr><td>Staging the Question</td><td>Show students this optical illusion (faces or a vase?), then ask students to share what they see. After exploring the illusion, ask students if they can see both images.</td></tr>
</table>

Supporting Question 1	Supporting Question 2	Supporting Question 3
Why do people sometimes get upset?	How might people react to the changes in their lives?	How do we let people know how we feel?
Formative Performance Task	**Formative Performance Task**	**Formative Performance Task**
Students record reasons for disagreement in the story and then make a text-to-self connection.	Students complete a chart diagramming the changes and corresponding emotions for each character in the story.	Students pick a character in the story who expressed a problem, then answer questions about its resolution.
Featured Sources	**Featured Sources**	**Featured Sources**
Source A: Knuffle Bunny by Mo Willems	**Source B**: The Terrible Thing That Happened at Our House by Marge Blaine	**Source C**: The Day the Crayons Quit by Drew DeWalt

<table>
<tr><td rowspan="2">Summative Performance Task</td><td>ASSESS Can two people see the same event differently? Construct an argument (e.g., a sentence with a picture, a drawing, an answered question) that evaluates differing viewpoints using specific claims and relevant evidence from sources while acknowledging competing views.</td></tr>
<tr><td>EXTEND Students watch the final minute of a major sporting event (Packers, Brewers, Badgers, Bucks, Herd, etc.) and discuss the reactions of fans from both teams.</td></tr>
</table>

Measuring What Matters: IDM Assessment
Beau Dickenson and John Hobson

What we measure shows what we think *matters* in the classroom. Unfortunately, students in social studies have historically been assessed on low-level and often random bits of knowledge, rather than what they can actually *do* with that knowledge.[28] This situation has often produced a tedious curriculum that focuses on memorizing discrete facts and teachers "teaching to the test." Ultimately, this approach has been boring for students and bad for social studies.

Educators have found creative ways to navigate these obstacles during the No Child Left Behind era, and after more than a decade, their creative energies coalesced into a new paradigm in the form of the C3 Framework[29] and the ensuing Inquiry Design Model.[30] IDM provided an ideal framework to fundamentally change the social studies classroom and finally move beyond the discipline's persistent content dilemma: **curricula** was made more viable through an emphasis on conceptual understandings and authentic source material; **instruction** was backwards-designed, thoughtfully scaffolded, and framed through compelling questions; and **assessments** were skills-based so that content knowledge could be used as *evidence* in support of student reasoning.

Consider the following assessment items students encountered in Virginia over the past 20 years—the first one is a multiple-choice question about the Harlem Renaissance adapted from the Virginia Standards of Learning test for seventh graders; the second is an inquiry-based assessment about the same content which was implemented in Albemarle County Public Schools. The multiple-choice question simply asks, *What was the literary and artistic movement centered on African-American culture during the 1920s known as?* followed by the typical options of A, B, C, and D with three distractors and the correct answer. The second assessment asks students to respond to the open-ended question, *"How can art be used as a tool for resistance?"* Both questions assess student knowledge of the Harlem Renaissance, however, the first trivializes the content while the latter deepens understanding and connects to universal themes such as resistance and cultural expression, all the while engaging students in a rich exploration of an artistic movement. The implications for teaching and learning are dramatic if our assessment items challenge students to actually do something with the content.

The backwards design, formative assessment, and instructional scaffolding embedded within IDM ensures that the summative assessment of an inquiry is a valid measure.[31] Framing this summative exercise through a compelling question that challenges students to make evidence-based claims further elevates the learning experience by making the assessment *authentic.* Valid and authentic assessment should matter in a classroom because it will support better instruction. If we teach through inquiry and then assess through a knowledge-based multiple-choice test, a fundamental disconnect will persist, and the principles of the C3 Framework will never fully be realized in the social studies classroom.

Over the past few years, Virginia has been leading the way in shifting towards a more authentic assessment model. In 2015, the Virginia Social Studies Leaders Consortium (VSSLC) worked with legislators to eliminate the traditional Standards of Learning (SOL) tests in third grade, U.S. History I, and U.S. History II and replace them with locally-developed performance-based assessments.[32] While this was a welcome change, there was little infrastructure to support such a fundamental shift toward C3 principles. The Virginia Social Studies Leaders Consortium continued these efforts in 2020 by working with the Virginia Department of Education in consulting with C3 Teachers to utilize the IDM as a framework for performance assessment across the Commonwealth. This has since evolved into menus of inquiries as state assessments through which students can obtain high school credits in social studies courses.

Virginia's journey has shown that teacher advocacy is essential in working with legislators and policymakers to realize the inherent value of these assessment practices, as well as how they have the potential to finally unlock the historic barriers to instructional innovation in the social studies classroom. And, if best practice is any indicator, we should always begin with the end in mind and first ensure that what we *measure* reflects what truly *matters.*

What's Better than One IDM Inquiry?

Nick Stamoulactos

Inquiry needs to be more than a once-in-a-while experience. After all, inquiry is the essence of social studies, and we know students need lots and lots of practice to get better at it. But social studies is typically a hard sell for elementary teachers; adding inquiry to the mix could create some serious resistance. And yet, elementary classrooms are perfect for both. Our youngest citizens are filled with curiosity and hope and they want to make a difference in the world. In the Syracuse City School District, we used the Inquiry Design Model (IDM) to revolutionize our third-grade curriculum.

Like many districts across the country, social studies gets short-shrift in elementary classrooms. Social studies often shares time with science, and so teachers toggle between the two in eight-week units. One of the things we wanted to do in Syracuse is make the third-grade content more relevant and interesting. To that end, we created an inquiry loop of three units and nine IDM inquiries around powerful topics to brighten up social studies for our third graders.[33] We focused our efforts on three core topics: World Geography, Human/Civil Rights, and Economics/Government.

In the World Geography unit, we focus on maps, water, and garbage—three essential elements of geography and ones students can relate to. In the final inquiry of the unit, "How does garbage hurt us?" students learn about the journey that garbage takes once it is thrown away, including its local and/or global destination, the impact it has on water supplies, and its influence on human populations. The culminating inquiry asks students to take informed action by conducting a waste audit of their school, generating solutions to reduce waste, and proposing a school-wide initiative.

In the Human/Civil Rights unit, students work through four inquiries. The first three look at children who have stood up for a cause: children marches during the Civil Rights Movement; Ruby Bridges and the dangers she faced; and children who are activists in their communities around the world. Together, these three inquiries set the stage for students to complete the fourth inquiry, "How do I make change?" where they investigate how they can make an impact on their community. Students examine an issue that is important to them, assess what can be done to help with the issue and the challenges that might ensue and plan ways they can take action on their issue.

In the last unit on Economics and Local Government, students complete three inquiries investigating food deserts. In the first, students consider what causes an area to be classified as a "food desert," the detrimental impacts food access problems can have on populations, and the need and means to advocate for a "food oasis." In the second inquiry, students synthesize what they have learned by investigating Syracuse's food deserts. Students research the factors impacting the health of the city and then begin to evaluate how they can contribute to addressing this concern. The final inquiry enables students to take action and address Syracuse's food environment with school or city stakeholders.

Third grade teachers and students love the new curriculum for several reasons. First, throughout the inquiries, students read a variety of texts including trade books, informational texts, photographs, and maps. This intentionality around sources helps them with their literacy goals. Second, the focus on culturally relevant topics (e.g., food deserts) and real opportunities for action makes the curriculum authentic in the very best sense of that word. With inquiry at the helm, there is always a question; answering that question with evidence-based arguments and informed actions gives students a real-word experience. Finally, at this point in our inquiry journey, I do not have to say to our teachers or students, "we are going to do inquiry" because, at this point, inquiry *is* social studies and social studies *is* inquiry.

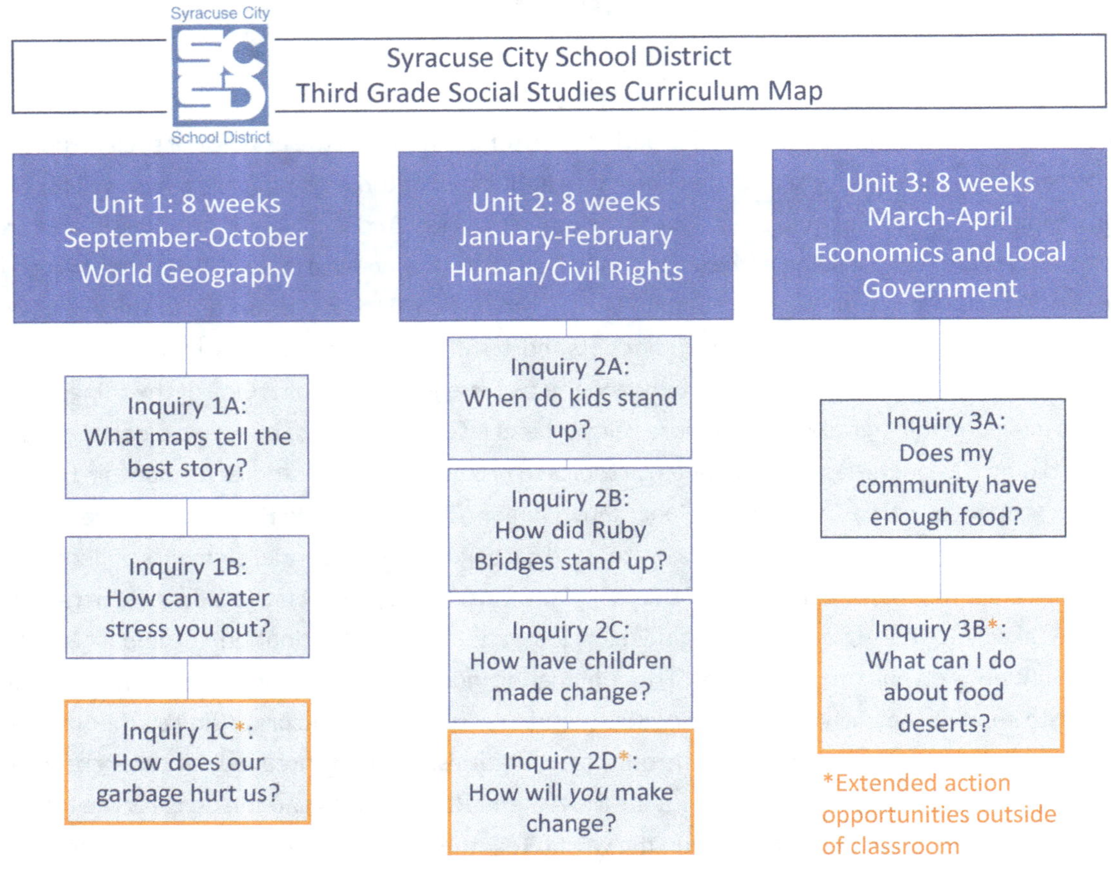

Zoom in, Focus, and Take the Shot: Reflections on Teaching Inquiry

Lauren Colley, Emma Thacker, and Rebecca Mueller

As we reflect on our past decade working with K-12 pre-service and in-service social studies teachers, we notice three shifts in how we help teachers learn to teach with inquiry.

Zooming In to Zoom Out: Questions, Tasks, and Sources

Teachers are often overwhelmed by the breadth and depth of the social studies content and skills needed for their students to complete a full inquiry. We have found this to be particularly true with our pre-service teachers who are learning how to effectively design instruction for the first time. In order to tackle this challenge, utilizing focused inquiries or the *"essence of inquiry"* allows teachers to zero in on a lesson-sized piece of inquiry construction and implementation before scaling up to the full IDM.[34]

Centering on questions, tasks, and sources within a focused inquiry, allows teachers to narrow the cognitive load by shrinking the question and amount of formative and summative work thereby creating a more manageable inquiry.[35] In a focused inquiry, there is still a compelling question to be answered by an evidenced-based argument, but the question is narrower in scope and the argumentative task could consist of a single claim and counterclaim. It also allows them time to practice inquiry design and implementation in ways that more closely mimic their everyday classroom praxis. Once they feel more experienced with focused inquiries, scaling up to a full-sized IDM feels less daunting because teachers have built skills they can apply in the IDM. Teachers can then zoom out and ask broader compelling questions and build more complex sourcework for their students in the IDM.

In and Out of Focus: The Importance of Questions

Questions can prove especially tricky for teachers, and both compelling and supporting questions provide unique challenges. Many teachers overcomplicate the compelling question in the desire to promote deep thinking. The compelling question should inspire and focus the inquiry, but an array of instructional decisions contribute to the intellectual rigor of the inquiry. When implemented effectively, a simple question can be the most compelling. Teachers may be more comfortable crafting supporting questions, but it is easy to think of them in isolation and lose focus on how the questions work together.

Compelling question types provide a useful scaffold.[36] Teachers can draft and stress-test different types of questions for the same topic and consider which best brings their instructional goals into focus. We have also learned that an important step in developing a cohesive inquiry is prompting teachers to share how they would explain the question logic to students.[37]

Questions are tough, and we have found that workshopping questions with colleagues often produces the best results. We use example inquiries on C3teachers to support teachers in understanding compelling and supporting questions and question logic and to model the reality that questions can and should evolve throughout the inquiry-development process.

Taking the Shot: Classroom Realities

Inevitably, when we introduce teachers to the idea of teaching with inquiry, we are met with a healthy dose of skepticism. Sure, the IDM seems like a useful tool and inquiry sounds good in theory, but who has time to actually use it in the classroom when we barely have time to go to the bathroom? We invite teachers to suspend disbelief and try it.

We model teaching with inquiry in our methods classes so students experience the IDM as learners prior to being asked to design inquiry-based instruction. Before jumping into the steps of designing inquiry, we now invite teachers to explore existing inquiries on C3teachers.org. There is little point in re-creating the wheel when there are strong existing resources out there, and we have shifted to supporting teachers to adapt existing inquiries to meet the needs of their students and curricular contexts. We are still happy to support teachers in designing inquiries from scratch but have found that it has been helpful to familiarize them with practical examples prior to doing so.

Shifting how we approach preparing teachers to teach with inquiry has helped us prepare a more attractive canvas for teachers, and we will continue reflecting and trying new approaches. The more examples of inquiry that teachers can experience for themselves, the better.

What's Ahead? Trusting Inquiry and Teaching with the Inquiry Design Model

Trust has surfaced in every conversation with an inquiry teacher and in every classroom visit as evidenced in each of the previous Portraits. Why trust? Students need space to figure things out in an inquiry. Teachers need to trust students and give them that space. And students need to trust teachers to make that space meaningful and to be there when they lose their way. Sometimes that space is uncomfortable and teachers will need to nurture students and scaffold the process so that they can ultimately embrace that intellectual freedom.

Arriving at trust has been a *Eureka!* moment for us further deepening our curiosity about trust and its relationship to inquiry. But trust is one of those words that is kind of squishy, and a platitude like, "just trust your students" seems unsatisfying and possibly frustrating for teachers wanting to engage with inquiry-based instruction. So, *trust* us, you are going to want to read on!

We have landed on three key inquiry processes that build a culture of trust in the classroom: deliberation, collaboration, and production.[38]

Deliberation involves instructional practices that enable students to listen to each other's ideas and speak about their own. These practices might include a Harkness Discussion, Think-Pair-Share, Take a Stand debate, or Socratic Discussion. These types of deliberative experiences engender respect for others and an appreciation for a pluralistic democracy where people hold different perspectives on life. Deliberative exercises build trust by fostering respect for ideas and *empathy* between students and between teacher and students because they show that teachers trust their students to think about big ideas.

Collaboration involves instructional practices that allow students to work with others to problem solve through teamwork. These practices might include a Jigsaw task, a Question Formulation Technique exercise, or a Structured Academic Controversy. During collaborative experiences, students negotiate with others and learn to respect other ways of knowing and doing. If a task is "group worthy," students learn to value team members' strengths and to value their own contributions to the whole. These kinds of experiences build trust by creating *interdependence* between students and demonstrating that a teacher trusts their students to work with others.

Production involves instructional practices that allow students to construct meaningful work. These practices could include an evidentiary argument or a summative project (e.g., public service announcement, museum exhibit) or it could include important formative work like a map, timeline, or T-Chart. When students produce work, they risk putting their ideas out there and cultivate *agency* in the process. Healthy inquiry cultures allow students to explore frontiers and create forgiving spaces to learn and grow. In doing so, they build classroom trust.

By allowing students space to think (**deliberate** ideas), talk (**collaborate** around ideas), and do (**produce** ideas), teachers build a culture of classroom trust with their students that engenders key attitudes of empathy, interdependence, and agency that can accelerate inquiry-based learning in the classroom. While these processes and attributes are not exclusive to social studies, they do connect deeply to the mission of preparing students for civic life.

So, fellow inquiry travelers, stay tuned! We will expand on the three processes above with specific guidance on instructional exercises that enable a trust-worthy classroom in an upcoming book. In the meantime, let's keep trusting inquiry!

Notes

1. *The College, Career, and Civic Life (C3) Framework for Social Studies State Standards* (Silver Spring, MD: National Council for the Social Studies (NCSS), 2013).

2. Ryan New, Kathy Swan, John Lee, and S.G. Grant, "The State of Social Studies Standards: What is the Impact of the C3 Framework?" *Social Education* 85, no. 4 (2021): 239–246; S.G. Grant, John Lee, and Kathy Swan, "The State of the C3 Framework: An Inquiry Revolution in the Making," *Social Education* 87, no 6 (NovDec 2023).

3. S. G. Grant, Kathy Swan, and John Lee, *Inquiry-based Practice in Social Studies Education: Understanding the Inquiry Design Model* (Routledge, 2017); Kathy Swan, S.G. Grant, and John Lee, *The Inquiry Design Model: Building Inquiries in Social Studies* (Silver Spring, MD: NCSS, 2018); Kathy Swan, S.G. Grant, and John Lee, *Blueprinting an Inquiry-Based Curriculum* (Silver Spring, MD: NCSS, 2019).

4. Grant, Swan, and Lee, *Inquiry-based Practice in Social Studies Education*.

5. Swan, Grant, and Lee, *The Inquiry Design Model*.

6. Leona Tyler, *The Psychology of Human Differences* (D. Appleton-Century Company, 1947); Grant Wiggins and Jay McTighe, *Understanding by Design*, expanded 2nd ed. (Alexandria, VA: ASCD, 2005).

7. Walter Parker, "Projects as the Spine of the Course: Design for Deeper Learning," *Social Education* 82, no. 1 (2017): 45–48.

8. Swan, Grant, and Lee, *Blueprinting an Inquiry-Based Curriculum*.

9. John Lee, Alicia McCollum, and Mary Beth Yerdon, with testimonials from C3 Teachers, "C3 Teachers: The Heart of the Inquiry," *Social Education* 87, no 6 (NovDec 2023).

10. Margaret Wertheim, interview with Krista Tippett, *On Being*, podcast audio (April 23, 2015). https://onbeing.org/programs/margaret-wertheim-the-grandeur-and-limits-of-science-feb2017/

11. Walter Parker and Diana Hess, "Teaching with and for Discussion" *Teaching and Teacher Education* 17 (2001): 273–289.

12. Grant, Swan, and Lee, *Inquiry-based Practice in Social Studies Education*.

13. Christy Cartner, Kathy Swan, and Ryan Crowley, "What can Women Teach us about Equality? An Inquiry-Based Curricular Approach to a Gender and Women's Studies Course," *Social Education* 87, no.3 (2023): 184–190.

14. Who's to Blame for the Cold War? On C3 Teachers: https://c3teachers.org/inquiries/cold-war.

15. Swan, Grant, and Lee, *The Inquiry Design Model*.

16. Why Was the US on the Winning Side of World War II? On C3 Teachers: https://c3teachers.org/inquiries/world-war-ii.

17. Swan, Grant, and Lee, *The Inquiry Design Model*.

18. Who's to Blame for the Cold War? On C3 Teachers: https://c3teachers.org/inquiries/cold-war

19. Grant, Swan, and Lee, *Inquiry-based Practice in Social Studies Education*; Swan, Grant, and Lee, *The Inquiry Design Model*; Swan, Grant, and Lee, *Blueprinting an Inquiry-Based Curriculum*.

20. Swan, Grant, and Lee, *Blueprinting an Inquiry-Based Curriculum*.

21. E. Aronson and S. Patnoe, *Cooperation in the Classroom: The Jigsaw Method*, 3rd ed. (London: Pinter & Martin, Ltd., 2011).

22. *The College, Career, and Civic Life (C3) Framework for Social Studies State Standards*; Grant, Swan, and Lee, *Inquiry-based Practice in Social Studies Education*.

23. Kathy Swan, Ryan Crowley, Nick Stamoulacatos, Bonnie Lewis, and Grant Stringer, "Countering the Past of Least Resistance: A Hard History Inquiry-Based Curriculum," https://c3teachers.org/wp-content/uploads/2022/01/SE-JanFeb2022-C3.pdf.

24. Grant, Swan, and Lee, *Inquiry-based Practice in Social Studies Education*.

25. Sarah Shear, C.M. Tschida, E. Bellows, L. Brown Buchanan, and E. E. Saylor, eds., *(Re)Imagining Elementary Social Studies: A Controversial Issues Reader* (Information Age Publishing, 2018).

26. Grant, Swan, and Lee, *Inquiry-based Practice in Social Studies Education*; Swan, Grant, and Lee, *The Inquiry Design Model*; Swan, Grant, and Lee, *Blueprinting an Inquiry-Based Curriculum*.

27. A. Tyner and S. Kabourek, "How Social Studies Improves Elementary Literacy," *Social Education* 85, no. 1 (2021): 32-39.

28. S.G. Grant, ed., *Measuring History: Cases of State-Level Testing in the United States* (Greenwich, CT: Information Age, 2010) and Paul Fitchett and Tina Heafner "A National Perspective on the Effects of High-Stakes Testing and Standardization on Elementary Social Studies Marginalization," *Theory and Research in Social Education* 38, no.1 (2010): 114–130.

29. *The College, Career, and Civic Life (C3) Framework for Social Studies State Standards* (Silver Spring, MD: NCSS, 2013).

30. Grant, Swan, and Lee, *Inquiry-based Practice in Social Studies Education*; Swan, Grant, and Lee, *The Inquiry Design Model*; Swan, Grant, and Lee, *Blueprinting an Inquiry-Based Curriculum*.

31. Swan, Grant, and Lee, *Blueprinting an Inquiry-Based Curriculum*.

32. #276-21 Commonwealth of Virginia, Virginia Department of Education Superintendent's Memo #276-21 Revisions to the Guidelines for Locally Awarded Verified Credits to Allow for the Use of Performance Assessments to Verify Credits in History and Social Science (2021), www.doe.virginia.gov/home/showpublisheddocument/3376/638119607672230000.

33. Swan, Grant, and Lee, *Blueprinting an Inquiry-Based Curriculum*.

34. Swan, Grant, and Lee, *Blueprinting an Inquiry-Based Curriculum*.

35. Swan, Grant, and Lee, *Blueprinting an Inquiry-Based Curriculum*.

36. Swan, Grant, and Lee, *The Inquiry Design Model*.

37. Swan, Grant, and Lee, *The Inquiry Design Model*.

38. Swan, Grant, and Lee, "Trusting Inquiry: Teaching with the Inquiry Design Model," *Social Education* 89, no.2 (2023).

Social Education **87, no. 5** (2023): 328–331.

Trusting Inquiry:
Teaching with the Inquiry Design Model

Kathy Swan, S.G. Grant, and John Lee

Trust is a firm belief in the reliability, truth, ability, or strength of someone or something.[1]

It is one thing to build an inquiry-based curriculum, it is quite another to make an inquiry come to life in a classroom. If curriculum is a recipe, then how do teachers move from being line-cooks to inquiry chefs? How do they get students to eat their inquiry vegetables and keep coming back for more? What is inquiry's instructional secret sauce? We argue that trust is how inquiry teachers "kick it up a notch!"

Why trust? Recently, we co-directed a documentary film project, *Making Inquiry Possible (MIP)*, featuring four films that explore how innovative teachers, schools, and districts are shifting to inquiry-based instruction.[2] At the core of each documentary is the question: What does it take to make inquiry *possible* in social studies? The answer has become unmistakable: trust. Like a song that gets stuck in our brains, once we start to hear it, we couldn't *un*-hear it.

For example, when we asked one of the teachers in the project how inquiry had changed his teaching, he responded this way:

> So my role as a teacher has changed. What I've noticed with the use of compelling questions and using IDM in my classroom is that it is absolutely incumbent on the student to answer that question for themselves. Now, that doesn't seem wild when we say that, but in the moment of teaching, many of our students have been accustomed to being able to find an answer, rather than simply create one.

Do you hear it? Did you notice how he needs to trust the students to answer the compelling question "for themselves"? Let's listen again. When we asked a teacher about scaffolding inquiry, this was the response:

> Students need enough support in order for them to even put the pieces together. What I've noticed is that it's almost like holding an egg. If you grip it too tightly, it's going to break. But if you truncate everything too much for the student, what you get on the other end is, is simply just not a robust answer. It kills the process. So because of that, I have to be the support, but also have to like, kick the kid out in the pasture a little bit to kind of figure things out on their own.

Surely you heard it this time—how the teacher needs to hold (or trust) the inquiry "egg" by not gripping too tight? Or how he needs to "kick the kid out in the pasture a little bit to figure things out on their own" as an act of pedagogical trust? While we would never suggest or condone literally kicking a kid, metaphorically (*and only metaphorically*), it does make sense for inquiry. Students need space to wrestle with questions, tasks, and sources. Teachers need to trust students and give them that space. And, students need to trust teachers to make that space meaningful and to be there when they lose their way. Sometimes that space is uncomfortable and teachers will need to nurture students and scaffold the process so that they can ultimately embrace that intellectual freedom.

Arriving at trust has been a *Eureka!* moment for us, further deepening our curiosity about its relationship to inquiry. But trust is one of those words that is kind of squishy; and a platitude like, "just trust your students" seems really unsatisfying and possibly frustrating for teachers wanting to engage with inquiry-based instruction. So, *trust* us, you are going to want to read on!

Cultivating Trust in the Inquiry Classroom: Processes and Attitudes

We have landed on three key inquiry processes that build a culture of trust in the classroom: deliberation, collaboration, and production.

Inquiry Processes and Attitudes
that build a classroom culture of trust

Deliberation
trust students to work with big ideas

Collaboration
trust students to work with others

Production
trust students to create meaningful work

Deliberative practices build trust by fostering empathy. Students listen to others' ideas and speak about their own. The types of experiences engender respect for one another and an appreciation for a pluralistic democracy where people come from differing perspectives.

Collaborative practices build trust through interdependence. When students collaborate, they learn how to problem solve through teamwork. Students negotiate with others and learn to respect other ways of knowing and doing. If a task is "group worthy," students learn to value team members' strengths and to value their own contributions to the whole.

Production practices build trust by enabling student agency. When students produce work, they risk putting their ideas out there — healthy inquiry cultures allow students to explore the space and value their contributions. In doing so, they increase student confidence.

Deliberation involves instructional practices that enable students to listen to each other's ideas and speak about their own. These practices might include a Harkness Discussion, Think-Pair-Share, Take a Stand debate, or Socratic Discussion. These types of deliberative experiences engender respect for others and an appreciation for a pluralistic democracy where people hold different perspectives on life. Deliberative exercises build trust by fostering respect for ideas and *empathy* among students and between teacher and students because they show that teachers trust their students to think about big ideas.

Collaboration involves instructional practices that allow students to work with others to problem solve through teamwork. These practices might include a Jigsaw task, a Question Formulation Technique (QFT) exercise, or a Structured Academic Controversy. During collaborative experiences, students negotiate with others and learn to respect other ways of knowing and doing. If a task is "group worthy," students learn to value team members' strengths and to value their own contributions to the whole. These kinds of experiences build trust by creating *interdependence* between students and by demonstrating that teachers trust their students to work with others.

Production involves instructional practices that allow students to construct meaningful work. These practices could include an evidentiary argument or a summative project (e.g., public service announcement, museum exhibit) or it could include important formative work like constructing a map, timeline, or T-Chart. When students produce work, they risk putting their ideas out there and cultivate agency in the process. Healthy inquiry classrooms allow students to explore frontiers and create forgiving spaces to learn and grow. In doing so, they build classroom trust.

By allowing students space to think (**deliberate** ideas), talk (**collaborate** around ideas), and do (**produce** ideas), teachers build a culture of classroom trust with their students that engenders key attitudes of empathy, interdependence, and agency that can accelerate inquiry-based learning in the classroom. While these processes and attributes are not exclusive to social studies, they do connect deeply to the mission of preparing students for civic life.

An Invitation

We have a book in the works about building trust that will expand on the three processes above with specific guidance on instructional exercises that enable a trust-worthy classroom. We would like to invite you into the C3 Teachers' studio by sharing your insights about the role of trust in inquiry. Consider the following:

- When did I start trusting inquiry?
- How do I create a trust-worthy classroom?
- How do I show my students that I trust them?
- What does it look like when students trust each other?
- What strategies accentuate trust and what differences do they make in students' attitudes toward your class?
- How does a trust-worthy classroom accelerate learning?

And then, drop us a line at info@c3teachers.org and tell us your ideas about building trust for inquiry and how you think it happens. We look forward to hearing from you.

In the meantime, let's keep trusting inquiry!

Notes

1. Adapted from www.merriam-webster.com/dictionary/trust.
2. Kathy Swan, Ryan Crowley, S.G. Grant, John Lee, and Gerry Swan, *Making Inquiry Possible* film project (2020): https://makinginquirypossible.org.

Section 3: Conclusion

This section would not be complete without expressing our deep gratitude to the educators who have committed to C3 inquiry *and* committed to sharing their experiences. One of our favorite poets, Wendell Berry writes about the value of living in a commonwealth:

> A proper community, we should remember also, is a commonwealth: a place, a resource, an economy. It answers the needs, practical as well as social and spiritual, of its members—among them the need to need one another.[1]

We are thankful that our C3 Teachers network has engaged in this proper inquiry commonwealth so that we all might learn, adjust, and grow together. More than that, we know that we have needed them to help us understand the myriad of practical, social, and spiritual (cultural) issues around inquiry. Without their actions, this revolution of ideas would have been good words on paper—a declaration that went nowhere. This teaching community has enacted the ideas which have sustained the ongoing C3 revolution.

In the next section, we dive deeper into one of the most vexing of inquiry topics—assessment. We examine five articles from the "Teaching the C3 Framework" archive that describe innovations, challenges, and practices around assessment using the Inquiry Design Model.

Note

1. Wendell Berry, *The Hidden Wound* (Berkeley: Counterpoint Press, 2010), 135.

Section 4: Assessment

Section 4: Assessment

Assessment is the third rail of the academic lives of teachers and students. Ideas, in the form of curriculum, matter; so, too, does instruction. In some ways, however, it is assessment that matters most, for it is through assessment—both formative and summative—that we learn if and how curriculum and instruction matter.

If this argument makes sense, it seems ironic that assessment is far less researched than its partners.[1] And of the empirical work done on assessment, most work focuses on standardized testing. Standardized testing can influence what is taught and how, but it is an uncertain presence.[2] Far more evident are classroom-based assessments. Yet Torrez & Claunch-Lebsack note that "there is a paucity of empirical research focusing specifically on assessment in the social studies classroom."[3] Curriculum and instruction are important, but their importance can only be validated through assessment. And therein lies the problem. To reach full flower, curriculum and instruction demand that we know—with a considerable degree of confidence—what students know and can do.

The qualifier, "with a considerable degree of confidence," is key because no assessment type offers a full range of insight into students' knowledge and skills. Each option has advantages—even multiple-choice tests. But each assessment option comes with distinct challenges to our confidence that we know what students know and can do.[4]

Much clearer is the need to pair formative assessments with summative. Formative measures offer the advantage of understanding students' emergent strengths and challenges as an inquiry unfolds. With this information, teachers can make instructional shifts that will better advantage their students before the summative task.

A revolution of ideas in terms of standards, curriculum, and instruction is all well and good. But assessment provides the opportunity to know if that revolution is gaining ground.

The six articles from the "Teaching the C3 Framework" archive suggest that the challenges of classroom-based assessment are being met. We have a long way to go, but navigating the relationships between formative and summative tasks within an inquiry framework gives us hope that the revolution will succeed, *and* we will know when it does!

* * * * *

The first piece, "IDM as an Assessment System," by S. G. Grant, Kathy Swan, and John Lee sets the essential assessment challenge: knowing what students know and can do with a high degree of confidence. The authors explain how the Inquiry Design Model (IDM) offers teachers and their students a systematic approach to track their academic growth in three different ways.

Creating evidence-based argument is the gold standard of inquiry-based teaching and learning. But there is much for teachers and their students to do in order to hit that mark. The third and fourth articles in this section address argument making. But the second piece, "Don't Forget the Tasks: Why Formative Tasks Are Key to Deliberation" by Bonnie Lewis, Kathy Swan, and Ryan Crowley, demonstrates the importance of building up students' knowledge and skills through formative tasks.

Many classroom observers can believe that secondary students can produce thoughtful and persuasive arguments. Patricia Krizan, in "So We *Want* Kindergartners to Argue? Developing Argumentation Skills in the Kindergarten Classroom," illustrates the point that kindergarten teachers and their students can produce evidence-based arguments as well.

As students gain familiarity and experience with making arguments, teachers can help in the refinement process by focusing on claim making. At heart, an evidence-based argument consists of a *stance* and one or more *claims* that support that stance.[5] This seemingly simply definition can result in several kinds of mayhem in students' hands. The

Persuasive Claim Framework that Ryan Lewis describes in "What's in a Claim? A Framework for Helping Students Write Persuasive Claims" offers considerable help in managing that mayhem.

One of the delightful outcomes of working with the C3 Framework and the Inquiry Design Model has been learning about the different ways educators have used the documents in innovative and ambitious ways. Paula McAvoy and her colleagues Arine Lowery, Nada Wafa, and Christy Byrd exemplify this trend in their article "Dining with Democracy: Discussion as Informed Action." Taking Informed Action is one of the signature features of the C3 Framework, and the myriad ways that students demonstrate their ability to make a difference in their worlds demonstrates the importance of making social studies relevant. The authors do so by chronicling the efforts of North Carolina teachers Russell McBride and Jeremy Thomas and their students to bring the local community into their inquiry around discussion of three policy questions.

The final piece in this section, "Can the Civics Test Make You a Good Citizen? Reconciling the Civics Test with Inquiry-Based Instruction" by Jennifer Fraker, Carly Muetterties, Gerry Swan, and Kathy Swan, deals with the perceived tensions between content and skills and inquiry-based practices and high-stakes testing. After taking the Civic Education Institute's 100 multiple-choice-question exam, students work through an IDM-rooted inquiry that enables them to think about and evaluate the test in terms of its capacity to promote good citizenship.

* * * * *

1. S. G. Grant, Kathy Swan, and John Lee, "IDM as an Assessment System," *Social Education* 87, no. 2 (2023): 108–113.
2. Bonnie Lewis, Kathy Swan, and Ryan Crowley, "Don't Forget the Tasks: Why Formative Tasks Are the Key to Deliberation," *Social Education* (in press, 2024).
3. Patricia Krizan, "So We *Want* Kindergartners to Argue? Developing Argumentation Skills in the Kindergarten Classroom," *Social Studies and the Young Learner* 35, no. 1 (2022): 26–31.
4. Ryan Lewis, "What's in a Claim? A Framework for Helping Students Write Persuasive Claims," *Social Education* 85, no. 2 (2021): 116–120.
5. Paula McAvoy, Arine Lowery, Nada Wafa, and Christy Byrd, "Dining with Democracy: Discussion as Informed Action," *Social Education* 84, no. 5 (2020): 289–293.
6. Jennifer Fraker, Carly Muetterties, Gerry Swan, and Kathy Swan, "Can the Civics Test Make You a Good Citizen? Reconciling the Civics Test with Inquiry-Based Instruction," *Social Education* 83, no. 6 (2019): 334–339.

Notes

1. Sarah Bonner, "Validity in Classroom Assessment: Purposes, Properties, and Principles," in *Sage Handbook of Research on Classroom Assessment*, ed. James McMillan (Thousand Oaks, CA: Sage, 2013), 87–106.
2. S. G. Grant, "An Uncertain Lever: The Influence of State-Level Testing in New York State on Teaching Social Studies," *Teachers College Record*, 103, no. 3 (2001): 398–426.
3. Cheryl Torrez and Elizabeth Claunch-Lebsack, "Research on Assessment in the Social Studies Classroom," in *Sage Handbook of Research on Classroom Assessment*, ed. James McMillan (Thousand Oaks, CA: Sage, 2013), 462.
4. S. G. Grant, "The Problem with Knowing What Students Know: Classroom-Based and Large-Scale Assessment in Social Studies," in *Handbook of Social Studies Research*, ed. Cheryl Mason Bolick and Meghan McGlinn Manfra, (New York: Wiley-Blackwell, 2016), 461–476; S. G. Grant and Cinthia Salinas, "Assessment and Accountability in Social Studies," in *Handbook of Research in Social Studies Education*, ed. Linda Levstik and Cynthia Tyson (Mahwah, NJ: Lawrence Erlbaum Associates, 2008), 219–238.
5. Kathy Swan, S. G. Grant, and John Lee, *Blueprinting an Inquiry-Based Social Studies Curriculum* (Silver Spring, MD: National Council for the Social Studies, 2019).

Social Education 87, no. 2 (2023): 108–113.

IDM as an Assessment System

S.G. Grant, Kathy Swan, and John Lee

Emerging from the *College, Career, and Civic Life (C3) Framework* , the Inquiry Design Model (IDM) was initially intended as an approach to curriculum development. Although curriculum is often treated as an independent element of teaching and learning, it is a distinction without a clear difference. As we work with teachers, we now see assessment as the next frontier for IDM.

Although considered the third leg of the curriculum-instruction-assessment triangle, assessment has never gotten the attention that the first two have. Torrez and Claunch-Lebsack note, "There is a paucity of empirical research focusing specifically on assessment in the social studies classroom."[1] Curriculum and instruction are important, but their importance can only be validated through assessment. And therein lies the problem. To reach full flower, curriculum and instruction demand that we know—with a considerable degree of confidence—what students know and can do.

The qualifier, "with a considerable degree of confidence," is key because no assessment type offers a full range of insight into students' knowledge and skills. Each option has advantages—even multiple-choice questions. But each assessment option comes with distinct challenges to our confidence that we know what students know and can do.

In this column, we describe how IDM offers a systematic approach to assessment, one that builds in complexity and nuance. IDM as an assessment *system* is built into the IDM blueprint in such fashion that it attends to the four qualities that Torrez and Claunch-Lebsack argue define "good" assessment practices.[2] We conclude with a call for teachers to think beyond their individual classroom assessments and toward grade-level, department-level, and even school-level approaches to understanding what students know and can do.

IDM as an Assessment System

Far too often, assessment is an afterthought in the instructional design process. Given the many challenges of assessment design—and the lack of ready solutions—teachers may fall back on familiar forms of assessments and hope for the best. As a result, the problem is not a lack of will on the part of teachers. Instead, it is the lack of design approaches and systematic ways for thinking that undercut more ambitious approaches to assessing students.

Backward design reminds us that the goal of assessment is to understand what students know and can do. Toward that end, assessment should be diagnostic and aimed at improving student learning. As a result, assessments are typically divided into *formative* (learning in process) and *summative* (the product of learning). This distinction reflects the longstanding push and pull between the products of learning and the processes resulting in those products. When measuring discrete products of learning, we gain limited insight into the means by which students develop knowledge and are thus limited in knowing how to support their growth. In models where learning is continuous, and students are active learners who construct their own knowledge, we have opportunities to track the progress of learning and gain more insight into how students learn. Formative assessments provide opportunities for teachers to map and track the progress of their students' learning within an inquiry, while summative assessments allow them to focus on the outcome, which, in the case of IDM, is argumentation.

The diagnostic opportunities of each kind of assessment are considerable, but planning for successful assessment diagnostics is challenging. And to make matters even more complicated, rather than using assessment information for diagnosing student challenges, it may be used for accountability purposes—to rank order students for sorting and labeling them as high and low achievers.

Missing from many assessment approaches is a systematic approach to assessment. Shepard notes the need for systematic approaches where the content of assessment is aligned with the curricular and instructional goals of the learning being assessed.[3] In such a holistic approach, curriculum, instructional, and assessment elements of the system work in tandem.

This interactive dynamic is front and center in the Inquiry Design Model. Within IDM, there is a three-part assessment system that positions formative and summative assessments as key elements in the overall IDM approach of questions, tasks, and sources. In effect, the tasks students complete become (a) the opportunities to know what they know and can do and (b) the structure for providing diagnostic feedback to them. Such iterative opportunities to engage in task-based assessments give shape to an inquiry curriculum.

Anatomy of IDM as an Assessment System

In order to demonstrate the first two components of the three-part IDM assessment system, let's look at a middle-level blueprint with the compelling question, "What is the greatest cost of water?" This question takes advantage of students' intuitive sense that water is "free." (See Figure 1)

The supporting questions push students to think about issues of access to water and who has it. Then they ask students to consider the idea of water as a "stressed" resource and how conflicts can develop over its availability and cost. (The inquiry is available for download at: https://c3teachers.org/inquiries/cost-of-water.)

Part one of the IDM assessment system centers on the relationship between *formative* and *summative* performance tasks. When students work through tasks related to the cost of water (e.g., geography, populations, scarcity) and the outcomes of that change (e.g., water- stressed areas, conflict), teachers can chart their growth in the knowledge and skills relevant to the inquiry topic. Scaffolding that knowledge and those skills enables students to then synthesize their understandings into the evidence-based arguments called for in the summative performance task. With the summative task as the goal, the interconnected formative tasks provide a vital series of experiences that enable students to reach that end. Evidence-based arguments can come in many forms, but they provide teachers with powerful insights into their students' knowledge and skills.

The second part of the IDM assessment system takes shape after the summative task. Generally speaking, an inquiry can end as students complete their arguments. But most teachers will seize any opportunity to know more about what their students know and can do in spaces both personal and civic. *Extension* tasks offer the occasion for students to present different versions of their arguments to new audiences both in and outside school and through a variety of mediums. For example, in the Cost of Water inquiry, students can extend and deepen their understandings by using the Popplet tool to describe the foci of their arguments. Students can push their understandings even further through *taking informed action* exercises. As the Cost of Water blueprint demonstrates, taking informed action tasks address the perennial student complaint about social studies: what am I supposed to do with this stuff we are learning? Public service announcements, letters to the editor, community surveys, and the like enable students to use their classroom-based learning to address and act on current issues in real-world fashion. In the featured inquiry, students direct their taking informed action energies toward a school-wide campaign related to issues of local water usage.

Part three of the IDM assessment system moves from a single blueprint to a curriculum map. Tracking students' inquiry knowledge and skill growth over time is key because one-off assessments can lead to false conclusions. Teachers can begin tracing their students' development through an individual inquiry. But any growth that occurs needs continual nurturing and regular checkpoints throughout the school year.

Figure 1. The Cost of Water Blueprint 7th Grade Water Inquiry

What is the Greatest Cost of Water?			
Georgia Performance Standard & C3 Framework Indicator	**SS7G6.** Explain how water pollution and the unequal access to water impacts irrigation and drinking water. **D2.Geo.9.6-8.** Evaluate the influences of long-term human-induced environmental change on spatial patterns of conflict and cooperation.		
Staging the Question	"When the well is dry we know the value of water" — Ben Franklin As a class, discuss the quote from Franklin, identifying factors that may impact the value of water.		

Supporting Question 1	Supporting Question 2	Supporting Question 3	Supporting Question 4
Who has access to water in the Middle East?	How do countries in the Middle East get water?	How is being "water stressed" impacting populations?	Why are conflicts arising over water?
Formative Performance Task	**Formative Performance Task**	**Formative Performance Task**	**Formative Performance Task**
Complete a map of the Middle East showing geographic features, population density, and water sources.	Create a chart that identifies and describes the effects of water collection methods used in the Middle East.	Write 1-2 paragraphs describing how being "water stressed" impacts populations in the area, citing specific supporting evidence.	Make a claim supported by evidence about why conflicts are arising over water.
Featured Sources	**Featured Sources**	**Featured Sources**	**Featured Sources**
Source A: *Aqueduct: Water Risk Atlas* accessible at **www.wri.org/aqueduct**	**Source A:** *AQUASTAT Database* **Source B:** Excerpt from "Finding the Balance"	Sources from SQs 1 and 2 **Source A:** *The Water Project*	**Source A:** Clip from *Global Public Square*, "The Coming Water Wars?" **Source B:** Excerpts from: "Mideast Water Wars" accessible at http://e360.yale.edu/feature/mideast_water_wars_in_iraq_a_battle_for_control_of_water/2796 **Source C:** "'Islamic State' Using Water as a Weapon" accessible at www.dw.com/en/islamic-state-using-water-as-a-weapon/a-19093081

Summative Performance Task	**ARGUMENT** What is the greatest cost of water? Construct an argument (e.g., detailed outline, poster, essay) that discusses the compelling question using specific claims and relevant evidence from contemporary sources while acknowledging competing views.
	EXTENSION Use a mindmap tool, such as Popplet, to illustrate the relationship between issues of water access in the region.
Taking Informed Action	**UNDERSTAND** Research your community's water supply. **ASSESS** Determine the most pressing water-related issue affecting your community. **ACT** Create a school-wide campaign to address this concern.

There are any number of ways to chart the progress of students' knowledge and skill development. Our favorite is through curricular looping. Drawing on Walter Parker's (2018) work,[4] we define looping as "offering students opportunities to engage in inquiry in regular intervals and in a coherent fashion within and across grade levels." As an example of looping across the school year, see Figure 2. In social studies, "racial justice" provides a powerful organizing topic for a set of five inquiries that take students from the post-Civil War period to the present. By keeping the compelling question the same in each inquiry—"What does it take to counter racial injustice?"—students have regular opportunities to compare and contrast the actions of historical figures with those of today.

Figure 2. Curricular Loop on Racial Justice

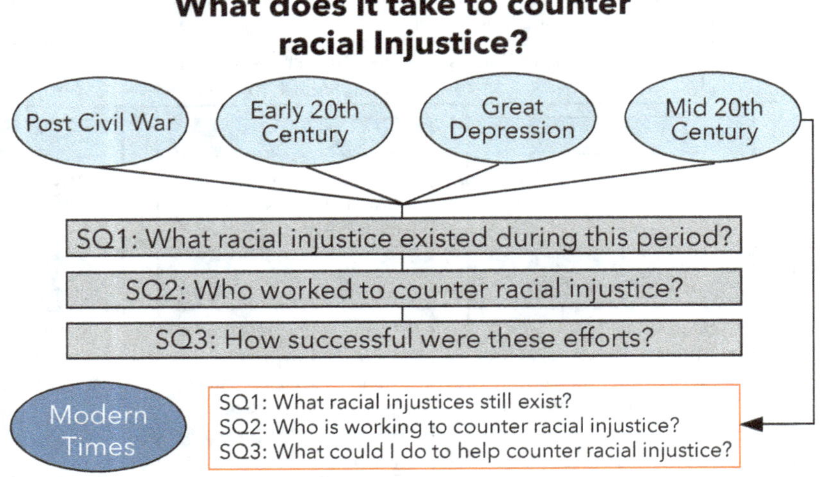

What does it take to counter racial Injustice?

Looping inquiries has curricular and instructional value: It also has considerable assessment value. Working through the various formative performance tasks, students show what they know and can do and their teachers can offer extensive feedback. Moreover, because the inquiry is still in progress, if teachers determine that their students need more practice, they can develop additional assessment tasks. Summative performance tasks, situated in the construction of evidence-based arguments, also give teachers several opportunities to track their students' growth as they work through each of the looped inquiries.

Torrez and Claunch-Lebsack conclude that "good" classroom assessment practices share four qualities: (1) they inform both students and teachers, (2) they illuminate and enhance the learning process, (3) they must be varied and ongoing, and (4) they should reflect authentic social studies activities.[5] The approaches to assessment built into IDM provide teachers and students with opportunities to be successful in all four of these areas. Formative performance tasks are intentional opportunities for students to learn as they are doing and for teachers to intentionally guide that process. Acting on the information gathered through the formative task process enables teachers to course correct students as they move toward constructing solid, well-supported summative arguments.

IDM-based assessments are ongoing and intimately connected to the curriculum and instruction that is built into each inquiry. Through IDM, the curriculum-instruction-assessment triangle has three equally long and sturdy legs. Moreover, the range of assessment tasks offers students authentic opportunities to act in ways that reflect their interests in and their energies toward the world around them.

Building an Inquiry-Based Assessment Approach

In the previous section, we highlighted IDM as a three-part assessment system that features a sustained approach to inquiry. But what happens when teachers band together to make an inquiry-based assessment approach to social studies within *and* across grade-levels? In our book on blueprinting a curriculum, we described districts that are moving toward *horizontal* and *vertical* curricular loops.[6] Doing so creates multiple opportunities for students to engage in inquiry and to catalog students' knowledge and skills growth over time.

As noted above, looping means offering students regular opportunities to engage in inquiry within and across grade levels. In a *horizontal* loop, students engage with complex ideas (e.g., human rights, progress, power) using challenging inquiry skills (e.g., questioning, source work, argumentation) over a single course of study. Each time students revisit the idea and/or process, it is reinforced and solidified until they begin to demonstrate a degree of facility with the relevant ideas and with the requisite skills. In the previous section, we saw a horizontal loop in action. Students in the sixth grade worked with the ideas of progress and unintended consequences over a series of six inquiries across an ancient history course (e.g., Was agriculture good for humans? Does development mean progress?). By developing intentionally sequenced inquiries, teachers can gauge student growth around a big idea (progress) and through the development of particular skills (e.g., evidentiary claim-making).

Vertical looping allows educators to build out their horizontal curricular loops so that students experience inquiry consistently across grade levels. In other words, sixth-grade students shouldn't have all the fun! In the example that follows, we can see that horizontal looping across grade loops creates a clear vertical loop (See Table 1). Middle school educators worked together to develop six inquiries per grade-level with each anchored in a powerful construct that defines the course of study (6th grade— progress; 7th grade—power; 8th grade—justice).

Inquiry as an assessment approach becomes coherent when it loops across a course of study and even more so when it loops across grade levels. We say this because when a group of teachers commits to inquiry, they also commit to emphasizing the skills that are foundational to inquiry—questioning, sourcing, argumentation, communication, and action. These core skills become the north star of the social studies curriculum. That's a powerful idea, as teachers are then able to calibrate their assessment criteria to focus on the content *and* the skills of inquiry. Moreover, once they commit to looping inquiry, teachers can see students' skill development and growth over time as they practice the same set of important skills in a variety of content contexts.

Looping sets teachers up for meaningful assessment, grading, and reporting. This is good news for schools, departments, and districts that are moving to proficiency-based, competency-based, and/or standards-based grading and reporting models. In each of these models, teachers determine a common set of criteria to report student progress. Social studies educators often resist developing such criteria because they struggle to pinpoint the content and skills that emerge in a course, and then across courses. As we discussed in the section above, IDM allows this criterion setting to become much more explicit and coherent. If sixth-, seventh-, and eighth-grade teachers are all having students read and evaluate sources, craft evidentiary claims and arguments, express these arguments in a variety of mediums, and take informed action, we see the potential for common criteria to surface.

Table 1. **Horizontal and Vertical Middle School Loops**

Middle School Horizontal and Vertical Loops							
Course Grade Level	Concept	September	October	November/December	January	February	March/April
World History 6th Grade	Progress	Was agriculture good for Humans?	What do pyramids tell us about the past?	Does development mean progress?	Did Shi Huangdhi improve China?	How did democracy change the world?	Did the Roman Empire fall?
Civics 7th Grade	Power	How powerful should the Congress be?	How powerful should the Courts be?	How powerful should the President be?	How powerful should the People be?	How powerful should the States be?	How powerful should the ____ (local) be?
US History 8th Grade	Justice	Did the return of Bruce's Beach bring justice?	How did the U.S. manifest Westward Expansion?	How did Reconstruction lead to retaliation?	What is the legacy of Japanese internment?	How should we remember Brown v. Board of Education	How should Syracuse make peace with redlining?

Conclusion

Assessment and grading expert Rick Stiggins writes, "Students can hit any target that they know about and that stands still for them."[7] IDM helps teachers to set a consistent and steady set of targets around the skills essential to inquiry. But even when those targets are clear, assessing student work is far from simple. Assessment involves a set of complex factors including assessment validity, students' experiences and motivation with the task, and the ever-present challenge of knowing what students know with a high degree of confidence. With all these imperfections, social studies educators need a systematic assessment approach that helps to mitigate the challenges and amplifies the outcomes of a meaningful social studies education. We think that IDM offers just such an approach.

Notes

1. Cheryl A. Torrez and Elizabeth Ann Claunch-Lebsack, "Research on Assessment in the Social Studies Classroom," in *Handbook of Research on Classroom Assessment*, ed. James H. McMillan (Thousand Oaks, CA: SAGE, 2013), 461–472.
2. Ibid.
3. Lorrie A. Shepard, "The Role of Assessment in a Learning Culture," *Educational Researcher* 29, no. 7 (2000), 4–14.
4. Walter Parker, "Projects as the Spine of the Course: Design for Deeper Learning," *Social Education* 82, no. 1 (2018), 45–48.
5. Torrez and Claunch-Lebsack.
6. Kathy Swan, S.G. Grant and John Lee, *Blueprinting an Inquiry-Based Curriculum: Planning with the Inquiry Design Model* (NCSS and C3 Teachers, 2019)
7. Richard J. Stiggins, Judith A. Arter, Jan Chappuis, and Stephen Chappuis, "Classroom Assessment for Student Learning: Doing it Right, Using it Well," Assessment Training Institute, 2004, 57.

Don't Forget the Tasks: Why Formative Tasks Are Key to Deliberation

Bonnie Lewis, Kathy Swan, and Ryan Crowley

"You really just need to gather a few sources around a good question," Mr. Morelli responded when we asked how he used inquiry in his practice. Mr. Morelli teaches 11th grade U.S. History and is familiar with the C3 Framework[1] and IDM blueprints.[2] We observed him teach in the fall of 2022 during a broader study about teaching contentious social studies using IDM inquiry. Mr. Morelli clearly understood the elements of inquiry-based instruction—questions, tasks, and sources—and was able to operationalize them in his day-to-day instruction. Still, we wondered when, in describing inquiry, he left out the thing that connects questions to sources: tasks. His comment made us wonder if gathering sources around a good question naturally led to students doing formative tasks and if those tasks produced the kind of meaningful deliberation necessary to complete an inquiry's summative performance task. So, we began asking ourselves: Can you *just* do inquiry by gathering a set of sources around a compelling question? After reflecting, however, we feel that doing inquiry only through questions and sources fails to recognize that inquiry-based learning relies on what students *do* with those questions and sources. If teachers want their students to engage in meaningful deliberation around a compelling question, they must focus on explicitly connecting questions and sources with formative and summative performance tasks. Deliberation and inquiry go hand-in-hand. Inquiry-based learning calls on teachers to facilitate student-led discovery, something that can only happen when students ask questions

Supporting Question 1	Supporting Question 2	Supporting Question 3
What is *eminent domain* and *common good*?	Why was the Chickamauga Dam built?	What were the costs and benefits of building the Chickamauga Dam?
Formative Performance Task	**Formative Performance Task**	**Formative Performance Task**
Create a class definition of *eminent domain* and describe how it impacts the common good.	Annotate on a photograph of the Chickamauga Dam and include a caption about why the dam was built.	Construct a class T-chart and list the costs and benefits of building the Chickamauga Dam.
Featured Sources	**Featured Sources**	**Featured Sources**
Source A: Definition of *eminent domain* **Source B:** *Unintended Consequences: Eminent Domain Video,* IzzitEDU, video	**Source A:** *Chickamauga Dam,* Tennessee Valley Authority **Source B:** *75 years of the Chickamauga Dam: 1938,* Chattanooga History **Source C:** *Workers of the Chattanooga Dam Project,* Chattanooga History	**Source A:** *The lost town of Old Harrison,* WRBC, 2021. **Source B:** *Harrison, Tennessee: Hamilton County's hidden Atlantis,* News Channel 9, 2017 *Students should also use sources from Supporting Question 2*

and weigh possible answers before settling on *a plausible and evidentiary* answer. John Dewey noted that "only by wrestling with the condition of the problem at first hand, seeking and finding his own way out, does [the student] think."[3] Teaching through inquiry is about setting students up to wrestle with the issue at hand using sources so that they can communicate their conclusions. For this outcome to happen, deliberation must be front and center in the progression from compelling question to summative performance task.

3rd Grade Geography Inquiry

Was the Chickamauga Dam worth it?	
C3 Framework Standard	**D2.Geo.9.3-5.** Analyze the effects of catastrophic environmental and technological events on human settlements and migration.
Staging the Question	Imagine that three students brought bags of M&Ms to class to eat at recess. None of the other students had a similar tasty treat. The teacher decides to take the candy and divide it evenly so that each student has a little bit of candy instead of just three. Discuss: Is that fair? Who benefits from the teacher's decision? Who doesn't benefit from the teacher's decision?

In this article, we discuss how a sequence of tasks supports meaningful deliberation within an inquiry. Specifically, we look at an upper elementary inquiry that features a cost-benefit analysis on a dam project in Tennessee. "Was the Chickamauga Dam worth it?" asks students to assess the common good of a public works project. We use this inquiry to show how formative and summative tasks promote individual and group deliberation. Then, we discuss what would happen if the tasks were not explicit and the Chickamauga Dam inquiry was just "a few sources around a good question." Ultimately, we challenge teachers to think about the ways that tasks surface deliberative moments in a classroom by allowing students to engage in the issue featured in an inquiry.

The Importance of Deliberative Formative Work

Within IDM inquiries, tasks bind together the questions and sources by requiring students to *do something*. Task work provides students with opportunities to engage in the deliberative process in which they interpret sources, weigh them

Supporting Question 2
Why was the Chickamauga Dam built?
Formative Performance Task
Annotate on a photograph of the Chickamauga Dam and include a caption about why the dam was built.
Featured Sources
Source A: *Chickamauga Dam,* Tennessee Valley Authority   **Source B:** *75 years of the Chickamauga Dam: 1938,* Chattanooga History   **Source C:** *Workers of the Chattanooga Dam Project,* Chattanooga History

Summative Performance Task	**ARGUMENT** *Was the Chickamauga Dam worth it?* Construct an oral argument using the "taking a stand" protocol and answer the compelling question—Was the Chickamauga Dam worth it?
Taking Informed Action	Students ask a member of the local zoning board into class to discuss eminent domain cases that have impacted or will impact the community. Discuss the costs and benefits of eminent domain and determine whether students should take a stand in an upcoming case.

against one another, and communicate their conclusions. In this process, deliberation moves from something that is happening internally—where students are thinking through what the sources mean and how they speak to the issue at hand—to something that happens externally, where students engage in discussion with one another to explore possible arguments before communicating their own conclusions. In inquiries, formative performance tasks require students to engage in deliberation by wrestling with the issue raised by the compelling question through analysis of the featured sources. However, the deliberation that happens in the formative performance tasks fits into a larger skill-building process that requires students to understand the featured sources in addition to completing a summative performance task. Although not all task work in an inquiry is deliberative, it all contributes to meaningful deliberation by providing space for students to engage in each step.

Understanding sources. The featured sources in an inquiry speak to the issue featured in the compelling question. The sources should help students understand the issue and its nuances in addition to providing evidence students might use later to construct arguments. Understanding what the sources communicate is an important first step in deliberation, and formative tasks should facilitate this process. Often, tasks that explicitly ask students to understand the sources are included in the beginning of an inquiry. But students need to understand that sources are more than just a means to address the tasks. Rather, teachers should ensure this step is happening with each featured source throughout an inquiry, regardless of whether the formative task calls for an explicit demonstration of comprehension.

For example, in the Chickamauga Dam inquiry, the second formative performance task asks students to annotate an image of the dam with information about the dam's context and to write a description explaining why the dam was built. This task emphasizes a meaningful and nuanced understanding of the source as students conceptualize why the dam was built in the first place. Simply viewing the picture of the modern dam and then moving on to deliberation would mean that students missed important information relevant to the issue they were deliberating. For example,

Supporting Question 3
What were the costs and benefits of building the Chickamauga Dam?
Formative Performance Task
Construct a class T-chart and list the costs and benefits of building the Chickamauga Dam.
Featured Sources
Source A: *The lost town of Old Harrison*, WRBC, 2021. **Source B:** *Harrison, Tennessee: Hamilton County's hidden Atlantis*, News Channel 9, 2017 *Students should also use sources from Supporting Question 2

by using the information from the Tennessee Valley Authority to annotate the picture of the dam, students are able to understand why Tennesseans chose to build the dam in the first place. Understanding this piece of information sets students up for further task work that asks them to weigh the costs and benefits of the dam on Tennesseans. Therefore, understanding what the source says is an important first step towards meaningful deliberation. But we should not stop there.

Weighing the evidence. Formative performance tasks provide instructional space for students to deliberate ideas within the featured sources. Students must be given the chance to demonstrate that they understand the sources in relation to one another and in relation to the stances they may take in response to the compelling question. Here is where students engage in disciplinary skills around causation, contextualization, comparison, change over time, and corroboration. Deliberation at this stage can be both internal and external as students think through how the sources fit together, whether they address the issue on their own or with their classmates. Students are not drawing conclusions at this point in the deliberative process, but rather exploring possible conclusions based on the body of credible evidence they are examining.For example, in the Chickamauga Dam inquiry, the third formative task asks students to construct a T-chart enumerating the costs and benefits of the dam. In constructing the graphic, students engage with the sources through the disciplinary skill of cause and effect by evaluating the effects of the dam's construction on Tennessee and the surrounding communities. Students use the featured sources as a set, focusing on how they speak to one another and how they relate to the compelling question. Tasks that are explicitly focused on deliberation—such as the construction of the T-chart—encourage students to think about the compelling question and how one might answer it. Evaluating the impact the Chickamauga Dam had on Tennessee and the community encourages students consider the stances they might take when answering the question, "Was the Chickamauga Dam worth it?"

Communicating Conclusions. Only after students have understood the sources and deliberated over possible answers to the compelling question, do they take an evidence-based stance and communicate their conclusions. This final step in the deliberative process calls on students to share the conclusions that arose from the process of understanding and evaluating the featured sources through formative task work. Inquiries culminate in students constructing an evidentiary argument that addresses the compelling question. These arguments represent the intellectual work and deliberation that occurred throughout the inquiry process. By the time they reach this step, students should be aware of the nuances of the issue they are deliberating as well as the possible ways they might answer the compelling question. If students possess this understanding, they can craft informed and evidentiary conclusions.

For example, in the inquiry about the Chickamauga Dam, the summative performance task asks students to engage in a debate by first participating in a "Take a Stand" activity where they position themselves along a continuum drawn in the classroom in relation to how they intend to answer the compelling question. After visualizing the different stances, they and their classmates might take, they are asked to engage in a debate based on evidentiary arguments and addressing counterclaims. The formative task work undertaken by students should prepare them for this final deliberative exercise.

Summative Performance Task	ARGUMENT *Was the Chickamauga Dam worth it?* Construct an oral argument using the "taking a stand" protocol and answer the compelling question—Was the Chickamauga Dam worth it?

What Happens When We Leave Deliberative Formative Tasks Out?

For deliberation to be meaningful, inquiries must include all stages of the deliberation process—understanding the sources, weighing the options, and then communicating conclusions. In our years of observing lessons using IDM inquiries, we have noticed that teachers may leave out a stage of the deliberation process in their task work or rely too much on one stage to the detriment of other elements. When this happens, several things can occur that undercut meaningful deliberation. First, students might develop uninformed arguments by failing to understand the evidence offered in the sources. Second, rather than finding their own stances on an issue, students may copy other students' responses because they have not weighed the evidence themselves. Finally, students might fail to see how the tasks they complete in an inquiry connect to a broader issue that holds significance outside the classroom.

When we forget to understand the sources. Teaching through IDM inquiries can take more instructional time than simply telling students what they need to know about a topic or issue. Sometimes, to compensate for the time spent engaging in source analysis and argumentation, teachers skip over the tasks that ask their students to understand the featured sources in an inquiry. This situation might happen because teachers assume their students already understand the sources or, rather than having students grapple with comprehension tasks, teachers might simply tell students what each source means. Each of these approaches takes away the chance for students to develop understandings of the sources and how those sources relate to the issue raised by the compelling question. When students engage in deliberation and communication without knowing what the sources say about the issue, their final arguments can lack nuance and complexity. Worse, failing to understand the sources, students' final arguments can be uninformed or inaccurate, even if they attempt to refer to the sources as evidence. The featured sources within an IDM speak to the issue featured in the compelling question in ways that encourage students to think and rethink what they know about the issue. Doing the work to understand the sources sets the groundwork for the analysis and synthesis that happens when students weigh the evidence and communicate their claims.

When we forget to weigh the evidence. In observing teachers implement IDM inquiries, the most common mistake we see is for teachers to skip formative tasks that ask students to weigh the evidence. Perhaps they assume this action is happening by the nature of working with sources and questions. Or, as is the case with many novice teachers we have observed, they may be hesitant to give up control over how students engage with the sources. Yet, inquiry-based learning requires teachers to give students the space they need to wrestle with issues independently and collectively. In an inquiry, this wrestling primarily happens during the formative performance tasks. We acknowledge that a classroom where students engage in deliberation and argumentation for themselves is inherently more risky and less controlled. But we also know that such classrooms are where meaningful deliberation takes place. If students skip steps in the deliberation process, their stances in response to the issue will not come from their own reasoning and may become unclear and/or inaccurate.[4] Worse, they may simply copy the argument of a classmate or adult that they then match up with pieces of evidence. Although this approach may be a good scaffold for students as they learn the elements of an argument, it is not how meaningful deliberation around issues takes place because it does not encourage students to think critically for themselves.

When we skip communicating conclusions. One last mistake we see teachers make is to focus only on understanding the sources and engaging in skill work without connecting both to enduring themes and big ideas in the field through compelling questions. While explicit skill work—where teachers center instruction on a disciplinary skill for the sake of learning the skill—can be helpful, without connecting these tasks to a compelling question and summative argument, we lose the "so what" of our instructional practice.

Formative tasks around comprehending and deliberating sources become significant when tied to a compelling question for two reasons. First, when guided by a compelling question, the task work completed in an inquiry directly sets up the summative performance task through which students answer the compelling question. This process requires students to use the work they did throughout the inquiry and contextualizes that work in the larger task of crafting an evidentiary argument. Second, having students communicate their conclusions in response to a compelling question after completing formative task work makes clear the connection between the work they are doing in their classroom and enduring issues within society at large. Without this connection, lessons can feel like an endless "to do" list with no clear purpose. Further, failure for students to see how comprehension and deliberation skills relate to their lives outside of school is a lost opportunity for teachers to model what engaged citizenship can look like through inquiry-based learning. Communicating conclusions at the end of the inquiry cycle drives the point home that working with sources through deliberative tasks is a means to an end, and that the end holds significance for both our classrooms and our communities.

Conclusion

In a recent article by a colleague and fellow inquiry teacher Meghan Hawkins, she reinforced the idea that formative performance tasks support every step of the inquiry process and that the work students do in the formative performance tasks is so much more than what it appears:

> Formative performance tasks may not be glamorous. They may appear simple. Yet this seeming simplicity belies the integral role of formative performance tasks in getting students to really grapple with the questions, wrestle with sources, and find their voice in summative performance tasks.[5]

Although not the flashiest part of the inquiry, formative performance tasks are integral to the deliberation process. Looking at formative and summative tasks through the lens of meaningful deliberation means featured sources move from being something students simply read and interpret to being pieces of evidence used to communicate conclusions. Formative performance tasks become less like drill work and more like the necessary steppingstones to reach an argument.

The reality of inquiry-based instruction is that it is *all* important—what we teach and how we teach it. Mr. Morelli wasn't wrong when he summarized inquiry as a good question and a few sources. What we have learned in our own practice, however, is that the deliberative tasks layer on opportunities to grapple and that the grappling is where the real inquiry magic happens.

Notes

1. National Council for the Social Studies, *College, Career, and Civic Life (C3) Framework for Social Studies State Standards* (Silver Spring, MD: NCSS, 2013).
2. Kathy Swan, S. G. Grant, and John Lee, *Blueprinting an Inquiry-Based Curriculum* (Silver Spring, MD: NCSS, 2019).
3. John Dewey, *Democracy and Education* (Norwood, MA: Macmillan, 1916), 188.
4. Ryan Lewis, "What's in A Claim? A Framework for Helping Students Write Persuasive Claims," *Social Education* 85, no. 2 (March/April 2021): 116–120.
5. Kathy Swan, S. G. Grant, and John Lee, "The Art of the Blueprint: Inquiry in the Classroom," *Social Education* 87, no. 6 (November/December 2023): 373.

Social Studies and the Young Learner 35, no. 1 (2022): 26–31.

So We *Want* Kindergarteners to Argue? Developing Argumentation Skills in the Kindergarten Classroom

Patricia Krizan

What exactly are argumentation skills?
How do the Toolkit inquiries help to develop these skills?
What does this look like in a kindergarten classroom?

Argumentation, both oral and written, has long been recognized as a necessary skill[1] and has even been dubbed "an essential instrument for a free society."[2] Mastering this skill allows us to thoughtfully consider evidence, weigh various options, and reach sound decisions. But, despite its recognized importance, too often argumentation is overlooked or minimized in the social studies curriculum where speaking and writing have been predominantly expository in nature as students compile or summarize information.[3] Argument discourse calls upon students to make claims, provide reasoning and relevant textual evidence, and address counterclaims. Although argument is often thought to be the purview of secondary educators, skills associated with argumentation can be introduced and nurtured in primary school. These skills include formulating an opinion, stating a claim, articulating reasoning, and citing evidence, as well as understanding other perspectives and evaluating arguments of others.

Welcome to the *Teaching Young Learners with the C3 Framework* column, a new feature in *Social Studies and the Young Learner*. Our mission is simple—to promote the ideas and practices of inquiry-based teaching and learning in younger grades. The *C3 Framework* fosters the notion of inquiry for all, that elementary and secondary students alike benefit from opportunities to engage deeply with social studies content and with one another.

The *Teaching Young Learners with the C3 Framework* column will include a wide range of articles and authors. Many will present classroom-based inquiries ready to download and teach. We hope many articles will highlight student and teacher experiences with inquiry in the elementary classroom. Others will offer insights into the various elements of an inquiry—compelling questions, formative performance tasks, sources, and taking informed action activities. And still others will highlight the benefits and challenges of teaching and learning with inquiry. The authors will vary as well—classroom teachers, school administrators, curriculum specialists, and university professors.

We expect you will find much of value in this issue's column and those that follow. We also encourage you to consider authoring a column as many voices make a powerful song. If you have even the germ of an idea, let us know and we will look forward to working with you to bring it to print.

—Column Editors: Emma Thacker, Kathy Swan, John Lee, & S.G. Grant

In this article, I examine how the *New York State Social Studies Resource Toolkit (Toolkit)*[4] supports argument discourse in social studies and then explore a primary teacher's curricular and instructional decisions regarding the development of children's argumentation skills. My study provides insights into how teachers can involve some of our youngest students in authentic, inquiry-based social studies learning that fosters argument discourse. While some may believe that primary students are too young for argumentation, we will see how one kindergarten teacher used the *Toolkit* inquiries to accomplish this lofty but attainable goal.

Social Studies Standards and *Toolkit* Inquiries Focus on Argument

In an effort to highlight the importance of and encourage instruction in argument discourse, recently adopted standards in both English Language Arts (ELA) and social studies include argumentation and argument writing expectations. The publication of *The College, Career, and Civic Life (C3) Framework for Social Studies State Standards*[5] incorporates the *K–12 Common Core State Standards for ELA/Literacy for History/Social Studies, Science & Technical Subjects* (CCSS)[6] and explicitly cross references common language and expectations for student learning. The Inquiry Arc, a key feature of the *C3 Framework*, focuses social studies teaching and learning on four dimensions which contribute to the development of argumentation skills: (1) developing questions and planning inquiries, (2) applying disciplinary concepts and tools, (3) evaluating sources and using evidence, and (4) communicating conclusions and taking informed actions. The recently released *Toolkit* provides inquiry-based curriculum materials to develop not only social studies concepts but proficiency in argumentation as well.[7]

The structure of each K–12 *Toolkit* inquiry is the Inquiry Design Model (IDM),[8] which offers students opportunities to engage with and practice the skills prioritized in the Inquiry Arc.[9] The IDM consists of eight components, beginning with a compelling question that is intended to spur further investigation and ending with the summative performance task where students construct an argument that answers the compelling question "using specific claims and relevant evidence."[10] The *Toolkit* inquiries scaffold argumentation for students, and the K–2 compelling questions problematize the traditional expanding environment topics of self, family, and community. Each compelling question requires students to state a claim, whether distinguishing needs and wants, evaluating a rule, or identifying responsible behaviors. The supporting questions and formative performance tasks scaffold students' thinking and call upon young learners to investigate, analyze evidence, take a stand, and provide reasoning as teachers encourage the development of these argumentation skills. The child-friendly featured sources included in each inquiry, whether an image bank, text, picture book, or video, provide evidence to support a student's stance on the compelling question, and thus, foster the process of argumentation. The IDM affords spaces for students to reason through various perspectives as they learn to substantiate their claims with textual evidence.

To better understand teachers' instructional decision- making and how they facilitate the development of argumentation skills with young learners, I recruited veteran kindergarten teacher Olivia Martin to offer insight on the implementation of one of the Toolkit inquiries. At the time of my study, Olivia had taught kindergarten for 26 years at Treetops School, a low-needs public primary school in a suburban district located approximately 30 miles from a major metropolitan area in New York State, and the district was in its second year of implementation of the *Toolkit* inquiries.[11] The Kindergarten inquiries include the following topics and compelling questions:

- Identity—Is Everyone Unique?
- Holidays—What Makes Holidays Special?
- Wants and Needs—Can We Get Everything We Need and Want?

- Maps and Globes—Which Is Better, a Map or a Globe?
- Civic Ideals—Why Do I Have to be Responsible?
- Rules—Are All Rules Good Rules?

During the course of the school year, Olivia used all or parts of these social studies resources with her class of twenty students, the majority of whom were English language learners.

Kindergarteners Participate in Argument Discourse

Although developing argumentation skills with primary students may appear daunting, Olivia employed a dialogic approach to scaffold instruction and attain this goal. Scholars contend that dialogue is a key factor in mediating students' construction of knowledge in general[12] and, specifically, in supporting students' acquisition of argumentation skills.[13] Olivia recognized the importance of dialogue in advancing students' argumentation skills and emphasized that students need encouragement to support their oral responses: "They have to feel comfortable that they are able to do this, so that's a big thing. They know they have a voice." Although she did not use the term *argument* initially, the idea of taking a position and articulating reasons began early on. Olivia introduced argumentation by focusing on *opinions*. As she explained to her kindergarteners, "This is opinion when you tell us how you feel or what you think about something." The following vignette illuminates the processes by which her young learners began to acquire argumentation abilities.

Figure 1

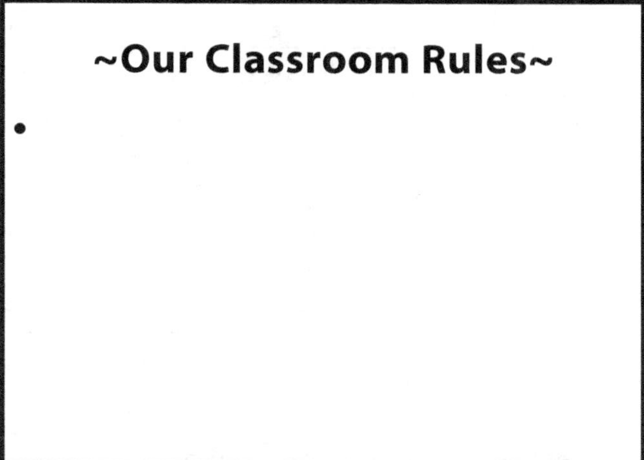

In September, Olivia implemented the *Toolkit* Rules inquiry since it aligned with a typical start-to-the-school-year activity—establishing classroom rules. This inquiry poses the compelling question, "Are all rules good rules?," which provides opportunities for students to understand, analyze, and evaluate rules while considering multiple perspectives. Students first explored the supporting questions, "Who makes the rules?" and "What does it mean to follow the rules?," using the inquiry image bank. They completed the formative performance tasks by discussing real world rules and rule makers (lifeguard, parent, police officer, and school principal) as well as by drawing rules being followed and not followed. At the same time, Olivia read fiction and nonfiction books involving rules, which often depicted reasons for particular regulations or practices and consequences when the rules are or are not followed.[14] As student understanding of rules deepened, Olivia constructed a graphic organizer (Figure 1) with the class: "'How can we build a classroom community?' 'What do we need to do?' and 'How should we behave?' They come up with the rules, and I make a chart. The rules become their rules, and ownership goes back to them." Based upon student suggestions of what they shouldn't do, the teacher discussed with the class the positive behaviors to be exhibited, which then became the classroom rules (see Figure 2).

Olivia then posed Supporting Question 3, "Can the rules ever change?," and applied it to classroom procedures, thereby giving students an opportunity to evaluate and revise: "Remember, these are *your* rules that you told me what you wanted—you talked about the rules you thought were important in here...So, we can change them, if you feel that they are not working; we can always change rules. That's always an option." Olivia indicated that many of the complaints in a kindergarten classroom center on taking turns. What may have appeared equitable in September may be met with objections and choruses of "it's not fair!" a month later. After a few weeks of school, her students began to grow frustrated with the *weekly* selection of the class meteorologist as they realized that some would not have the opportunity to announce the weather until December or January, a much-too-long wait for such a coveted position! Olivia convened a class meeting; student dialogue was at the heart of this activity: "'Do you think that would be a better rule? What do you think?,' and let them talk it out." Based upon student input, the morning calendar activity was modified so that children took turns being the meteorologist on a daily, rather than weekly, basis. Encouraging student agency, Olivia reminded the class, "If we see it's not working, we change our rules. Rules are made to be changed according to your needs."

Figure 2

Student Suggestions	Classroom Rules
No hitting, no punching, no pushing	Keep our hands to ourselves
Don't yell	Talk in our indoor voices
Don't talk when the teacher is talking (or another kid either)	Raise your hand to talk Listen when others are speaking
No budging	Wait until it's your turn
No grabbing a toy or book	Ask to share or for a turn
Don't say mean things	Walk in the classroom and halls
No running in school	Run in the gym or on the playground only

So too, students became disenchanted with the lining up procedure in which they were called by rows to the front of the class. Again, Olivia opened the topic for discussion, allowing students to voice their dissatisfaction with the current process: "I'm always last!" "Conner keeps trying to budge!" "We never get to be next to other friends." The class then brainstormed possible solutions: "The tallest can go first then the next one and the next one." "No, it should be the littlest!" "If it's your birthday, you should be first." Olivia offered other possibilities—by hair color, by birth date, or in alphabetical order. The class discussed the various options and then voted. Results deemed that children would be called alphabetically by their first names. One student immediately amended the new procedure and proposed that sometimes they would be called starting with A and at other times "backwards—starting with Z so the As don't always go first." The class concurred, and Olivia altered the lining up process accordingly. Olivia chuckled as she related the discussion, knowing full well that some of the same problems regarding position would surface with the alphabetical solution, but she would provide an opportunity for the class to revisit the situation and rethink possible options. The teacher emphasized reasoning as students identified what was and was not working, provided their rationales for change, and suggested a new rule.

Olivia continued to use this approach during the year when students expressed complaints with other routines ("I didn't get a turn!" "I never get a chance to go on the SMARTBoard!"). Again, she "let them talk it out" and propose a solution: "'Yeah, that may be a better idea. We could try that; we could have a better system to make life better and work smoother, and we can change what we do.' And, they have to buy into that. They have to have ownership of rules." Olivia created space for discussion and encouraged student problem-solving. Olivia then expanded the concept of changing rules to include a larger context: "In the United States, too, with grown-ups. If the rules don't work, we can change them and that's why we have people work for us in the government to change the rules to make them acceptable to everyone." Lessons involved civic mindedness and prepared these young citizens to consider laws of the larger community.

Mrs. Claire Cumberbatch leading her students in the Pledge of Allegiance. Cumberbatch was the leader of the Bedford-Stuyvesant group protesting school segregation.

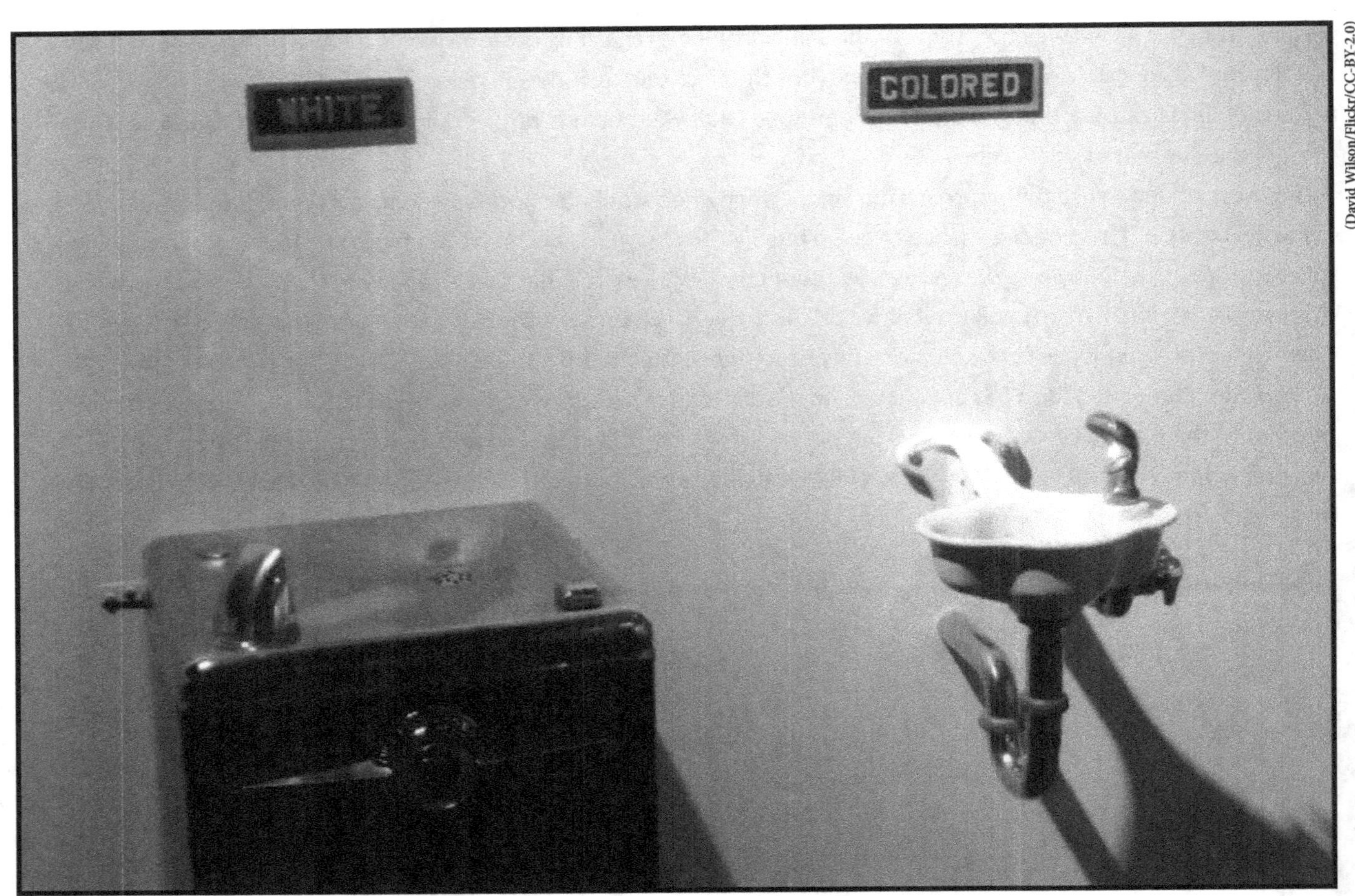

An exhibit at the Levine Museum of the New South showing segregated drinking fountains.

Later in the school year, Olivia revisited the compelling question, "Are all rules good rules?," and introduced historical sources from the Civil Rights era in conjunction with Martin Luther King Jr. Day. Olivia supplemented the inquiry with the book, *Happy Birthday, Dr. King*, as well as segregation visuals (such as the photograph on this page) and laws. She informed students: "There were rules back then too that were real rules for real people to follow, and they found that they didn't work at all. And the whole country was angry with one another, so he [Dr. King] worked for peace and tried to change, and he did change some of the rules." Next, kindergarteners examined and discussed pictures of children in school:

They see *white, colored,* and say, "How come? Why?" There were rules that only white kids could drink, and it said that on the water fountain. And only kids of color can drink over here....It grabs them right away. In their verbiage, "It's not fair! Why can't they? Why would there be such a rule like that?," and "Playing on a playground and you can't play with who you want to? What?"

Olivia noted that the inquiry and civil rights component resonated with kindergarteners: "So that one [inquiry] was a great one for changing rules and why we need to change rules....They're interested, they really are. This is right on with them—they get it and it's at their level."

Meeting the Challenges

Although Olivia possessed well-designed curriculum materials and age-appropriate pedagogical strategies, she noted challenges. Students, even at this young age, were overly concerned with producing the "correct" answer. Olivia reassured her kindergarteners, "It's okay, there's no right or wrong—it doesn't mean you were the winner or loser." Also, children often mirrored the stance of their teacher or classmates. Olivia related instances of pupils aligning themselves to whatever position was being discussed at the moment: "Some students just go with the flow, and if the teacher says it, that's it!" Another challenge mentioned was students' difficulty in articulating reasons. Olivia shared that kindergarteners can make a claim, but when probed, "'Can you tell me why you think it's this?' Some go, 'Hmm, I don't know.'" Others, she noted, may provide reasons that were tangential or disconnected from the claim.

Olivia indicated that continued dialogue, brainstorming, and creating class t-charts with reasons supported her students' development of argument skills. She passionately expressed: "You have to get them there. So you change the scenario, change the vocabulary, change the words…feel them out so [they] can't just say, okay, you didn't get it and then move on. You have to probe deeper." Despite these challenges, Olivia confirmed growth in students' cognitive and argument abilities as reflected in their improved capacity to state a claim and offer reasons that were well- aligned to the claim by the end of the school year.

Children's Literature

Candell, Arianna. *Mind Your Manners: In School.* Hauppauge, NY: Barron's Educational Series, Inc., 2005.

Cook, Julia. *A Bad Case of Tattle Tongue.* Chattanooga, TN: National Center for Youth Issues, 2006.

dePaola, Tomie. *Strega Nona.* New York: Aladdin Books, 1975.

Henkes, Kevin. *Lilly's Purple Plastic Purse.* New York: Scholastic, Inc., 1996.

Jones, Kathryn D. *Happy Birthday Dr. King!* New York: Aladdin Books, 1994.

Lionni, Leo. *It's Mine!* New York: Alfred A. Knopf, Inc., 1986.

O'Neill, Alexis. *The Recess Queen.* New York: Scholastic Press, 2002.

Williams, Rozanne. *Cat and Dog at School.* California: Creative Teaching Press, 1996.

Argumentation and Young Learners

As the vignette illustrates, kindergarteners are quite capable of participating in meaningful argument discourse. Olivia recognized the importance of dialogue to support student learning: Through discussion and cooperative learning tasks, students appropriated argumentation skills as they articulated claims, practiced reasoning skills, and evaluated information with their peers. These conversations reinforced argumentative reasoning and promoted higher level thinking as children learned to express their ideas and consider classmates' responses.[15] While inquiry instructions advise teachers that "class discussion or a combination of drawing and writing" is an appropriate response for the summative argument at the primary level, the Treetops first- and second-grade curricula require that children produce written responses. Research emphasizes the importance of dialogue in supporting argument writing,[16] and Olivia's primary colleagues noted students' improved ability to make a claim and supply reasons while learning to write arguments. Kindergarten lessons in argumentation carried forth into first and second grades and laid a firm foundation for argument writing tasks.

Studies also indicate that the teacher is of primary importance in mediating concepts and skills through the design of the learning experience—by selecting and scaffolding appropriate curriculum materials and instructional strategies, to promote children's cognitive development.[17] As we have seen, Olivia adeptly used the *Toolkit* inquiries as well as supplemental graphic organizers, visuals, and texts to foster argument discourse. Although she initially expressed apprehension regarding children's abilities to fully participate in inquiry tasks, Olivia was pleased with her kindergarteners' development of argumentation skills, and since implementing the *Toolkit*, has become more intentional about incorporating argument discourse across the curriculum, specifically in ELA and science. Ultimately, her young learners were successful in their efforts to articulate their arguments by stating a claim, supporting the claim with evidence, and recognizing other perspectives—certainly not the skills one typically ascribes to a social studies learning experience in kindergarten!

Notes

1. R. Andrews, *Narrative and Argument* (Milton Keynes, UK: Open University Press, 1989); R. Andrews, *Teaching and Learning Argument* (New York: Cassell Education, 1995); D. Kuhn, *The Skills of Argument* (Cambridge, UK: Cambridge University Press, 1991); D. Kuhn, "Thinking as Argument," *Harvard Educational Review* 62, no. 2 (1992): 155–178.

2. T. M. McCann, "Argumentative Writing Knowledge and Ability at Three Grade Levels," *Research in the Teaching of English* 23, no. 1 (1989): 63.

3. G. Graff, *Clueless in Academe* (New Haven, CT: Yale University Press, 2003); L. Levstik, "What Happens in Social Studies Classrooms? Research on K–12 Social Studies Practice," in *Handbook of Research in Social Studies Education*, eds. L. S. Levstik and C. A. Tyson (New York: Routledge, 2008), 50–62.

4. New York State Education Department, *New York State K–12 Social Studies Resource Toolkit* (2015).

5. National Council for the Social Studies, *The College, Career and Civic Life (C3) Framework for Social Studies State Standards* (Silver Spring, MD: National Council for the Social Studies, 2013).

6. National Governors Association Center for Best Practices, Council of Chief State School Officers, *Common Core State Standards for English Language Arts and Literacy in History/Social Studies, Science, and Technical Subjects* (Washington, DC: National Governors Association Center for Best Practices, Council of Chief State School Officers, 2010), https://www.thecorestandards.org/ELA-Literacy/

7. The *Toolkit* is comprised of six curriculum inquiries (one annotated and five abridged) for Grades K–11. The inquiries for Grade 12 are presented in two sets—six for Economics and six for Participation in Government. The *Toolkit* inquiries are available at https://c3teachers.org/new-york-hub/.

8. S. G. Grant, J. Lee, and K. Swan, *Inquiry Design Model—Blueprint* (C3 Teachers, 2014).

9. The IDM template can be accessed at http://www.c3teachers.org/inquiry-design-model/

10. S. G. Grant, J. Lee, and K. Swan, *Inquiry Design Model—At a Glance* (C3 Teachers, 2014), 1, http://www.c3teachers.org/wp-content/uploads/2015/06/Inquiry-Design-Model-glance.pdf

11. This kindergarten example is part of a larger study on inquiry and argumentation in K–2 classrooms. P. I. Krizan, "K–2 Social Studies: Vygotsky, Inquiry, and Argumentation," doctoral dissertation, Binghamton University, 2018 (ProQuest Dissertations and Theses Global, publication no. 13421534).

12. L. S. Vygotsky, *Mind in Society: The Development of Higher Psychological Processes* (Cambridge, MA: Harvard University Press, 1978); L. S. Vygotsky, *Thought and Language* (Cambridge, MA: Harvard University Press, 1986); J. V. Wertsch, *Voices of the Mind: Sociocultural Approach to Mediated Action* (Cambridge, MA: Harvard University Press, 1991).

13. M. Goldstein, A. Crowell, and D. Kuhn, "What Constitutes Skilled Argumentation and How Does It Develop?" *Informal Logic* 29, no. 4 (2009): 379–395; A. Reznitskaya, R. Anderson, and L. Kuo, "Teaching and Learning Argumentation," *The Elementary School Journal* 107, no. 5 (2007): 449–472; C. R. Wolfe, "Argumentation Across the Curriculum," *Written Communication* 28, no. 2 (2011): 193–219.

14. Selections included *A Bad Case of Tattle Tongue* by Julia Cook, *Cat and Dog at School* by Rozanne Williams, *It's Mine!* by Leo Lionni, *Lilly's Purple Plastic Purse* by Kevin Henkes, *Mind Your Manners: In School* by Arianna Candell, *The Recess Queen* by Alexis O'Neill, and *Strega Nona* by Tomie dePaola

15. D. Kuhn, Thinking Together and Alone. *Educational Researcher* 44, no. 1 (2015): 46–53; N. Mercer, R. Wegerif, and L. Dawes, "Children's Talk and the Development of Reasoning in the Classroom," *British Educational Research Journal* 25, no. 1 (1999): 95–111; Wertsch, *Voices of the Mind*.

16. Graff, *Clueless in Academe*; D. Kuhn and A. Crowell, "Dialogic Argumentation as a Vehicle for Developing Young Adolescents' Thinking," *Psychological Science* 22, no. 4 (2011): 545–552.

17. K. C. Barton, "'Oh, That's a Tricky Piece!': Children, Mediated Action, and the Tools of Historical Time," *The Elementary School Journal* 103, no. 2 (2002): 161–185; A. Kozulin, "Introduction to Vygotsky's 'The Dynamics of the Schoolchild's Mental Development in Relation to Teaching and Learning,'" *Journal of Cognitive Education and Psychology* 10, no. 2 (2011): 195–197.

Social Education **85**, no. 2 (2021): 116–120.

What's In A Claim?: A Framework for Helping Students Write Persuasive Claims

Ryan Lewis

With ten minutes left in class, my junior year sociology students sat quietly, full of controlled effort as they tackled the exit question on the overhead. The question was a simple supporting question that they had been working on as part of our latest inquiry. After a few minutes, I began walking the aisles, glancing over some shoulders, stopping here and there to look closely at student work. What was I looking for? Like many teachers, at this point in a lesson, I was hoping to see coherent answers to the question. However, over the last few years, I have come to look for something more specific. I was looking for a claim—a two- to three-sentence long response that would reveal what I needed to know about the depth of student learning. I stopped at the desk of one student who had finished her response. I picked her paper up, read it, and handed it back. "This is good, really good," I said. "A few months ago, you wouldn't have written this." She responded, "I know. After doing this all year, it's easy now."

After the C3 Framework was published in 2013, I remember attending a professional development on teaching through inquiry.[1] Although I thought I knew what to expect, I was not prepared for ideas that would forever change the way I taught. From the moment I heard the phrase "compelling question," I was hooked and I began to reorganize my courses. Bit by bit, I added focused inquiries, full inquiries, even compelling questions to assignments—all of the trappings of inquiry. I even made a "cycle of inquiry poster" and tacked it on my classroom wall.

After two years of working furiously to map out inquiry, however, I was stuck. Somewhere in the forest of questions, tasks, and sources, I felt I had missed something. I repeated the same processes: Questions, check; tasks, check; sources, check; argument, check. Students were learning. They were reading. They were challenged. All of the things that social studies educators say they want their students to be doing, mine were doing.

Yet, increasingly, it appeared that too many students were missing the boat. It was these students that kept me up at night. Somewhere, in my mind, a step had been missed, or perhaps overlooked. It wasn't until I began the next school year that my concerns began to coalesce around one word—claim. "Write an evidence-based claim…." That phrase pops up over and over in the C3 language and in the Inquiry Design Model (IDM) world.[2] As I sat one morning grading student claims, it hit me: Do my students really know what a claim is? Do *I* really know what a claim is? These questions have dominated my thinking for the past two years. These questions ultimately led me to a conviction that crafting persuasive claims is at the heart of what we do as social studies teachers. So, how do we get our students to write them, and write them well?

It turns out that words like "claim" are hard to nail down. As teachers, we throw the word around all the time. But what do we mean when we say a claim is "good" or "strong?" Not only is the term vague, so are its descriptors. Although "claim" as a concept first caught my attention in the language of the C3, frustratingly absent were the qualities and characteristics of claims. Claims required evidence, to be sure, but what does this even mean? I wanted guidance or some kind of tool that would help me clarify the components of a claim, be consistent in my feedback to students, and would prompt conversation between students about the nature of claims.

Spurred on by these questions, I began working on a tool to coach my students around better claim writing. I started by asking the question, "How do we teach students to write better claims?" I worked with my professors and teacher colleagues to develop what we all jokingly call The Lewis Framework, in which I outline four characteristics of a persuasive claim. In this article, I start by reviewing the literature that guided the framework's development and then I walk through the current iteration of the *Framework for Making Persuasive Claims*. From there, I describe student examples and how the framework is being used in my classroom to coach students in the writing process.

Ryan Lewis teaches claim writing to a group of students at Woodford High School, Kentucky.

Searching for Answers

Traditionally, claim making falls within the larger discourse of argumentation. In fact, VanSledright has argued that argumentation is what sets social studies apart from other forms of learning due to the specific demands of source work and evidence gathering.[3] Yet, argumentation instruction is consistently left out of the classroom in favor of more "traditional" instruction of textbook memorization and the presentation of simplified narratives devoid of discussion or critique.[4]

With so much already written on argumentation, why spend so much time thinking about claims? It turns out that making claims, both as a *product* and as a *process*, is integral to teaching argumentation.[5] As Monte-Sano notes, the possibility of learning is predicated on students' ability to understand arguments, which includes "the questioning and analysis of sources; the consideration of causation, change, perspective, or significance; [and] the construction of claims through corroboration of evidence."[6] Claim making, then, is a key part of the argumentation process, requiring teachers to be able to both articulate and to teach the process of constructing claims.

Teachers understand the challenges of teaching argumentation. It requires time, resources, and opportunities for students to participate in the process "as questions are framed, data gathered, and claims formed. Learning to produce a well-written, evidence-based argument is challenging work."[7] However, just as inquiry requires instructional shifts, so does teaching the process of argumentation, adding to the need for teachers to develop "specific instructional practices [to] support this shift."[8]

The C3 Framework and IDM have emphasized the centrality of argumentation through implementation of compelling questions and the explicit processing of sources through formative tasks.[9] What are currently needed are more instructional tools to assist teachers and students in doing inquiry. The *Persuasive Claim* framework links together a theoretical emphasis on argumentation and the daily act of working with students to become better writers and thinkers.

Introducing a Framework for Writing Persuasive Claims

According to Monte-Sano "claims are an end-product of discussion developed through honest consideration of sources."[10] The *Persuasive Claim* framework attempts to elaborate on this definition, parsing it down in order to better understand it. For our purposes here, I define a *persuasive claim* as an assertion that is supported with factual information and evidence from sources. A claim is often written in one or two sentences as it is meant to state a conclusion rather than be explanatory or expository. Claims can be a response to a question or they can be deduced by examining source(s). In either case, the key is that the claim is supported by the evidence that a student has interpreted and excerpted from sources, regardless of the conflicting nature and/or complexity of the source(s).

In order to better understand the nature of a claim, my colleagues and I settled on four important and integral dimensions of a persuasive claim. A persuasive claim is evidentiary, it is clear, it is accurate, and it is reasoned. In expanded form, these dimensions are explained as follows:

- **Evidentiary:** An *evidentiary* claim should be a convincing statement, supported by corroborating evidence from multiple sources, that accounts for evidentiary discrepancies or conflicting perspectives.

- **Reasoned:** A *reasoned* evidentiary claim should be logical and valid within the context of the question or task. Such a claim demonstrates students' thoughtful interpretation of sources in relationship to a question or task.

- **Clear:** A *clear* evidentiary claim should use unambiguous language to effectively communicate conclusions. Clarity enables the claim to speak to a wide audience who may not have examined the same sources as the author.

- **Accurate:** An *accurate* evidentiary claim presents factual information that is verifiable, is accepted as true, and reflects a plausible interpretation of a source(s). Such a claim is relevant to the question at hand and reflects a clear understanding of the relevant ideas and events.

Why these dimensions? These four dimensions add focus to what is often a messy process. This focus also creates increased clarity for teachers and students and streamlines feedback, assessment, and common language around claim making and argumentation.

Conceptualized in a more streamlined way, it is helpful to see these dimensions in rubric form. The same indicators are organized below in a single-point rubric.[11] This rubric was created by a C3 teacher and his students as a way to assess student argumentation during the summative task of an inquiry. Here it is repurposed, allowing students to clearly see the expectations for a per- suasive claim. Each side of the rubric allows for teacher feedback to show areas of student progress (Enhancers) and also areas in which students need to grow (Distractors). As we will see in the coming sections, having these clear expectations makes teacher feedback simple and concise.

The framework, like the rubric, is designed to be flexible in order to accommodate student needs and to provide structure and language that both guides students and assesses their learning. The four dimensions are likewise meant to pull double-duty—describing what is expected of students and helping teachers pinpoint what is going on in the students' writing.

Beta-Testing the Persuasive Claim Framework

But what does all of this look like in real time? Let's consider the following example. Some of my colleagues and I used a tenth-grade IDM inquiry on the French Revolution to beta-test the framework and its four dimensions. Focusing on the supporting question "Did Napoleon's rise to power represent a continuation of or an end to revolutionary ideals?" we drafted the following evidentiary claim:

> *Even though Napoleon's rise to power brought about order and an attempt at reform through his Code Napoleon, his reign was not a continuation of the Revolution due to his consolidation of power as Emperor and the suppression of critics and the press in France.*

Not bad, we thought. But we decided to use the framework to drill down on what is really going on here:

> **Evidentiary:** This claim is "evidentiary" because it weighs evidence. Napoleon was a "child" of the Enlightenment and believed in many liberal reforms. This point was taken into consideration, but it was weighed against Napoleon's actions as Emperor. The claim was informed by multiple sources of information.

Enhancers	Criteria/Dimension	Distractors
(Areas that show progress)	**Evidentiary** Claim is convincing. Author weighs evidence by corroborating multiple sources in order to support the claim. **Reasoned** Claim is logical and valid. It answers all parts of the question or task and conclusions follow a logical chain of reasoning. **Clear** Claim communicates conclusions effectively by using unambiguous language. Claim can be understood by a wide audience and avoids vague language. **Accurate** Information presented in the claim is factual and verifiable. Claim represents plausible interpretation of evidence.	(Areas that need improvement)

Accurate: This claim is "accurate" in that all of the actions mentioned in the claim are accepted as true and are both verifiable by and reasonably inferred from primary and secondary sources. The Code Napoleon was an actual law enforced in France that many historians recognize as important and significant. Napoleon did crown himself Emperor. There are several letters written by Napoleon discussing his political ideals showing that he was influenced by Enlightenment thought.

Reasoned: The claim is "reasoned" in that it answers and considers all parts of the question. The claim shows an attempt to arrive at a conclusion that is supported by the evidence. The claim is valid as it follows an historical attempt at comparing one series of events to another, looking for similarities or differences.

Clear: The claim is "clear" in that it uses language that is comprehensive and unambiguous. The author uses content specific vocabulary in order to add specificity, avoiding vague allusions to events or individuals.

The value of these dimensions lies not in simply articulating what makes a claim persuasive; rather it provides a coherent and consistent set of language that actually allows students to assess their own writing.

Writing Better Claims

So far, so good, right? To be sure, let's look at another, more likely, scenario based on the writing of some of my students. At the start of this year, I began my tenth-grade government classes with an inquiry into the potential problems with democracy. One of the supporting questions asks, "what challenges are currently facing American democracy?" What follows are four student claims. Using the *Persuasive Claim* framework above can you spot the places where the claims need help? Let's try it out! (*Note: The grammatical errors in the claims are as the students wrote them.*)

Claim 1: "Aside from an absence of participation, caused by a lack of respect within the judicial limits and constant fighting, the United States thrives with a flawless voting system, along with free speech and judicial limits on the executive."

The student does make an attempt to answer the question. But what does he mean by a "lack of respect with the judicial limits"? This part of the claim needs clarity. Using the framework, what suggestions would you make to this student?

Claim 2: "American democracy faces many challenges that will cause it to slowly erode. One of these challenges include that the constitution is based off of racist ideas considering it was written by people who supported slavery. This can prove to be a problem because if minorities feel undermined they won't feel encouraged to participate in the government thinking their voice doesn't matter. Democracy is also in danger because Americans were never adequately taught to participate as a citizen from a young age causing a lack of participation in citizens overall."

This student clearly wants to use a wide array of evidence to support her conclusion. But one wonders what question this student is answering. It probably lacks reasoning which also hurts the claim's accuracy. Knowing that this student needs help in possibly two areas, what suggestions would you make?

Claim 3: "Democracy today is facing many challenges such as people have less of an understanding of what democracy is, which leads to people thinking and saying that the constitution is not needed. Although we are not in imminent danger, if these challenges worsen, the American democracy would be in great danger."

This student provides us with a clear answer. Yet, to what "challenges" is he referring? Which people think the Constitution is not needed? This claim is begging for evidence. If you were standing next to this student, what evidence would you suggest they use?

Claim 4: "American democracy is built upon the practice of democratic institutions, such as elections. However, a lack of effective institutions, combined with partisan politics, has led to decreased participation in the democratic process, thus weakening America's democracy."

Good claim! More specifically the claim defines and provides examples (Evidentiary). It is well organized as it uses a counterclaim to emphasize its conclusion, giving a nod to competing evidence (Reasoned, Evidentiary). It is easy to understand and uses language that most academics would recognize (Clear, Accurate). The claim is also verifiable, connecting "partisan politics" to a struggling democracy (Accurate).

Claims represent a summation of student content knowledge and the depth to which a student comprehends a single question or a set of information. As claims represent the foundation of argumentation, claim writing becomes fundamental to the ways in which a teacher organizes instruction and a way for students to systematically reflect on their own learning. Much as a professional basketball player continues to improve through dribbling and shooting drills, continued experience in claim making enhances and expands students' ability to express evidence-based arguments. Monte-Sano and de la Paz emphasize the importance of these repeated opportunities for students to write, linking this practice to student success.[12] If the goal of inquiry is the pursuit and exploration of compelling questions, claim writing represents the way by which students actually grapple with the questions by weighing evidence and forming conclusions. In essence, claim making operationalizes students' level of understanding of the question and reflects the trajectory of their thinking about the compelling question. If inquiry is the road map, claim making is the vehicle. Therefore, teaching students to write better claims is worth our time.

Conclusion

The Framework for Making Persuasive Claims has shifted the way my students think, write, and talk about arguments. It has created a common language around inquiry. The terms clear, evidentiary, reasoned, and accurate now have a specific and permanent meaning for my students, simplifying my feedback and coaching.

By focusing on claim making, teachers take the first and most critical step in establishing a culture of inquiry with their students. While inquiry as a whole provides a consistent direction for scope and sequence in a curriculum, a focus on argumentation and, to a greater extent, claim making provides a skill focus for both teachers and students. This focus clarifies the question of what we are "doing" as social studies teachers. Rather than different skill sets across units, courses, or even teachers, classrooms that focus time and energy on claim making create a set of articulated student expectations, further stressing the salience of argumentation in social studies education.

Of course, claims do not represent the end goal of instruction. As someone who is still trying to "figure out" inquiry, my focus on helping students write better claims represents only one puzzle piece in the giant picture of social studies teaching. The next questions surface from our practices as teachers: How do claims help my students identify the arguments in a source? Can writing claims help my students think more clearly about controversial topics? In what other areas can I apply this framework? These are only questions that time and hard work with our students will reveal.

Notes

1. National Council for the Social Studies, *College, Career, and Civic Life (C3) Framework for Social Studies State Standards* (Silver Spring, Md., 2013).
2. S.G. Grant, Kathy Swan, and John Lee, *Inquiry-Based Practice in Social Studies Education: The Inquiry Design Model* (New York: Routledge, 2017).
3. Bruce A. VanSledright, "Fifth Graders Investigating History in the Classroom: Results from a Research- Practitioner Design Experiment," *The Elementary School Journal* 103, no. 2 (2002), 131–160.
4. Sam Wineburg, "On the Reading of Historical Texts: Notes on Breach Between School and Academy," *American Educational Research Journal* 28, no. 3 (1991), 495–519.
5. D. Walton and D.M. Godden, "Informal Logic and the Dialectical Approach to Argument," in *Reason Reclaimed*, eds. H. V. Hansen and R. C. Pinto (Newport News, Va.: Vale Press, 2007), 3–17.
6. Chauncy Monte-Sano, "Argumentation in History Classrooms: A Key Path to Understanding the Discipline and Preparing Citizens," *Theory into Practice* 55, no. 4 (2016), 316.
7. E.B. Moje, "Doing and Teaching Disciplinary Literacy with Adolescent Learners: A Social and Cultural Enterprise," *Harvard Educational Review* 85, no. 2 (2015), 265.
8. Ibid; Monte-Sano, "Argumentation in History Classrooms," 316.
9. Kathy Swan, John Lee, and S.G. Grant, "Questions, Tasks, Sources: Focusing on the Essence of Inquiry," *Social Education* 82, no. 3 (2018), 142–146.
10. Ibid; Monte-Sano, "Argumentation in History Classrooms," 316.
11. Kathy Swan, S.G. Grant and John Lee, *Blueprinting an Inquiry-Based Curriculum: Planning with the Inquiry Design Model* (National Council for the Social Studies, 2019), 164–165.
12. C. Monte-Sano and S. De La Paz, "Using Writing Tasks to Elicit Adolescents' Historical Reasoning," *Journal of Literacy Research* 44, no. 3 (2012), 273–299.

Social Education **84**, no. 5 (2020): 289–293.

Dining with Democracy:
Discussion as Informed Action

Paula McAvoy, Arine Lowery, Nada Wafa, and Christy Byrd

Jeremy Thomas and Russell McBride are social studies teachers in North Carolina and, until recently, were colleagues at a charter school outside of Raleigh, serving students in grades 6–12. After learning about the Inquiry Design Model (IDM),[1] both teachers implemented it into their classrooms and immediately saw how the blueprint helped deepen students' engagement, understanding of concepts, and ability to make and support arguments. The teachers even took the model to the next level by co-teaching an elective in which students learned to design their own inquiries and took turns leading classmates through their lessons. The course was student-centered and alive with discussion. As a result of their collaboration, Jeremy and Russell made the IDM blueprint a regular feature of their school's social studies program.

Like many teachers, Jeremy and Russell found that Taking Informed Action was the hardest aspect to put into practice. Moving student engagement beyond the classroom can be difficult to manage—it is both time consuming and logistically challenging. And, as Jeremy noticed, a lot of teachers "just throw it to the side." But an idea emerged when Jeremy attended a session at the North Carolina Social Studies Conference in 2019. The presenter shared an assignment he called "Dinner with Democracy," in which each student arranged to have a meal with someone to talk about their political views. The students then reported back about what they learned in their conversations. On the way home from the conference, Jeremy and Russell started brainstorming. Jeremy said they liked the idea because, "we wanted our students to learn that civil discourse can extend outside of the classroom and out into everyday life," but they also wanted a task that would require more public engagement.

By the time they arrived home, Jeremy and Russell had decided to host Dinner with Democracy as an evening event that would engage students and parents in multigenerational political discussions. Russell noted that this goal had been on their minds for a couple of years:

> In 2016, I think what we saw in the election more than anything is that kids did not see examples of how to engage each other when they disagree. So, we wanted to figure out a way to not just bring kids, but also bring parents and our larger school community together to try to model this for the whole community.

Later that semester, Jeremy and Russell facilitated their first Dinner with Democracy. They saw the civil discussion that unfolded as a type of informed action that could help alleviate the divisiveness of political polarization. It was a success to be sure. But it was also just the beginning of a journey with discussion and Taking Informed Action that would bring us into their work and unfold over the next several years.

Dinner with Democracy 2.0

In October of 2019, Jeremy and Russell hosted a gathering of about 60 people—tweens, teens, parents, teachers, administrators—and us, faculty and graduate students from nearby North Carolina State University. On the perimeter were tables filled with potluck contributions, and in the center were ten tables arranged with six seats each. The room was filled with the aroma of food and the anticipation of interacting with strangers about one's political beliefs and values. We were there to experience Jeremy and Russell's Dinner with Democracy 2.0.

Jeremy and Russell started by explaining the reasons for the event and the norms for the evening. The first round began with a student who provided a three-minute "TED talk" about gun violence. She ended with an invitation to discuss whether the U.S. should pass stricter gun control policies. Guests were randomly assigned to tables, which were set with jars of ice breaker questions (e.g., What is the scariest movie that you've seen?). The discussion began with participants introducing themselves and answering the question. Next, the format required that each person at a table share her or his perspective on the focal issue before the group engaged in open conversation. The room buzzed as people eagerly offered their ideas.

Arine Lowery records responses during the Dessert with Democracy tug-of-war activity.

Jeremy and Russell circulated, keeping watch for incivility, but mostly just enjoying the experience of seeing parents and students listening to each other. Gun violence was the first of three controversial political issues posed throughout the evening. In between each discussion, people rose to get their next course and then found a seat at a new table of participants.

Central to the idea of Taking Informed Action is that students should drive the activity. Jeremy and Russell had worked with students through a series of classroom inquiries that led to this Taking Informed Action task in which the students designed the questions and prepared the short talks that launched each discussion round. As Jeremy said, "we wanted them to create questions that they were going to feel comfortable engaging with and that they felt were relevant." The classes also worked together to generate the list of ice-breaker questions. Each table had a jar of these questions that they could pull from throughout the evening. The students also worked together to organize the event, recruit family and friends, and model the norms of discussion. In this way, the students' classroom learning extended to a new audience.

Discussion as Informed Action; Discussion as Inquiry

One challenge that teachers face today is how to engage students in political discussion without inviting the vitriol of polarization into the classroom.[2] Russell's students were similarly concerned, with one asking whether her dad *had* to be invited, because, "I don't think he can have this conversation." But, as this event showed, something remarkable happens when diverse groups are brought together, given norms and structure, and invited to share: They behave. The teachers reported that parents "were shocked" that middle schoolers could engage with complex questions, and the students were "impressed" (and relieved) that their parents listened and remained respectful.

Providing opportunities for students and the larger public to talk with one another normalizes disagreement as an essential feature of democratic life. Yet fear of disagreement is precisely why many teachers hesitate to bring political issues into the classroom.[3]

Ill-mannered disagreements can cause discussions in classrooms to go poorly. Fear of this result may be one reason why teachers shy away from designing inquiry-based discussions. The general focus of the C3 Framework's Inquiry Arc—investigating compelling questions, building knowledge, constructing arguments, and taking a stand—are the same building blocks for a good discussion. If the question is genuinely open to interpretation, students will naturally disagree as they read, evaluate sources, and construct evidence-based arguments. Because the students are consulting common materials to build understanding, they are engaged in a puzzle and not merely trying to win an argument. The discussions that result should contribute to the development of the participants' ability to listen to and discuss with others who may not agree.

Designing an inquiry that culminates in a discussion—within the classroom or at a public event—models several civic virtues that educators ought to be cultivating. First, discussion-as-informed action asks students to apply what they have learned to a current issue. Consider, for example, ending an inquiry on the history of voting rights and voter suppression with a discussion about whether ID cards should be required to vote. This discussion would be more informed because students could evaluate the issue within the larger historical context of restrictions on voting rights. In addition, it would offer students an opportunity to listen to how others reason about an issue that affects their lives and the larger community. Moving this conversation beyond the classroom to a public event, further broadens perspectives because young people hear how the issue affects parents, peers, and community members. Lastly, classroom and community discussions about political issues help students find their civic voice—they get practice speaking up and being heard.

Version 3.0: Dessert with Democracy

The graduate students who participated in Jeremy and Russell's Dinner with Democracy event were all members of a course at North Carolina State University that focused on classroom dialogue and deliberation, co-taught by Paula McAvoy and Christy Byrd. One of the major projects for the course was to develop and implement a similar event with two goals: (1) design the discussions to include the practices of dialogue and deliberation and (2) deepen the inquiry.

The result was a public event we named Dessert with Democracy.

From left to right: Paula McAvoy, Nada Wafa, and Christy Byrd pose after the Dessert with Democracy event.

On a November evening in 2019, over 100 people arrived at the NC State campus and were greeted by a bounty of cupcakes, fruits, cheese, and crackers. The audience included area teachers, pre-service teachers, faculty, elected officials, graduate students, middle and high school students and their parents. To meet our goals, we provided more structure to the event, and used the Taking Informed Action sequence (Understand, Assess, Act) as our guide. The Dessert with Democracy graphic (see Table 1) provides an overview of the structure and questions asked. There were three 25-minute rounds that each followed the same pattern.

Understand. Each round began with a five-minute background talk, following Jeremy and Russell's TED talk design. The talks were supported with slides and each presenter explained the background to the issue, relevant evidence (e.g., the gun issue included statistics about gun-related deaths in the U.S.), and set up a clear policy proposal. Table facilitators then invited everyone to answer the "opening share" question.

The sharing questions were designed to elicit a more personal response to the topic. For example, during the college affordability question (Round 2), the facilitator invited participants to share their responses to the question "how has paying or attempting to pay college tuition affected your life or the lives of people close to you?" During the sharing questions, facilitators made sure that everyone had the opportunity to speak without interruption and without comment from anyone else. Doing so allowed everyone to articulate a perspective that could not be questioned or challenged. The personal experiences became part of the group's common understanding about the issue.

These questions modeled aspects of intercultural dialogue.[4] Unlike deliberations, which are discussions that try to make a decision about a policy, dialogues provide spaces for participants to listen with the aim of understanding our different experiences within society. In its truest form, dialogue facilitates conversation among people who may have antagonistic socio-historical legacies due to unequal social power, stereotypes, or explicit and implicit bias.[5] The aim is to develop empathy and common understanding and to treat each other with dignity. Our sharing questions recognized the idea that to talk about a political issue with strangers can result in more open and honest discussions if everyone has a sense of how others are differently affected.

Assess. Next, facilitators invited their table participants to evaluate reasons for and against the policy proposal. To do this, we used the Tug-of-War strategy described in *Making Thinking Visible* by Ron Richart, Mark Church and Karin Morrison.[6] Each table in the room had a large sheet of paper on which they drew a horizontal line to represent the rope in a tug-of-war. On one side of the line, the group collectively generated reasons for the pro side of the proposal. After a few minutes they moved to the con side of the line.

This process was important for two reasons. First, it set a tone for discussion and not a debate by requiring everyone to work together to think of reasons. Second, it modeled inquiry by first asking participants if they could think through the issue from multiple angles before coming to a judgment. After listing reasons for and against, the group was invited to have a 10-minute open discussion about the proposal. This time period gave participants an opportunity to evaluate the ideas and arguments they generated.

Table 1: Structure of the Event

The Dessert with Democracy event is designed for three rounds of discussion. Each round follows the same structure and should take 30 minutes. Each table had a designated facilitator to help participants move through the inquiries.

Objectives	Develop a better understanding of the diverse views in our community. Express one's views and feel heard. Leave with a new understanding about the issues we discuss.
Staging the Question	1. **The Set Up. (5 mins)** Short talk delivered by a student or faculty member that gives sufficient background and provides enough evidence so that participants can understand the policy question and discuss it. 2. **Opening Share Around. (4-5 mins)** A warm-up introductory question for the group. This is not the policy question, but one that can give participants a sense of each other's experience with this issue. Each person can share their 1–2 sentence answer. <u>No comments from others are allowed</u>. See examples in the supporting questions below. 3. **Tug of War of Reasons. (5 mins)** Using the Tug-of-War Routine, groups can spend up to five minutes generating questions for the yes and no sides of the "rope." The facilitator may encourage participants to stay with one side before moving to the other side. 4. **Discussion. (10 mins)** The group engages in a free discussion of the policy question. 5. **Closing Share Around. (4 mins)** Each person shares her or his answer to the sentence "if I had to vote on this issue today, I'd say _____ because _____." No comments from others are allowed. 6. **Vote** with a show of hands.

The following is a snapshot of the Dessert with Democracy event.

Round 1	Round 2	Round 3
Policy Question: Should the voting age in the U.S. be lowered to 16?	**Policy Question:** Should North Carolina make college tuition-free for public universities?	**Policy Question:** Should North Carolina pass the School Security Act of 2019 (SB192) and allow teachers to be armed in school?
The set up (5 minutes) A moderator presents about the issue.	**The set up** (5 minutes) A moderator presents about the issue.	**The set up** (5 minutes) A moderator presents about the issue.
Opening Share (5 minutes) Begin with your name and something you value about living in the United States.	**Opening Share** (5 minutes) How has paying or attempting to pay college tuition affected your life or the lives of people close to you?	**Opening Share** (5 minutes) When I think about gun violence in the United States, I feel ____, because ___ .
Tug of War Activity (5 min)	**Tug of War Activity** (5 min)	**Tug of War Activity** (5 min)
Open Discussion (10 min)	**Open Discussion** (10 min)	**Open Discussion** (10 min)
Closing Share "If I had to vote on this issue today, I'd say ______, because ______."	**Closing Share** "If I had to vote on this issue today, I'd say ______, because ______."	**Closing Share** "If I had to vote on this issue today, I'd say ______, because ______."
Room votes with a show of hands.	**Room votes** with a show of hands.	**Room votes** with a show of hands.
Break/select a new table.	Break/select a new table.	Closing/Reflection.

Act. Each table concluded the round with a final share-out about the policy proposal. The facilitator invited each person to respond to the prompt "if I had to vote on this issue today, I'd say ____, because ____." Each person had up to one minute to speak. At the end of each round, we polled the room using a show of hands to see how many were for and against the policy.

Reflection

The purpose of any Taking Informed Action task is to help students develop the skills and confidence to be politically engaged. As Jeremy noted, one of the biggest takeaways for his students was learning that they "could speak about these things with their parents and with other adults." Furthermore, both teachers reported that the students felt heard, which reinforced the notion that young people "have a powerful voice and can have an impact on what [is] going on around them."

Deliberation should also help people become more informed about an issue and about how people are differently impacted. Evaluations taken at the Dessert with Democracy event overwhelmingly showed that participants "loved listening to different perspectives" and felt that the tight structure and use of the Tug of War activity were essential to bringing those out. The structure also helped set the right tone. Many commented that the room felt "calm," "comfortable," and "non-confrontational." Ultimately, students and the participants engaged in a deliberative inquiry that allowed them to do something fairly rare in today's political culture—engage in an open discussion about our differences.

Notes

1. Kathy Swan, John Lee, S.G. Grant, *Inquiry Design Model: Building Inquiries in Social Studies* (National Council for the Social Studies, 2018).
2. Paula McAvoy and Diana Hess, "Classroom Deliberation in an Era of Political Polarization," *Curriculum Inquiry* 43, no. 1 (2013): 14–47.
3. Ronald W. Evans, Patricia G. Avery, and Patricia Velde Pederson, "Taboo Topics: Cultural Restraint on Teaching Social Issues," *The Clearing House* 73, no. 5 (2000): 295–302.
4. Donna Rich Kaplowitz, Shayla Reese Griffin, and Sheri Seyka, *Race Dialogues: A Facilitator's Guide to Tackling the Elephant in the Classroom* (New York & London: Teachers College Press, Columbia University, 2019).
5. David Schoem and Sylvia Hurtado, *Intergroup Dialogue: Deliberative Democracy in School, College, Community, and Workplace* (Michigan: University of Michigan Press, 2001).
6. Ron Richart, Mark Church, and Karin Morrison, *Making Thinking Visible: How to Promote Engagement, Understanding, and Independence for All Learners* (Jossey-Bass, 2011).

References

1. Hess, Diana E., and Paula McAvoy, *The Political Classroom: Evidence and Ethics in Democratic Education.* Routledge, 2015.
2. Swan, Kathy, S.G. Grant, and John Lee, *Blueprinting an Inquiry-Based Curriculum* (National Council for the Social Studies, 2019).

Social Education **83**, **no. 6 (2019): 334–339.**

Can the Civics Test Make You a Good Citizen? Reconciling the Civics Test with Inquiry-Based Instruction

Jennifer Fraker, Carly Muetterties, Gerry Swan, and Kathy Swan

Students' knowledge of civics is bleak. As evidenced by National Assessment of Education Progress (NAEP) civics assessment data, only 23 percent of students performed at or above the *proficient* level on the 2014 civics assessment.[1] Whether eroded by the effects of the *No Child Left Behind* Act of 2001 (NCLB) or the ever-shrinking footprint of social studies in K-12 schooling, educators across the political and pedagogical spectrum agree that students' lack of civic knowledge is problematic.

Two recent initiatives have tried to combat this lack of civic understanding among students. Some educators have championed the legislative efforts of the Civics Education Initiative that focuses on foundational civic knowledge through the testing of civics-related content. To date, roughly 30 states have adopted this 100-question multiple-choice test as a high school graduation requirement.[2] Other educators have joined the National Council for Social Studies (NCSS) in advocating for the C3 Framework, an approach for reframing the study of civics around inquiry in the hopes that anchoring citizenship in the compelling questions of social studies might help students acquire deeper understanding and operationalize civic ideas.[3]

But many teachers are confused by the mixed signals that surround these two efforts. In our home state of Kentucky, high school teachers are required to help students pass the fact-based civics test, now a high school graduation requirement. At the same time, social studies teachers are reorienting their instruction around inquiry-based practices that are at the center of the new social studies standards. Although content is important in the inquiry process, teachers also are emphasizing disciplinary processes and inquiry skills that help students argue with evidence about thorny questions. Understandably, teachers want to implement both sets of requirements (testing and inquiry), but they wonder if they should be teaching just the "facts" or a deeper level of understanding of civic ideas.

In this article, we tackle this tension between a fact-based civics test and inquiry-based teaching and learning. We begin with a short history on the civics test and the new standards in Kentucky before turning our attention to one approach to the civics test using an Inquiry Design Model (IDM) inquiry— "Does the civics test make you a good citizen?" In doing so, we confront the pervasive content versus skills debate that so often balkanizes social studies educators.

The Rise of the Civics Test

As part of the Joe Foss Institute's Civic Education Initiative, legislation was proposed across the nation, asking states to require high school seniors take and pass an exam based on the U.S. Citizenship and Immigration Services (USCIS) Naturalization test.[4] The 100 fact-based questions about U.S. history, geography, and civics "were chosen specifically because they constitute the bare minimum of knowledge a person needs to begin understanding how our government works and who we are as a people."[5] Examples of questions include: What are the first three words of the Constitution? How many amendments does the Constitution have? What is the economic system in the United States? Since the Joe Foss Institute launched the Civics Initiative in 2014, roughly 30 states have adopted some sort of requirement related to the passage of a civics test.[6]

In 2017, the Kentucky General Assembly passed a law requiring students to pass a civics test composed of 100 questions in order to graduate from a public high school.[7] Kentucky's test is derived from the USCIS naturalization process. Students must have a passing score of 60% or higher (USCIS requires an oral examination in which immigrants seeking naturalization pass six out of 10 questions correctly) and may retake the exam as many times as needed. For Kentucky legislators, like those across the nation, the requirement was seen as a much-needed step toward addressing society's lack of basic civic knowledge. The struggle Kentucky educators now face, as a result of implementation efforts, is how they can balance this mandate with best instructional practices. In other words, it's one thing to "know" basic civics, but another to actually "do" civics.

The Rise of Inquiry

Inquiry-based learning is not new but the College, Career, and Civic Life (C3) Framework for Social Studies State Standards codified a language around inquiry into a standards document meant to provide states with guidance for upgrading their existing social studies standards.[8] The most obvious difference between the C3 Framework and past standards efforts is the Inquiry Arc, "a set of interlocking and mutually reinforcing elements that move from developing questions and planning inquiries to communicating conclusions and taking informed action."[9] Many states from Vermont to Hawaii are revising their academic standards around the core inquiry practices outlined by the C3 Framework.

Kentucky adopted new social studies standards in July 2019.[10] The standards place four inquiry practices—Questioning, Investigating Disciplinary Concepts, Using Evidence, and Communicating Conclusions—at the center

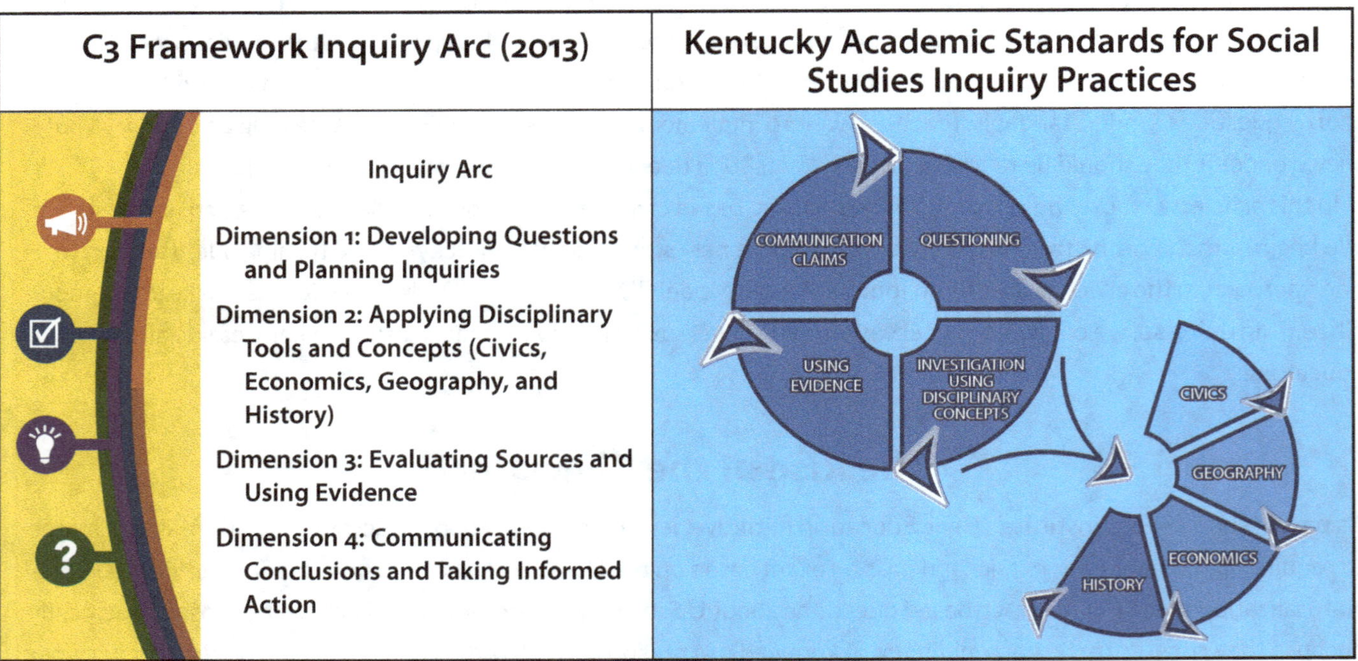

of good social studies. Based largely on the C3 Framework's Inquiry Arc, the inquiry practices require teachers and students to ask questions that drive student investigation of the subject matter and eliminate the "skills vs. content" dilemma in social studies as both are needed to successfully engage in inquiry. However, this shift presents a new struggle for teachers with regard to building inquiry-based curriculum: How do I teach my content through inquiry?

C3 Framework Inquiry Arc (2013) Kentucky Academic Standards for Social Studies Inquiry Practices

In an effort to support teachers seeking to use inquiry in their classrooms, the lead writers of the C3 Framework co-created the Inquiry Design Model (IDM). The IDM is a curricular scaffold for teachers and students wanting to do disciplinary inquiry. At the core of the IDM is a one-page blueprint that articulates the questions, tasks, and sources that define a curriculum inquiry.[11] Teachers using the IDM can essentially teach the entirety of the Inquiry Arc and hit on all four inquiry practices within a week's worth of instruction.

A Time of Reconciliation

So, is there a way to teach the factual knowledge needed to pass the civics test using an inquiry approach? We have been exploring just this question. Using the IDM process, we built an inquiry framed by the compelling question— Does the civics test make you a good citizen? For this inquiry, we use an *embedded action* inquiry blueprint where the Taking Informed Action sequence—understand, assess, and act— is embedded within the supporting questions and summative performance task, rather than occurring entirely at the end of the blueprint.[12] In the sections that follow, we walk through the anatomy of the inquiry, demonstrating the questions (compelling and supporting), the tasks (both formative and summative), and the sources (both primary and secondary) that are featured on the blueprint.

Questions

The compelling question for the inquiry— Does the civics test make you a good citizen?—frames a study of the civics exam itself and what it means to be a "good citizen." As part of the inquiry, students take the test and evaluate whether the knowledge within the test is necessary or sufficient as they consider the notion of citizenship, and more importantly *good* citizenship. In other words, the inquiry puts students in the center of a policy dilemma—how do educators help students prepare for civic life and what role should the civics test play in that endeavor?

In addressing the compelling question, the inquiry structures students' work as they proceed through the series of supporting questions, formative performance tasks, and featured sources. The supporting questions are sequenced to progressively build students' understandings of the civics test's content and to explore other kinds of civic learning and the role that each play in preparing students to be good citizens.

The supporting questions help students break down the compelling question and, simultaneously, prepare them for the exam:

- What is on the civics test?
- How did the class perform on the civics test?
- What is the most important material on the civics test?

- What other kinds of civic learning could be on the test?

Understanding the civics test content, as well as how it can complement being a good citizen, illuminates the intersection between the civics test and the knowledge, skills, dispositions, and experiences needed to prepare students for informed participation in civic life.

Sources

The main source propelling this inquiry is the civics test itself. Although each Kentucky school district can create its own civics tests, all exams must be based upon the 100 questions from the USCIS Citizenship Exam.[13] This inquiry employs the *Digital Driver's License* online platform, a resource available to all Kentucky districts, to administer and collect results to the test.[14] Students use the test and test result data to answer supporting questions 1, 2, and 3.

To help students grapple with the idea of a "good citizen" and the test content, the staging task includes sources that describe the test, showing both positive and negative perspectives. We included the Joe Foss Institute's reasoning for supporting civics exam legislation, noting specifically that the test's content includes the "things every student should know to be ready for active, engaged citizenship."[15] Other sources supporting the staging task include excerpts from the *Chicago Tribune* and *The Atlantic*. Both articles provide arguments for and against the exam, specifically related to how it prepares students for active citizenship. (See Table 1).

For supporting question 4, where students evaluate the test content's utility and contributions to civic learning, we provided a list of online civic education resources (e.g., iCivics, Center for Civic Education, Mikva Challenge). Teachers can pull excerpts from these resources or have students explore them on their own, considering what each says about preparing students for civic life.

Table 1. Supporting Question 4 Source Excerpts

"Critics: Civics Test Not Designed to Judge High School Knowledge." —*Chicago Tribune*	"Why Civics is About More Than Citizenship." —*The Atlantic*
National Council for the Social Studies: Students should learn by doing—with teachers fostering active discussions, highlighting opposite viewpoints and encouraging them to actively learn how government works. Illinois Sen. Dennis Kruse, R-Auburn: "I think it's in the lack of basic education in our schools. We've got a generation of people who don't know where we came from…. Something is not connecting, the kids, they are not connecting and retaining the information."	Fordham Foundation's Robert Pondiscio: "The more educated you are, the more likely you are to be civically engaged." Joseph Kahne in *Education Week*: "There's not any evidence base to show that this will be effective…. It's something state legislators can pass and feel good about." He argued that the testing approach to civic education is the equivalent of "teaching democracy like a game show."

<table>
<tr><td colspan="4" align="center">Kentucky Civics Test Inquiry</td></tr>
<tr><td colspan="4" align="center">Does the civics test make you a good citizen?</td></tr>
<tr><td>Kentucky Academic Standards</td><td colspan="3">HS.C.RR.2 Explain how active citizens can affect the lawmaking process locally, nationally and internationally.

HS. C.I.CC.2 Engage in disciplinary thinking and construct arguments, explanations or public communications relevant to meaningful and/or investigative questions in civics.</td></tr>
<tr><td>Staging the Question</td><td colspan="3">Create a mind map to list, organize, and connect associated ideas, actions, and/or people to the central concept: "good citizen."</td></tr>
<tr><td>Supporting Question 1</td><td>Supporting Question 2</td><td>Supporting Question 3</td><td>Supporting Question 4</td></tr>
<tr><td>UNDERSTAND</td><td>UNDERSTAND</td><td>UNDERSTAND</td><td>UNDERSTAND</td></tr>
<tr><td>What is on the civics test?</td><td>How did the class perform on the civics test?</td><td>What is the most important material on the civics test?</td><td>Should the civics test include other kinds of civic learning?</td></tr>
<tr><td>Formative Performance Task</td><td>Formative Performance Task</td><td>Formative Performance Task</td><td>Formative Performance Task</td></tr>
<tr><td>Take the school or district's civics test.</td><td>Draft a report identifying the class's area of strength and weakness with reference to specific questions.</td><td>Using a Kanban board, deliberate and rank the importance of different test items for engaging in civic life.</td><td>Create a claim, or series of claims, supported by evidence, about whether the test should include other kinds of civic learning.</td></tr>
<tr><td>Featured Sources</td><td>Featured Sources</td><td>Featured Sources</td><td>Featured Sources</td></tr>
<tr><td>Source A: School or district's civics test

Source B: Civics Test from the Digital Drivers License (DDL)

Source C: US Citizenship and Immigration Services, 100 Civics Questions</td><td>Source A: Civics Test Results Matrix from the Digital Drivers License (DDL)

Featured Sources from Supporting Question 1</td><td>Source A: Civics Test Question Cards

Featured Sources from Supporting Questions 1–2</td><td>Source A: List of civic education resources

Featured Sources from Supporting Questions 1–3</td></tr>
<tr><td>Summative Performance task</td><td colspan="3">ARGUMENT Construct an argument (e.g., detailed outline, poster, essay) that discusses the compelling question using specific claims and relevant evidence from contemporary sources while acknowledging competing views.

EXTENSION Analyze how individual test items connect to issues facing students' communities. Identify which content will help address their chosen issue, as well as additional information they would need in order to take informed action.</td></tr>
<tr><td>Taking Informed Action</td><td colspan="3">ASSESS Evaluate the district's civics test and consider the extent to which the test supports student's preparation for "good citizenship."

ACT Create a proposal about the needs of the civics test and/or preparation for citizenship to share with the local school district, school board, state official, or national organization.</td></tr>
</table>

Tasks

The formative performance tasks help scaffold students' evaluation of the civics test, building their understandings of its content and its potential role towards creating good citizens. To introduce students to the inquiry, the staging the compelling question task asks students to create a mind map where they connect ideas, actions, or people around the central concept "good citizen." Within the inquiry, we provided resources to familiarize teachers and students with scholarly understandings of "good citizenship." The central criticism of the civics test is that it focuses on memorization of individual facts, rather than having students engage in civic practices. The inquiry's sources explain the dimensions of a rigorous and meaningful civic education, notably the need for teachers to develop students' *civic knowledge*, as well as *civic skills* and *civic dispositions*, and provide opportunities to take action in a *civic experience.* We selected excerpts from the C3 Framework and Westheimer and Kahne's 2003 article titled "What Kind of Citizen?"[16] With teacher guidance, the staging task introduces students to the compelling question and bridges the concept of a "good citizen" to the remainder of the inquiry.

In the inquiry, students answer the supporting questions by completing four formative performance tasks, building towards the summative argument task:

- Take the school or district's civic test.
- Draft a report identifying the class's areas of strength and weakness with reference to specific questions.
- Using a Kanban board, deliberate and rank the importance of different test items for participating in civic life.
- Create a claim, or series of claims, supported by evidence about whether the exam could include other kinds of civic learning.

To answer the first supporting question, students take the school or district's civics test. The second task has them reflect upon their collective test results and draft a report identifying the class's areas of strength and weakness with reference to specific questions. The intention of this task is to have students organize the content knowledge contained within the civics test, and likewise, reflect upon areas of needed growth in order to be successful on the test. In the third task, students connect the test back to the compelling question by considering how the content helps prepare them for participation in civic life. Students deliberate and rank test questions' importance using a Kanban organizational board. Kanban boards help visually represent information or tasks by evaluating and organizing items in relation to one another. (See Figure 1). These tasks prepare students for the final supporting task where they create evidence-based claims about whether the test could include other kinds of civic learning needed to be an active participant in civic life.

In this inquiry, the task logic is designed to help students build their understanding of the civics test by progressively developing their assessment of its content. The task sequence prepares students to construct complex and evidence-based arguments in response to the compelling question, "Does the civics test make you a good citizen?" Students' arguments will likely vary, but could reflect any of the following:

- The civics test's content includes important information needed to participate in civic spaces.
- Even though the information on the civics test is valuable, the test only assesses memorized content and not the skills, dispositions, and/or experiences needed to be a good citizen.
- Though the test doesn't include action opportunities, the information does help create a knowledge base for good citizens to draw upon and take action.
- There is a lot of information on the test that could be seen as disconnected from modern civic issues. The test, and preparation for the test, doesn't necessarily connect those dots.

Figure 1. Kanban Board and cards

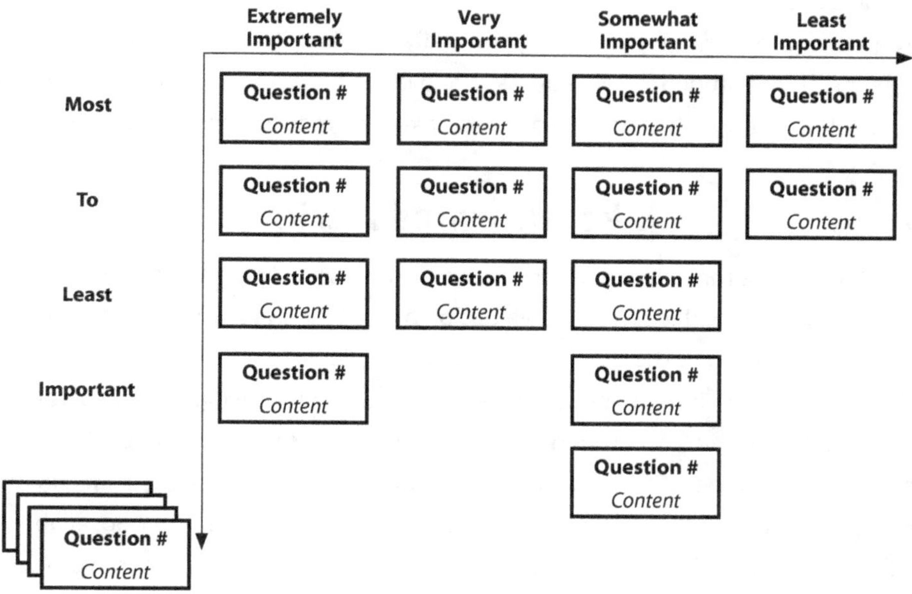

What is the supreme law of the land?	What does the Constitution do?
The idea of self-government is in the first three words of the Constitution. What are these words?	What is an amendment?
What do we call the first ten amendments to the Constitution?	What is <u>one</u> right or freedom from the First Amendment?
How many amendments does the Constitution have?	What did the Declaration of Independence do?

- Knowing a lot of facts doesn't necessarily mean you are positively impacting your community, so a test alone cannot make you a good citizen.

Students could extend their arguments by analyzing how individual test items connect to issues facing their communities. Using the test items, students select an issue and identify the exam content to help them address the issue, as well as additional information they need in order to take informed action on the issue.

Take Informed Action

After students have completed the formative and summative performance tasks and developed understandings of the civics test's content, they are ready to deepen their evaluation of the test and take informed action. Students evaluate their own district's civics test and assess the extent to which they believe the test supports preparing students to be good citizens. If students do not believe it adequately supports good citizenship, their evaluation should provide suggestions about a more authentic way for students to demonstrate civic learning. Suggestions must consider the civics test's requirements to follow the USCIS questions. Accordingly, suggestions can include ideas to supplement the test (e.g., a civic capstone project). To take informed action, students act by writing a proposal about the civics test's areas of need (or needs of civic education for the state in order to prepare students for active citizenship) to share with the local school district, school board, state official, or national organization.

To Inquiry and Beyond

In this article, we laid out an ambitious plan to combat the struggles teachers face when trying to implement the civics test in a meaningful way. In a future article, we hope to talk about how the implementation of the inquiry actually went, from both teacher and student perspectives. For now, we know many teachers in many states face the same kind of incongruence around inquiry and a fact-based test. Our hope is that this column might start a conversation about how we move with educational policy, making the best of what seems like just one more thing.

Notes

1. The Nation's Report Card, www.nationsreportcard.gov/civics/
2. Joe Foss Institute, https://civics.asu.edu/JFI
3. C3 Framework, www.socialstudies.org/standards/c3
4. Joe Foss Institute, https://civics.asu.edu/JFI
5. Diana Hess, Sam Stone, and Joseph Kahne, "Should High School Students Be Required to Pass a Citizenship Test?" *Social Education* 79 (2015): 173–176.
6. Joe Foss Institute, https://civics.asu.edu/JFI
7. https://apps.legislature.ky.gov/recorddocuments/bill/17RS/sb159/bill.pdf
8. Kathy Swan and Susan Griffin, "Beating the Odds: The College, Career, and Civic Life (C3) Framework for Social Studies Standards," *Social Education* 77 (2013): 317–321.
9. S.G. Grant, Kathy Swan, and John Lee, *Inquiry-Based Practice in Social Studies Education: Understanding the Inquiry Design Model* (London: Routledge, 2017).
10. Kentucky Academic Standards, https://kystandards.org/standards-resources/cs-docs
11. S.G. Grant, Kathy Swan, and John Lee, Ibid.
12. Kathy Swan, S.G. Grant, and John Lee, *Blueprinting an Inquiry-Based Curriculum: Planning with the Inquiry Design Model* (National Council for the Social Studies and C3 Teachers, 2019).
13. Kentucky Department of Education, Civics Test, https://education.ky.gov/curriculum/conpro/socstud/Pages/citizenshipassessment.aspx
14. Kentucky Department of Education, Digital Citizenship, https://education.ky.gov/school/diglrn/digcitizen/Pages/default.aspx
15. Civics Education Initiative, www.ecs.org/clearinghouse/01/19/46/11946.pdf

16. National Council for the Social Studies. *The College, Career, and Civic Life (C3) Framework for Social Studies State Standards: Guidance for Enhancing the Rigor of K-12 Civics, Economics, Geography, and History* (Silver Spring, Md.: NCSS, 2013); J. Westheimer and J. Kahne, "What Kind of Citizen? The Politics of Educating for Democracy," *American Educational Research Journal* 41, no. 2, (2004) 237–269.

Section 4: Conclusion

A directionless revolution serves no one's purpose. But neither does a revolution that cannot tell success from failure. The revolution of ideas initiated by the C3 Framework shows multiple signs of taking root: in standards, in curriculum, in instruction, and—as we will see in the next section—in teacher education. All have presented challenges, though none can draw on as thin a research base as assessment. The third leg of the curriculum-instruction-assessment stool, then, continues to be a bit wobbly. The articles in this section, however, suggest a brighter—and sturdier—future.

Section 5:
Teacher Education

Section 5: Teacher Education

As we have seen in the previous sections, the publication of the C3 Framework ushered in an inquiry revolution of ideas for social studies. But the stages of this revolution have unfolded in ways that have surprised and challenged us. With the birth of the inquiry revolution in 2013, work on state standards commenced and has continued apace with energy and vigor that has surprised many. The development of curriculum innovations has challenged us to imagine social studies classrooms where children are the center of our attention and our actions as teachers are committed to supporting their intellectual growth. Implementing these innovative inquiry curriculum plans with ambitious and connected assessment systems proved to be another challenge and opportunity as the revolution of ideas grew and came of age. But how do we sustain this revolution?—that was a question that, in the adrenaline rush of the unfolding events of the last decade, lurked in the background, never quite gaining the headlines that the standards, curriculum, instructional and assessment activities garnered, but critically important nonetheless.

As social studies professionals, we have seen this movie before. We know that innovative educational practices and policies (even those revolutionary ones) must be nurtured and strengthened, even institutionalized, to stand the test of time. But how? What are the mechanisms? Who are the players? What are the means to sustain the inquiry revolution? As Benjamin Franklin is said to have commented on September 18, 1787, to the question of an American future—now you have a republic, if you can keep it. Perhaps we also thought that the day after publishing the C3 Framework on September 17th, 226 years later. Can we keep inquiry in social studies? We think so, but not without a long-term commitment to a strong system of support. New standards, innovative curriculum, and instructional/assessment practices are not enough. We need teachers and teacher preparation programs committed to preparing future teachers to keep the inquiry revolution of ideas alive.

Fortunately, the social studies community had an opportunity to think in earnest about how to sustain the move toward inquiry in 2017 with the publication of *National Standards for the Preparation of Social Studies Teachers* from the National Council for the Social Studies. This work, led by Alex Cuenca, put forward a view of ambitious teaching and a vision for social studies teaching and teacher education. We were asked to provide a foreword for this publication. We did so in a way that positioned teacher educators front and center in the effort to grow the inquiry revolution. Below is our call to action for teachers or, as we envisioned at the time, our call for a collaborative C3 concert series!

Standards work is not for the faint of heart. When the *College, Career, and Civic Life Framework for Social Studies State Standards* ("C3 Framework") was published in 2013, the writers knew that there would be a long road ahead if the document was to make a difference for social studies. First, state departments of education would need to incorporate the C3 Inquiry Arc into what is often an arduous state standards adoption process. And, they would need to do this against the backdrop of Common Core fatigue and without a national mandate or external incentive to do so. Second, even if a quorum of states adopted the C3 Framework in some shape or form, the ideas put forth in the document (e.g., inquiry, civic action, disciplinary and interdisciplinary practices) required additional systemic supports. Teachers would need to have clear curricular models and instructional materials that would help them do C3 inquiry, and social studies students would need to be evaluated on the disciplinary thinking skills animated within the inquiry arc. In other words, it wasn't enough to create a hit song; we need an entire catalog of music, a variety of venues, lighting and sound experts, and marketing to pull off a concert series that could usher in a new genre of social studies.

    The good news is that the C3 concert series is taking shape. Under the capable leadership of Alex Cuenca and his team, these new national standards for teacher preparation explicitly reinforce the ideas that are outlined in the C3 Framework. In the introduction, they write, "As the statement on what meaningful and powerful social studies instruction ought to look like, the C3 Framework served for the 2016 committee as the milestone for the kinds of knowledge, skills, and dispositions social studies teacher preparation programs are required to cultivate" (p. 8). Thus, each of the five anchor standards, or core competencies, outlined in the document is infused with the language and ethos of the C3 Framework. For example, in defining the Content Knowledge—Standard 1—the writers included the content and skills from the core social studies disciplines (Dimension 2) as well as the inquiry practices essential to a meaningful social studies education (Dimensions 1, 3, 4). In doing so, this writing committee has sent a clear and cohesive message to teacher educators, the pre-service teachers they work with, and the larger social studies community that the C3 Framework is not a one-hit wonder but a broader, more ambitious initiative that aims to impact every facet of social studies education.[1]

Two years later, Pat Krizan penned a thoughtful article that moved our thinking forward regarding how we engage social studies educators through professional development on inquiry. Krizan describes her approach to PD with teachers as anchored by an exploration of the *why* of inquiry, pushing teacher educators to reckon with the power of inquiry with working with their colleagues while also honoring teachers' prior knowledge and expertise. With a focus on teacher collaboration, Krizan maps the terrain of professional development for teaching with inquiry anchored in an unpacking of the Inquiry Design Model, the exploration of exemplary inquiries, and the planning and implementation of inquiries, including those designed by other educators and those newly designed by teachers with whom she was engaging.

    Energy grew over the next two years as we published what we viewed as a foundational article on how teachers and teacher educators might sustain and grow the inquiry revolution. In this piece, "The Signal and the Noise: Coaching Pre-Service Candidates to Teach With Questions, Tasks, And Sources," Kathy Swan, Ryan Crowley, and Gerry Swan describe an approach to coaching pre-service teachers to teach with *Questions, Tasks, and Sources (QTS)*. What began as a seemingly straightforward representation of the Inquiry Design Model's emphasis on questions, tasks, and sources became a touchstone for recognizing high-quality inquiry design and implementation and a useful entry point for pre-service teachers to learn about IDM and develop their own inquiry design skills.

    With the inquiry revolution of ideas in full swing as more states began to incorporate the C3 Framework into social studies standards and as inquiry development continued at a steady pace, we felt the pull of our teacher colleagues who wanted visions of what is possible for inquiry teaching. Our 2021 article on the *Making Inquiry Possible* films answered the call. In this article, Kathy Swan, Ryan Crowley, S. G. Grant, John Lee, Gerry Swan, Callaway Stivers, and Gates Sweeney describe what was perhaps our most ambitious project to date, a film series designed to help educators understand how their collaborative efforts could make inquiry-based curriculum and instruction achievable. Central to the *Making Inquiry Possible* films is the notion that an individual teacher, committed to the inquiry cause, is necessary, but not sufficient to make inquiry a broad reality. What's needed is an educational community of designers, teachers, their students, and supportive administrators. In this article and through the films, we explore why we need inquiry, what inquiry looks like, and what makes inquiry possible.

    That same year, in 2021, we invited Alex Cuenca to reflect on the 2017 *National Standards for the Preparation of*

Social Studies Teachers standards and how they were impacting social studies teacher education. In his article, Cuenca describes a set of inquiry-based core practices for social studies teacher education. Using inquiries from our collection on C3Teachers.org, Cuenca puts forward seven core practices that serve as "conversation points to help reorient the overt focus on curriculum toward a more appropriate balance with teaching method" (p. 213).

More recently, Ryan Lewis, Kathy Swan, and Ryan Crowley offer a new perspective in the inquiry revolution and in our unfolding understanding of how to prepare teachers for inquiry teaching with their article "Turning Student Teachers into Claim Makers." In this work, Lewis, Swan, and Crowley put forward a framework for how teachers might support students to do the hard work of inquiry, what they call the *Persuasive Claim Framework*. As a theory for how making claims—the core business of inquiry—works in practice, Lewis, Swan, and Crowley provide teachers with firm footing for enhancing their inquiry teaching practices and give teacher educators substance to ground their work in preparation for new teachers to support their students in doing inquiry.

* * * * *

1. Patricia Krizan, "Engaging Social Studies Educators: Professional Development on Inquiry," *Social Education* 83, no. 3 (2019): 160–163.
2. Kathy Swan, Ryan Crowley, and Gerry Swan, "The Signal and the Noise: Coaching Pre-Service Candidates to Teach with Questions, Tasks, and Sources," *Social Education* 84, no. 2 (2020): 100–107.
3. Kathy Swan, Ryan Crowley, S. G. Grant, John Lee, Gerry Swan, Callaway Stivers, and Gates Sweeney, "Making Inquiry Possible: A Film Project on Building a Culture of Inquiry," *Social Education* 85, no. 1 (2021): 26–30.
4. Alexander Cuenca, "Inquiry-Based Core Practices for Social Studies Teacher Education," *Social Education* 85, no. 6 (2021): 382–386.
5. Ryan Lewis, Kathy Swan, and Ryan Crowley, "Turning Student Teachers into Claim Makers," *Social Education* (in press, 2024).

Note

1. Kathy Swan, John Lee, S. G. Grant, foreword to *National Council for the Social Studies National Standards for the Preparation of Social Studies Teachers*, ed. Alexander Cuenca, Antonio J. Castro, Brandie Benton, Andrew Hostetler, Tina Heafner, and Emma Thacker (Silver Spring, MD: National Council for the Social Studies, 2016), 5.

Social Education 83, no. 3 (2019): 160–163.

Engaging Social Studies Educators: Professional Development on Inquiry

Patricia Krizan

Social studies teachers often have a love-hate relationship with inquiry. The possibilities of a dynamic and engaging approach to learning labor against time constraints imposed by a content-heavy curriculum. In that scenario, how can professional development (PD) on inquiry inform educators and encourage skeptical teachers to implement this practice? How can those responsible for teacher learning opportunities plan meaningful, inquiry-based PD?

Recent research on effective professional learning links PD experiences, teacher practice, and student outcomes, and has identified remarkably similar features.[1] These studies suggest that effective PD "is content focused, incorporates active learning, supports collaboration, uses models of effective practice, provides coaching and expert support, offers feedback and reflection, and is of sustained duration."[2] Interestingly, these seven features align to the very factors that teachers themselves value in PD.[3]

In this article, I share my approach to professional development on inquiry design. I begin by honoring the "why" of both social studies and inquiry and recognizing participants' prior knowledge. Next, I collectively establish a common understanding of inquiry based on standards and pedagogical experts. Convening in grade-level teams, I ask teachers to examine and deconstruct models of inquiry practice and to collaboratively plan and pilot an inquiry-based learning experience for their students. These professional learning opportunities occurred over time, providing opportunities for feedback, analysis of student work, and revisions based upon student outcomes.

Honoring the *Why* of Inquiry

Before delving into inquiry-based lessons, it is crucial that participants understand the purpose of both inquiry *and* of the PD sessions. Framing the initial PD meeting so that teachers become invested in inquiry results in more productive and meaningful learning. I find that posing a few questions at the onset focuses participants on the topic and allows educators to reflect upon their practices. I ask teachers to consider the larger questions that transcend district mandates or state testing requirements: Why teach social studies, anyway? What are your goals for students this year? What are your hopes for students in five years? Teachers often cite lofty ambitions such as cultivating critical thinking skills or developing informed citizens. I then inquire about their objectives for this PD: What are *your* goals for these sessions? What do *you* hope to learn? Exploring teachers' thinking regarding the value of social studies and learning takes little time and the responses provide a purpose for *their* professional learning.

Activating Teachers' Prior Knowledge

These initial questions trigger teachers' prior knowledge and offer insights into what participants know: Who are novices to inquiry? Who has experimented with inquiry-based lessons? I have learned that differences among the participants often become a strength of the PD sessions in that many voices and diverse experiences are offered.

Likewise, working with multiple grade levels provides opportunities for vertical articulation of inquiry skills and practices.

With this opening in place, participants then discuss their ideas about the advantages and disadvantages of an inquiry approach. Both positive and negative viewpoints matter if teachers are to trust that a realistic view of inquiry-based learning will be presented. In the discussion, I balance the time teachers think individually with opportunities to talk with a partner or in small groups and then share with the entire group. Positive teacher responses typically include: "[Students] achieve a deeper understanding of content (vs. chalk and talk), and connect with material," "Encourages development of inquisitive students," "Promotes critical thinking," and "More meaningful learning—[students] take the driver's seat, develop own questions."

We then turn to perceived disadvantages. Teachers discuss their concerns about using inquiry in their small groups for five minutes and then come to consensus regarding their top three issues. Typical comments include: "Too much content—pressed for time, even though it's worthwhile," "Content knowledge—do they have enough to engage?" "Do students have the skills?" and "Student impulsivity—not utilize time wisely."

These frank conversations serve to inform me of teachers' misconceptions regarding inquiry learning. A common misunderstanding is the belief that framing instruction with a question equates to "doing inquiry." In fact, some ask, "How is this different than using an essential question?" Subsequent sessions build a common understanding of inquiry, including the vocabulary to foster accurate and knowledgeable communication with colleagues, students, and parents.

Establishing a Common Understanding

After teachers voice their initial perspectives, it is time to establish a common understanding of inquiry based on the standards and research. Delving into the standards, inquiry research, and models helps participants gain a solid foundation in this pedagogical practice and assure future decisions on inquiry learning are well-informed.

I begin with the National Council for the Social Studies publication *The College, Career, and Civic Life Framework for Social Studies State Standards* (C3 Framework, 2013), so teachers can examine a standards framework and understand the Inquiry Arc.[4] This standards framework highlights conceptual understandings and capitalizes on students' curiosity and questioning of their world. The Inquiry Arc, central to the C3 Framework, focuses on four dimensions: (1) Developing questions and planning inquiries; (2) Applying disciplinary concepts and tools; (3) Evaluating sources and using evidence; (4) Communicating conclusions and taking informed action. These dimensions promote a spirit of discovery and situate students as active participants in the learning process. During the PD, I ask participants to read and annotate the overview and to highlight two sentences that resonate with them. Teachers meet in groups to discuss their selected sentences and then share their comments with the class.

Next, I introduce the Inquiry Design Model (IDM), which offers teachers opportunities to engage with and practice the design thinking that can bring the Inquiry Arc to instructional life.[5] A tool like IDM at-a-Glance (www.c3teachers. org/wp-content/uploads/2015/06/Inquiry-Design-Model-glance.pdf) makes concrete the inquiry design process and serves as a blueprint to support teachers' efforts.[6]

Once again, I provide adequate reading and processing time. I often utilize a "Round the Table" activity, which invites each group member to explain a key design point and its importance in two minutes or less. This process allows everyone to contribute and encourages dialogue as teachers elaborate upon their ideas regarding the IDM. After 10 minutes, I ask groups to offer three agreed-upon design insights to the class and capture these for all to see. A word of caution: Teachers tend to love the IDM, and while it may be tempting to start with the IDM blueprint, developing a conceptual understanding of inquiry and its purpose cannot be underestimated.

After teachers become familiar with the components of the IDM, I introduce the conceptual foundations which delineate 10 assumptions regarding inquiry learning.[7] Whether participants read all the assumptions or their groups are assigned an assumption or two, I ask them to consider the "so what" questions such as "why does this matter for social studies." As teachers begin building deeper, multifaceted understandings of inquiry, I invite them to share their thoughts and make connections. Typically, I hear comments such as "Creates student-centered instructional model—but may be uncomfortable for teachers who are used to direct instruction" and "Have students make decisions based on valid sources, not just emotions." And, emphasizing the need for PD to assist with this shift in instruction, participants often note, "Teachers need training—be able to let go, feel the discomfort, allow students to take control."

Thomas Guskey and Kwang Suk Yoon as well as Linda Darling-Hammond, Maria Hyler, and Madelyn Gardner concur that effective PD includes expert support; but academics' perspectives are not readily accessible in most schools.[8] However, scholarly expertise *is* available through publications and websites. Using a range of articles such as Kathy Swan, John Lee, and S. G. Grant's "Questions, Tasks, and Sources: Focusing on the Essence of Inquiry" is perfect for a jigsaw and provides educators with processing time to manipulate ideas and gain exposure to multiple perspectives.[9] The C3 Teachers website provides several articles on inquiry as well as webinars on IDM. Teachers admit that they rarely, if ever, read and discuss research-based articles with colleagues during PD. Incorporating relevant research respects teachers' professionalism.

Examining Models in Grade Level Teams:

As previously noted, effective PD "focuses on teaching strategies associated with specific curriculum content … and uses curricular models of effective practice."[10] With a common understanding of inquiry and its components established, it's time to explore classroom lessons. The C3 Teachers website (c3teachers.org/inquiries) offers well-structured models of inquiry learning utilizing the foundations of inquiry including questions, tasks, and sources.[11] These inquiry-based learning experiences incorporate the dimensions of the Inquiry Arc and afford students opportunities to explore, analyze, apply, and evaluate social studies concepts, as well as to consider multiple perspectives.

While on the C3 Teachers website, I ask the teachers to choose topics that they are teaching in the upcoming weeks. Since the content in curriculum guides can vary, participants may want to check the grade level above and below their current assignment for relevant subject matter as well. Once teachers have chosen a focal inquiry, I encourage them to follow the steps below to unpack these resources:

- **Compare the inquiry to state standards**—What aspects of your state standards are addressed? What parts are missing? In my work with teachers utilizing the New York State inquiries, we find that an inquiry may be aligned to all or only part of a Key Idea, so teachers need to have a clear understanding of exactly what standards are addressed in a particular inquiry.
- **Place the inquiry in context**—What content topics precede the inquiry? What comes after? Embedding inquiry into an existing curriculum requires consideration of the content that precedes and follows the inquiry topic.
- **Determine prerequisites**—What skills and knowledge do students need to participate in this inquiry? The inquiries provide opportunities for interdisciplinary lessons as students read or listen to arguments and learn to participate in argumentative discourse, but teachers need to think about putting students in the best

position to do so.

- **Unpack the inquiry**—How is the compelling question staged? What are the supporting questions? Formative performance tasks? How is the summative task scaffolded? What types of featured sources are included? What suggestions for civic participation are provided in the taking informed action component? Participants can use the IDM blueprint to record their comments and questions.

Key to these discussions is recognizing teachers' expertise and experience by encouraging them to make connections: What is similar and different from teachers' current practice? What seems doable? What may be challenging? Teacher feedback enables me to address misunderstandings and to provide additional supports.

In my work with teachers, the C3 inquiries have been well-received. For elementary instructors, these educator-friendly resources increase the likelihood that teachers will provide inquiry learning experiences for their students. Teachers appreciate the rich and varied sources as well as the logical progression of questions and tasks that scaffold student learning. They also recognize the need for additional differentiated resources to meet the needs of diverse student populations.

A concern most often expressed by secondary teachers is the need for time to incorporate student-centered inquiry learning in a content-heavy and state-tested curriculum. I suggest teachers can begin by prioritizing the content: What are the non-negotiables? What are the top 10 concepts students should understand deeply after completing the course? Participants can then focus inquiry learning on these substantive topics so that students are spending time exploring the very content teachers want them to learn.

Planning and Implementing the Inquiry

After closely examining an inquiry, teachers collaboratively plan implementation. In particular, I ask teachers to examine the inquiry with *their* particular students in mind: Who would need extra support? What scaffolds would be appropriate? Are other resources needed? Remember, the inquiries are not prescriptive—teachers may well have a better visual or a more relevant text to replace or supplement the featured resources. Teachers may also want to develop additional graphic organizers, include sentence starters, or modify texts to meet the needs of their students.

Prior to implementation, I provide teachers with a feedback form to record impressions and reflections on each component as well as their curricular and instructional adaptations, student successes, and challenges. Teachers complete the feedback form while teaching so that details are captured in real time rather than from recall a month or two later. The standard format of the feedback form enables teachers to review their experiences in a systematic fashion during the post-implementation session. I also ask participants to bring samples of student work to the next PD session as well as student reactions to inquiry learning.

Reflecting upon Lessons Learned

"High-quality professional learning provides time for teachers to think about, receive input on, and make changes to, their practice by facilitating reflection and soliciting feedback."[12] Typically, the meeting after implementation of the first inquiry is an energy-filled event with participants sharing their experiences. The session begins with an open discussion in which participants share general impressions of their encounters with inquiry-based teaching and learning. Grade-level teams then debrief in a more structured fashion. Teachers can compare similarities and differences in their experiences with each component as collected on the feedback form. Adaptations and additional learning tools can be added to a grade-level Google document intended to preserve and share materials. There, teachers can also review and discuss student samples for further evidence of student learning.

Next Steps

After implementing their first inquiries, teachers have several options. I suggest that they explore another IDM inquiry and apply lessons learned or utilize the IDM blueprint to develop their own inquiries.

For example, a fifth-grade team of teachers, who implemented a few existing inquiries, decided to modify an inquiry with the compelling question, "What is the real cost of bananas?" They opened their investigation with: What is the real cost of ____? and then asked students to complete the query with a product of interest to them. Responses included cellphones, jeans, sports equipment, and video games—items with a real-world relevancy to the students' lives.

With a firm grounding, teachers become knowledgeable consumers of inquiry-based learning. Understanding of the relationships among questions, tasks, and sources enables participants to evaluate websites and inquiry-based lessons. Teachers appreciate that inquiry is more than using a question to frame learning, that it means opportunities for students to take a position, investigate and evaluate information, and make evidence-based decisions.

And to further make our work real, we have created a Rockland County page on the New York State C3Teachers hub (c3teachers.org/new-york-hub). There, we look forward to sharing our work with the larger social studies community.

Conclusion

Guskey and Yoon determined that "effective professional development requires considerable time, and that time must be well organized, carefully structured, purposefully important. The subheadings in this article can provide the focus for a session, but I always begin the next meeting with a short review—where we've been and where we're going. As with teaching students, however, I have to be sensitive to my participants' needs and make adjustments along the way. In the end, by applying the features of effective professional development to teachers' inquiry learning, I can see results develop for educators, which is the first step toward richer instruction for their students.

Notes

1. Linda Darling-Hammond, Maria E. Hyler, and Madelyn Gardner, *Effective Teachers Professional Development* (Palo Alto, Calif.: The Learning Institute, 2017); Laura M. Desimone, "A Primer on Effective Professional Development," *The Phi Delta Kappan* 92, no. 6 (March 2011): 68-71; Thomas R. Guskey and Kwang Suk Yoon, "What Works in Professional Development?" *The Phi Delta Kappan* 90, no. 7 (March 2009): 495–500.
2. Darling-Hammond, Hyler, and Gardner, *Effective Teachers*, v-vi.
3. Lisa Matherson and Tracy M. Windle, "What Do Teachers Want from Their Professional Development? Four Emerging Themes," *The Delta Kappa Gamma Bulletin* 83, no. 3 (2017): 28-32.
4. *The College, Career and Civic Life (C3) Framework for Social Studies State Standards: Guidance for Enhancing the Rigor of K-12 Civics, Economics, Geography, and History* (Silver Spring, Md.: National Council for the Social Studies, 2013).
5. S.G. Grant, John Lee, and Kathy Swan, *Inquiry-Based Practice in Social Studies Education* (New York: Routledge, 2017).
6. Grant, Lee, and Swan, "Inquiry Design Model (IDM)—at a Glance," C3 Teachers, www.c3teachers.org/wp-content/uploads/2015/06/Inquiry-Design-Model-glance.pdf; Grant, Lee, and Swan, "Inquiry Design Model Blueprint," *C3 Teachers*, www.c3teachers.org/inquiry-design-model/.
7. Grant, Lee, and Swan, "The Inquiry Design Model," C3 Teachers, https://c3teachers.org/wp-content/uploads/2014/10/IDM_Assumptions_C3-Brief.pdf.
8. Guskey and Yoon, "What Works"; Darling-Hammond, Hyler, and Gardner, *Effective Teachers*.
9. Kathy Swan, John Lee, and S.G. Grant, "Questions, Tasks, and Sources: Focusing on the Essence of Inquiry," *Social Education* 82, no. 3 (2018): 133–137.
10. Darling-Hammond, Hyler, and Gardner, *Effective Teachers*, v.

11. Grant, Lee, and Swan, *Inquiry-Based Practice.*

12. Darling-Hammond, Hyler, and Gardner, *Effective Teachers,* vi.

13. Guskey and Yoon, *What Works,* 499.

Social Education **84**, no. 2 (2020): 100–107.

The Signal and the Noise: Coaching Pre-Service Candidates to Teach with Questions, Tasks, and Sources

Kathy Swan, Ryan Crowley, and Gerry Swan

In his best-selling book, *The Signal and the Noise* (2012), Nate Silver investigates the art and science of predicting the future by finding a true signal in the noisy world of big data.[1] He interviews successful forecasters from a range of fields—from weather to sports to the stock market—trying to weave together a theory of what makes these individuals' predictions reliable. What becomes clear in the book is that these experts do not pay attention to all the data points and instead focus on the most salient variables.

Teacher educators are also inundated with "noisy data." We attend to what seems like a thousand standards documents (e.g., CAEP Standards, SPA standards, and InTASC standards) with what seem like a million discreet ideas about what our pre-service teachers should know and be able to do.[2] Against this backdrop, we have to make choices on where to place our focus in courses and clinical placements and how to attend to the many details of teaching and learning, while also imprinting our students with the big ideas of the social studies and effective classroom pedagogies.

Inquiry has become the clear signal in social studies. The publication of the *C3 Framework* in 2013 and the recent adoption of the new *Kentucky Academic Standards for Social Studies* underscore inquiry; so we are "all inquiry," all the time in our methods classes at the University of Kentucky.[3] We teach students about the foundations of inquiry—questions, tasks, and sources—and how to build inquiry-based curriculum and instructional strategies for social studies.[4] Students begin their student teaching experiences knowing the difference between a compelling and supporting question, the role of a formative and summative performance task, and how disciplinary sources should be curated and adapted for classroom use.

But student teaching placements can also be noisy places with competing and contradictory signals around inquiry. One of the most powerful of these signals is actually from within, consisting of the experiences of student teachers as learners. Most student teachers did not experience inquiry learning as students. Instead, they were likely in classrooms dominated by the lecture, and the read- the-book, and answer-the-questions pedagogies that have long dominated our field. This apprenticeship of observation presents unique challenges but may be countered with a recognition that how we learn may shape how they teach, along with consistent modeling and support for new inquiry-based approaches.[5]

For years, we used a clinical observation form that gauged general teaching strategies as a way to facilitate conversations between the pre-service teacher, the cooperating teacher, and the university supervisor. Not surprisingly, we struggled to stay on message about inquiry-based teaching. So, we asked ourselves: How do we amplify the inquiry signal when students move from our classes to their student teaching placements? We decided to focus our attention on the observation form, rebuilding it around key signals of inquiry: questions, tasks, and sources.

In this article, we introduce the Questions-Tasks-Sources (QTS) Observation Protocol that we have just deployed in spring 2020.[6] We begin with a short overview of our teacher education program and the curricular goals and outcomes of our core methods class. In doing so, we set the context for the QTS Observation Protocol and how the foundations of questions, tasks, and sources are operationalized in the instrument. We then walk through the four parts of the instrument, highlighting important criteria and the big ideas of each part. We end with a discussion of how we are using the instrument, early lessons we are learning, and suggestions for how the instrument might be used in schools.

Honing in on the QTS Signal

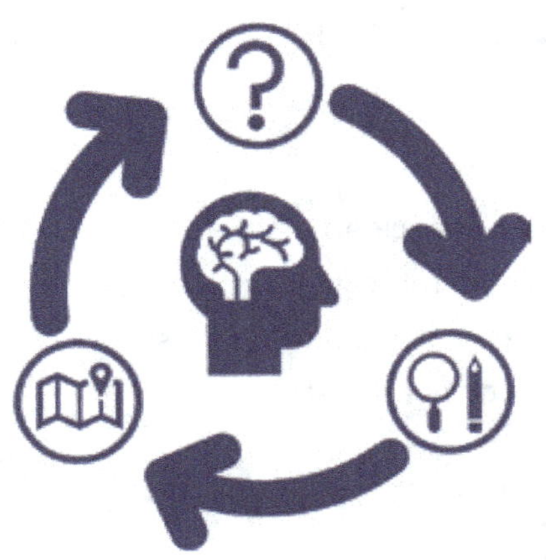

At the University of Kentucky, our secondary social studies students complete a three-semester sequence that earns them a master's degree along with teaching certification. The program includes two core methods courses and a student teaching seminar that allow us to focus on the curricular, instructional, and assessment aspects of an inquiry-based teaching practice. We do so through a series of projects that build our students' capacity to focus on "the signal"—questions, tasks, and sources (QTS). Further, the 2019 adoption of the *Kentucky Academic Standards for Social Studies*,[7] organized around the inquiry practices of questioning, investigating, using evidence, and communicating conclusions, provides even greater encouragement for our students—inquiry is now law in Kentucky!

In terms of curricular design and instructional implementation, our students practice crafting and teaching inquiry lessons, both using the more extensive format of the Inquiry Design Model and crafting smaller-scale inquiries guided by the QTS ethos.[8] We help students conceptualize how to make inquiry routine in their future classrooms, demonstrating how to anchor a curriculum map with inquiry design models (IDMs) and helping them to see how QTS can be the daily drumbeat of their practice. Even when we task our students with presenting or leading discussions in

Helena Jackson, student teacher in the College of Education at the University of Kentucky.

our methods courses, they are required to arrive with compelling and supporting questions, sources for students to discuss and analyze, and tasks to help organize the discussion and to scaffold interaction with the sources.

QTS also guides our assessment work. During their student teaching semester, our preservice teachers complete an action research project on improving and assessing claim-writing. Preservice teachers begin with a baseline analysis of initial evidentiary claims their students construct. They develop a series of lessons that target areas that need improvement (e.g., accuracy, clarity, reasoning of claims), implement those lessons, gauge the success of their instructional intervention, and then reflect on the experience. Students do an oral defense of the project as their summative examination, required for graduation from the program.

We also use inquiry as a way to operationalize the themes that guide our program. Our students explore constructivist approaches to teaching and learning by developing questions and tasks that draw out students' prior knowledge and that allow them to build understanding through peer interactions. We also push our students to use sources that represent multiple perspectives, particularly sources that introduce counternarratives and marginalized voices.[9] Whether we are helping students to develop concrete instructional practices or to grapple with big ideas related to equity and inclusivity, QTS guides the way. It is the backbone of everything we do. To bring this way of thinking into how we observe and coach our preservice teachers, we developed the QTS Observation Protocol.

The QTS Observation Protocol

The QTS Observation Protocol is reproduced on pages 203–204. It is comprised of four parts: (1) Use of Questions; (2) Use of Performance Tasks; (3) Use of Disciplinary Sources; and (4) Creates and Maintains Learning Environment. Each part of the instrument includes a set of indicators that describes both discrete and intersecting aspects of the overarching idea. While we consider every indicator to be important, we do not expect that all indicators will be demonstrated during each classroom observation. To address this factor without unduly penalizing our student teachers, the rating scale includes an 'N' option for noting that an indicator was not a focus for the lesson. At the end of this article, we delve more deeply into how the instrument is used in the evaluation cycle. In the sections that follow, we describe each part of the instrument, highlighting important criteria and the way in which they relate to one another.

Use of Questions

Pre-service teachers are expected to frame their instruction with compelling and supporting questions. In the QTS Observation Protocol, we acknowledge the explicit use of these kinds of questions, but also the quality of and relationship between the questions. For example, compelling questions should be academically rigorous, interesting to students, but also functional in the curriculum.[10] Compelling questions set students up for an argumentation task in which they construct evidentiary claims in response. Supporting questions are designed to build up students' understanding of content that is necessary for answering compelling questions. Student teachers are asked to clearly align supporting questions with the big ideas of the compelling question. In other words, student teachers should demonstrate that questions are an instructional compass providing direction and purpose for inquiry-based social studies.

Table 1: **Use of Questions**

?	Use of Questions
☐	Teacher uses compelling question/s to frame and guide instruction. The CQ is rigorous, relevant, and provides an opportunity for students to craft evidence-based arguments.
☐	Teacher builds students' knowledge through the use of supporting questions. SQs are intentionally sequenced and clearly related to the big ideas within the CQ.
☐	Teacher uses supporting questions aligned with tasks and sources.
☐	Teacher provides instructional space for student-generated questions.
☐	Teacher uses questions to check for students' understanding and to engage students in the content. Questions connect to prior knowledge, promote curiosity, and connect to out-of-classroom contexts.

We also acknowledge other kinds of questions that contribute to the culture of an inquiry-based classroom. For example, student teachers should create instructional space for student-created questions. In our methods classes, students learn about the Question Formulation Technique (QFT) and other questioning strategies that help students analyze sources, become curious about disciplinary ideas, and frame independent research projects. Additionally, we privilege formative checks for understanding and just-in-time questions that help teachers gauge students' prior knowledge as well as whether they are understanding the material.

Student teachers are asked to provide supplementary materials (e.g., lesson plans, ancillary materials) for a classroom observation to situate a particular lesson within the broader curriculum. In this way, an observer should see how a lesson focused on a supporting question relates to the other supporting questions as well as the compelling question. The criteria for *Use of Questions* are listed in Table 1.

Use of Performance Tasks

Pre-service teachers are expected to design formative and summative performance tasks that provide a feedback loop to inform and improve instruction. The tasks should be constructed as performances designed so that students practice argumentation (e.g., claim- making, evidentiary reasoning) and disciplinary thinking skills (e.g., reasoning spatially, analyzing cause and effect). Argumentation is central to inquiry so students need practice in evidentiary claim-making on a regular basis and they need to receive clear and consistent feedback on improving their argumentation skills.

Student teachers should also demonstrate that students extend their understanding by communicating the results of inquiry through expressive performance tasks (e.g., Socratic discussions, documentary making). Additionally, student teachers should include opportunities for their students to take informed action. These opportunities need not be elaborate; they could include something as simple as having an informed conversation with others about the civic ideas that surface during instruction.[11] The timing of class observations might preclude supervisors from seeing these types of experiences firsthand, so we expect that our student teachers demonstrate how their instruction is regularly leading students to authentic learning opportunities in social studies.

It is also expected that student teachers give thought to the balance between individual and collaborative tasks and that, over the course of the student teaching placement, there are different student grouping structures present during the observations (e.g., partners, small group). We also encourage our students to develop whole-group-worthy collaborative tasks that are open-ended, require problem solving, and promote both individual accountability and positive group interdependence.[12]

Table 2: **Use of Performance Tasks**

	Use of Performance Tasks
☐	Teacher uses a variety of formative performance tasks to provide students feedback on their progress and to check for understanding.
☐	Teacher uses formative tasks to target argumentation skills and other important disciplinary work within the social studies.
☐	Teacher uses argumentation as a cornerstone of the students' summative evaluation.
☐	Teacher is clear about the qualities of a good argument (evidentiary, reasoned, accurate, and clear) and helps students in building better arguments by providing meaningful feedback.
☐	Teacher provides opportunities for students to express their understanding through extension tasks and by taking informed action.
☐	Teacher provides opportunities for cooperative learning experiences that promote individual accountability and group interdependence.

These criteria represent the full plate of performance tasks. Realistically then, it is perfectly acceptable for a single, hour- long observation to only reveal 1–2 criteria. The larger goal of the observation instrument is to act as a set of cues for students to think about the individual parts of assessment (e.g., formative tasks), to connect them to the larger aims of assessment (e.g., summative assessment), and to hear a loud and unmistakable signal that argumentation should be at the center of their instruction. (See Table 2 for the *Use of Performance Tasks* criteria.)

Use of Disciplinary Sources

Preservice teachers are expected to provide a variety of sources (e.g., images, text, video) for their students to analyze in order to construct responses to compelling and supporting questions. Sources act as the raw material for every lesson the preservice teachers teach. Analysis of sources should be integral to the completion of the formative and summative performance tasks that ask students to engage in oral or written argumentation and other disciplinary thinking skills.

The QTS Protocol also emphasizes source selection and adaptation. Preservice teachers serve several masters in this process. Their source curation must demonstrate knowledge of the subject matter, inclusion of multiple and marginalized perspectives, understanding of the importance of instructional scaffolds and source modification, and utilization of different source modalities.

Table 3: **Use of Disciplinary Sources**

📖 Use of Disciplinary Sources
☐ Teacher uses a variety of source types to engage students (e.g., images, text, video).
☐ Teacher uses sources that demonstrate multiple perspectives (e.g., inclusion of marginalized perspectives, conflicting evidence on a topic).
☐ Teacher adapts sources (e.g., excerpt, annotate, modify) and creates instructional scaffolds to address learner needs.
☐ Teacher uses sources that help students complete formative and summative tasks in order to answer compelling and supporting questions.
☐ Teacher uses sources that demonstrate deep knowledge of the subject matter.

As an example, an inquiry lesson related to United States involvement in the Spanish-American War could include sources that capture significant events such as the sinking of the USS *Maine* or the role of yellow journalism in stoking fervor for war. Sources could also demonstrate anti-imperialist rhetoric within the United States and the experiences of those in Cuba or the Philippines who were impacted by the war. Student teachers also need to demonstrate the ability to adapt sources (e.g., excerpt, annotate) and scaffold them to meet the needs and abilities of the students in the classroom. Finally, sources should be varied in type, e.g., the text of a newspaper editorial, a political cartoon, historical photographs, or even a video clip of a historian discussing events related to the war. Table 3 lists the criteria for *Use of Disciplinary Sources.*

Creates and Maintains Learning Environment

The fourth component of the QTS Observation Protocol directs preservice teachers to consider the overall learning environment. Although we expect that questions, tasks, and sources will drive their lesson planning, we expect that knowledge of their students' unique characteristics, abilities, and backgrounds will drive their pedagogical decisions as well. Supervisors should note whether the preservice teacher relates to a wide array of students in a respectful and compassionate manner while communicating high expectations. They should also be able to see student teachers engage in positive redirections when students are off task as well as other community- building practices such as the facilitation of discussions and cooperative learning experiences.

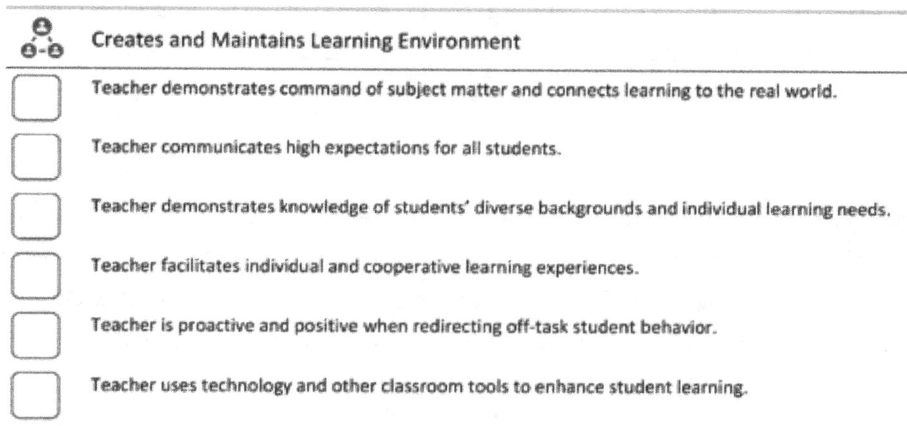
Table 4: **Creates and Maintains Learning Environment**

	Creates and Maintains Learning Environment
☐	Teacher demonstrates command of subject matter and connects learning to the real world.
☐	Teacher communicates high expectations for all students.
☐	Teacher demonstrates knowledge of students' diverse backgrounds and individual learning needs.
☐	Teacher facilitates individual and cooperative learning experiences.
☐	Teacher is proactive and positive when redirecting off-task student behavior.
☐	Teacher uses technology and other classroom tools to enhance student learning.

Although these indicators may seem more subjective than those in the previous three categories, we view the scores that student teachers receive here as conversation starters for post-observation conferences. We also view these aspects of teaching as aspirational rather than fixed destination points due to the complex human dynamics of high school classrooms. (See Table 4 for the criteria for *Creates & Maintains Learning Environment*.)

Coaching for Inquiry

The QTS Observation Protocol is meant to focus the conversations among members of the teaching triad (student teacher, cooperating teacher, and university supervisor) that occur before and after classroom observations. At the University of Kentucky, student teachers are required to have six documented observations during the field experience, at least four of which are completed by the university supervisor and two by the cooperating teacher over the 14-week school placement.

Table 5: **Scoring Options for the QTS Protocol**

N - Not a focus. If the item should have been present but was missing, mark it 1.
1 - Observed with implementation at a basic level
2 - Observed with implementation at a developing level
3 - Observed with implementation at a satisfactory level
4 - Observed with implementation at an exemplary level

The QTS Protocol has four levels of quality as scoring options—basic, developing, satisfactory, exemplary (see Table 5). There is also a "Not a Focus (N)" option that allows items to go unscored on a single observation. Student teachers have agency in this process, as they can ask the observer to focus on just one part of the instrument for an observation (e.g., use of questions). Although individual items are rated, no overall score or grade needs to be given to a student. Instead, the use of scores on individual indicators allows for the university supervisor or cooperating teacher to provide targeted rather than global feedback.

Looking Ahead

The QTS Observation Protocol is being piloted in our teacher education program, and early data tell us the instrument is helping student teachers (and their supervisors) focus on the signals, rather than the noise, of teaching. In a future column, we will share a case study on the "QTS Observation Protocol in Action," demonstrating the role the instrument is playing in improving our coaching in the field.

Going forward, we plan to engage with our university supervisors, student teachers, and cooperating teachers about possible revisions to the QTS Observation Protocol. We hope to use data generated from spring 2020 student teaching observations for purposes of program improvement as we refine aspects of the methods courses in our certification program. Additionally, we are in discussions with districts about using the QTS Observation Protocol for in-service teacher development, helping social studies educators and administrators as they engage in walk-throughs, peer observations, and instructional coaching.

The rollout of inquiry-based standards in Kentucky will drive changes in both pre-service and in-service teacher development. Our hope is that the QTS Observation Protocol adds to the dialogue about the nature of inquiry in social studies and instantiates a language of questions, tasks, and sources for our field.

Questions-Tasks-Sources (QTS) Observation Protocol

? Use of Questions

☐ Teacher uses compelling question/s to frame and guide instruction. The CQ is rigorous, relevant, and provides an opportunity for students to craft evidence-based arguments.

☐ Teacher builds students' knowledge through the use of supporting questions. SQs are intentionally sequenced and clearly related to the big ideas within the CQ.

☐ Teacher uses supporting questions aligned with tasks and sources.

☐ Teacher provides instructional space for student-generated questions.

☐ Teacher uses questions to check for students' understanding and to engage students in the content. Questions connect to prior knowledge, promote curiosity, and connect to out-of-classroom contexts.

🗺 Use of Disciplinary Sources

☐ Teacher uses a variety of source types to engage students (e.g., images, text, video).

☐ Teacher uses sources that demonstrate multiple perspectives (e.g., inclusion of marginalized perspectives, conflicting evidence on a topic).

☐ Teacher adapts sources (e.g., excerpt, annotate, modify) and creates instructional scaffolds to address learner needs.

☐ Teacher uses sources that help students complete formative and summative tasks in order to answer compelling and supporting questions.

☐ Teacher uses sources that demonstrate deep knowledge of the subject matter.

Swan, K., Crowley, R., & Swan, G. (2020).

Use of Performance Tasks

- Teacher uses a variety of formative performance tasks to provide students feedback on their progress and to check for understanding.
- Teacher uses formative tasks to target argumentation skills and other important disciplinary work within the social studies.
- Teacher uses argumentation as a cornerstone of the students' summative evaluation.
- Teacher is clear about the qualities of a good argument (evidentiary, reasoned, accurate, and clear) and helps students in building better arguments by providing meaningful feedback.
- Teacher provides opportunities for students to express their understanding through extension tasks and by taking informed action.
- Teacher provides opportunities for cooperative learning experiences that promote individual accountability and group interdependence.

Creates and Maintains Learning Environment

- Teacher demonstrates command of subject matter and connects learning to the real world.
- Teacher communicates high expectations for all students.
- Teacher demonstrates knowledge of students' diverse backgrounds and individual learning needs.
- Teacher facilitates individual and cooperative learning experiences.
- Teacher is proactive and positive when redirecting off-task student behavior.
- Teacher uses technology and other classroom tools to enhance student learning.

Comments:

Swan, K., Crowley, R., & Swan, G. (2020).

Notes

1. Nate Silver, *The Signal and the Noise: Why So Many Predictions Fail—But Some Don't* (New York: Penguin Books, 2012).
2. For examples of standards documents commonly used in teacher education programs, see CAEP Standards, https://caepnet.org/standards/2022-itp/introduction; SPA standards, http://www.socialstudies.org/standards/teacherstandards; InTASC standards, https://ccsso.org/resource-library/intasc-model-core-teaching-standards-and-learning-progressions-teachers-10.
3. C3 Framework, https://www.socialstudies.org/standards/c3; Kentucky Department of Education. *Kentucky Academic Standards for Social Studies*, https://education.ky.gov/curriculum/conpro/socstud/Pages/default.aspx
4. S.G. Grant, Kathy Swan, and John Lee, *Inquiry-Based Practice in Social Studies Education: The Inquiry Design Model* (New York: Routledge and C3Teachers, 2017); Kathy Swan, John Lee, and S.G. Grant, *Inquiry Design Model: Building Inquiries in Social Studies* (Silver Spring, Md.: National Council for the Social Studies and C3Teachers, 2018); Kathy Swan, S.G. Grant, and John Lee, *Blueprinting an Inquiry Based Curriculum: Planning with the Inquiry Design Model* (Silver Spring, Md.: National Council for the Social Studies and C3Teachers, 2019).
5. Alicia R. Crowe, Todd S. Hawley, and Elizabeth W. Brooks, "Ways of Being a Social Studies Teacher: What are Prospective Teachers Thinking?" *Social Studies Research & Practice (Board of Trustees of the University of Alabama)* 7, no. 2 (2012).
6. Kathy Swan, Ryan Crowley, and Gerry Swan, "The Questions-Tasks-Sources (QTS) Observation Protocol," www.c3teachers.org/qts-protocol/
7. Kentucky Department of Education. *Kentucky Academic Standards for Social Studies*, https://education.ky.gov/curriculum/conpro/socstud/Pages/default.aspx
8. Swan, Grant, and Lee, *Blueprinting an Inquiry Based Curriculum*.
9. Ryan Crowley and LaGarrett King, "Making Inquiry Critical: Examining Power and Inequity in the Classroom," *Social Education* 82 (2018): 14-17.
10. Grant, Swan, and Lee, *Inquiry-Based Practice in Social Studies Education*.
11. Swan, Grant, and Lee, *Blueprinting an Inquiry Based Curriculum*.
12. Elisabeth Cohen and Rachel Lotan, *Designing Groupwork: Strategies for the Heterogeneous Classroom* (Teachers College Press: New York, 2014)

**The authors would like to extend a special thank you to Carly Muetterties and Emily Rentschler, who provided input on the development of the QTS Observation Protocol.*

Social Education **85, no. 1 (2021): 26–30.**

Making Inquiry Possible: A Film Project on Building a Culture of Inquiry

Kathleen Swan, Ryan Crowley, S.G. Grant, John Lee, Gerry Swan, Callaway Stivers, and Gates Sweeney

"When I think of a culture, I think of something where people recognize certain elements. In a culture of inquiry, you may see lots of elements of a traditional classroom, but ultimately what you should see, and what you should, more importantly, hear, is how they're talking about their learning. I think if you don't have that shift in language, you're simply just going to try to repackage inquiry into something that it's really not."

—Ryan Lewis, Social Studies Department Chair, Woodford County High School

(Quote from the *Making Inquiry Possible* Film Project)

Introduction

Social studies has long had a bad rap as a "just the facts" school subject. That reputation isn't entirely deserved but it's been true long enough that far too many students have said "no thank you" when it's time for social studies. However, as Bob Dylan once wrote, "The times ... they are a changing.'"

The *College, Career, and Civic Life (C3) Framework for Social Studies State Standards* (NCSS, 2013) places inquiry at the center of good social studies teaching and learning.[1] Instead of social studies courses that emphasize rote memorization through the use of textbooks and lecture-based instruction, the C3 Framework asks teachers to reframe their content and instruction around important, compelling questions that we grapple with as citizens and within the social studies disciplines. A big takeaway from the framework is this: Inquiry shouldn't be a once-in-a-while experience in social studies classrooms. Rather, teachers need to think about orienting their classrooms so that inquiry is a consistent drumbeat that students hear and experience regularly.

We know this shift to inquiry can be challenging for social studies teachers, students, and administrators. Teachers are often reluctant to teach with inquiry because lecturing is efficient and social studies is a content-heavy field. Inquiry takes time and teachers understandably feel the pressure to cover wide swaths of social studies content. Beyond this, most educators and students have not learned social studies through inquiry-based approaches. Inquiry-based teaching and learning asks teachers to rethink their roles, their students' roles, and the nature of the classroom experience.

Making Inquiry Possible (makinginquirypossible.org) is an effort to help educators understand how the collaborative efforts of teachers, their students, and supportive administrators can make inquiry-based curriculum and instruction achievable. Our experience watching inquiry teachers is that an individual commitment is necessary, but not sufficient to make inquiry a broad reality.

Instead, teachers who shift to inquiry need supportive colleagues, ongoing professional learning opportunities, and time to reflect on and improve their practices. Students need time and support to adjust to new expectations and to new ways of expressing their ideas. Ironically, our best students often struggle with this "new deal" in social studies. No longer can they be passive learners; instead they need to marshal the energy to explore and investigate alongside their teachers. And, they need to get better at exercising the skills of inquiry—reading and evaluating sources, deliberating multiple sides of an issue, and crafting claims supported with evidence. Moreover, administrators need to do their walk-throughs and evaluations of social studies teachers with an understanding of these new techniques and expectations and knowing that repeated practice makes perfect. School leaders also need to find resources (time and money) to support teachers who are making these difficult changes in their instruction.

In other words, inquiry is not a solo endeavor. Although inquiry is worth the growing pains, it has its challenges and the more honest we can be in naming those challenges, the clearer we can be about tackling them. The Making Inquiry Possible (MIP) Project features four films that are accessible free of charge and show and tell educators about recent efforts in Kentucky to shift towards inquiry-based instruction in social studies. The project includes online professional development materials to accompany the documentaries that are designed to facilitate discussions about the triumphs and challenges that teachers, students, and districts experience as they implement the new standards.

In this article, we introduce the project and its component parts: the films, the professional learning modules, the connections to C3 Teachers, and the website that houses the project. We also preview plans for expanding the site and the films and our new efforts to help teachers and schools strengthen their inquiry cultures.

The Making Inquiry Possible Film Collection

"To be successful at inquiry you need colleagues. You need colleagues who are willing to try new things, who are willing to give you feedback…. And then even outside of that, you need administrators who understand that you're trying something new in your classroom and that it's not going to look like maybe traditional instruction that you've been doing."

—Summer Amro, Social Studies Department Chair, Woodford County High School
(Quote from the *Making Inquiry Possible* Film Project)

The documentary series at the center of the MIP Project explores how innovative teachers, schools, and districts are shifting to inquiry. At the core of each documentary, we ask: What does it take to make inquiry *possible* in social studies? We explore the role of the teachers, students, colleagues, and administrators in making the shift to inquiry-based teaching and learning in social studies.

All films focus on Kentucky social studies teachers and the systems that support them. In addition to being home base for three of the MIP Project directors, Kentucky provides a unique context for exploring what makes inquiry possible. In July of 2019, the state adopted new social studies standards with an emphasis on four inquiry practices: questioning, investigating using disciplinary concepts, using evidence, and communicating claims.[2] Kentucky's standards largely align with the C3 Framework[3] and resemble the shifts in the growing number of other states that have recently revised their social studies standards and incorporated more language supporting inquiry- based instruction. In this way, we hope the challenges and triumphs of the Kentucky teachers and administrators captured in the four films will feel familiar while also providing fresh perspectives for social studies teachers across the nation.

As the MIP Project team began conceptualizing the substance and feel of the documentaries, we knew the primary audience would be educators. But we also wanted the films to be digestible for those unfamiliar with the intricacies of K-12 classrooms. In other words, we wanted our parents, friends, and others to relate to the films and be inspired by a new kind of social studies. We partnered with Rapt Productions,[4] a film production company founded by two recent graduates of the University of Kentucky, out of appreciation for their technical expertise but also because they understood our vision to make something that spoke to a wide audience. For those of us all too familiar with the poor quality of most films related to education, we hope the MIP films will be a breath of fresh air due to their cinematic feel and the compelling insights of their characters.

The collection of films in the MIP Project include the following:

Why Inquiry? In this introductory film, we lay the groundwork for inquiry-based instruction in social studies classrooms. We tackle the foundational question: Why inquiry? We also outline the origins of the *Making Inquiry Possible* Project, preview the films that are featured on this website, and orient the viewer to the professional learning resources available to support educators in making inquiry possible in their own classrooms and districts.

What Makes Inquiry Possible? In this film, we look at one innovative high school in Woodford County, Kentucky, that is shifting to inquiry-based instruction. Social studies educators portrayed in this film show us how inquiry requires a common language, trust between teachers and students, and collaboration among colleagues. In doing so, they help us understand what makes inquiry possible.

What Does Inquiry Look Like? For teachers interested in implementing inquiry in their classrooms, it helps to see what inquiry looks like in action. In our second film, we feature two teachers implementing the same inquiry, *Can the Civics Test Make You a Better Citizen?*[5] The teachers lead students through an investigation of a state-mandated civics test, a current graduation requirement for Kentucky students, in order to evaluate the ways in which the test addresses the knowledge and skills needed to prepare students for active engagement in civic life.[6] See inquiry come alive as teachers take us through the instructional steps of implementing an inquiry.

How Do You Build an Inquiry Culture? Teaching with inquiry means honoring a teacher's expertise and individual craft while at the same time understanding that changing practice requires a collective effort. As teachers shift their instructional approaches to inquiry, they need support from colleagues and administrators. In this film, we feature one urban Kentucky district tackling inquiry by creating an inquiry culture that fits its unique context. The film, *How Do You Build An Inquiry Culture?*, is intended to be a mirror for educators who want to strengthen collaborative conversations when growing inquiry in schools.

Together these films examine different approaches for rolling inquiry out at the classroom, school, and district levels. In one approach, the featured high school is growing their inquiry culture with a bottom-up, grassroots approach. Teachers are in the lead using Professional Learning Communities, peer-to-peer mentoring, and limited external support. In the featured district, central administrators are building inquiry capacity through a system-wide approach providing structure through common curriculum documents and assessment systems that guide teachers with a larger vision of what inquiry should look like and building down to the classroom from there. What these educators demonstrate is that a healthy inquiry culture can grow from the bottom up beginning in teachers' classrooms and it can grow by district leadership building out an inquiry infrastructure for teachers to adopt.

The Professional Learning Modules—Digital Driver's License

"I absolutely don't think you can become an inquiry-based learning teacher overnight. I think that it is a very involved process."

—Jason Arnold, Woodford County High School Principal
(Quote from the *Making Inquiry Possible* Film Project)

The Digital Driver's License (DDL) is an online platform that enables teachers to earn badges or licenses for completing professional learning modules created for the *Making Inquiry Possible* Project.[7] There are four self-paced modules that correspond with the four MIP films:

Module 1: Why Inquiry?
Module 2: What Makes Inquiry Possible?
Module 3: What Does Inquiry Look Like?
Module 4: How Do You Build an Inquiry Culture?

Each module is broken down into several sections that align with important ideas explored in its related film. Educators can choose to watch the entire film via the MIP website or in featured clips within the sections of the DDL.

Individual sections of each module contain formative assessments known as a "Practice-It" in which teachers draw from what they learned in watching the documentary to answer a series of open-ended or multiple-choice questions. Many of the "Practice-It" questions also encourage teachers to connect their own teaching context to the experiences of the teachers in the films. At the conclusion of each module, teachers complete a summative assessment known as a "Prove-It." The closing assessments prompt teachers to develop action plans for how they can grow their own inquiry practice and for how they can initiate productive collaborations with colleagues.

Teachers can register for an account and begin to work through the modules by going to the Digital Driver's License launch page (idrivedigital.com) and signing in with Gmail or Office 365 email credentials. Teachers without these credentials can register for an account and will receive a username and login information. All modules can be completed asynchronously so individuals, Professional Learning Communities, departments, or other groups can watch the films and work through the professional learning materials at their own pace.

MIP Website and Connections with C3 Teachers

Galen Velonis: So, we're doing the judicial branch in our next unit and then are we thinking about wrapping it up with another inquiry? Or maybe just go with something we have time for?
Summer Amro: Yeah, I think I don't know if there is already any inquiry out there surrounding the state or local government?
Sarah Maynard: Yeah.

The *Making Inquiry Possible* films are accessible on our new website at http://makinginquirypossible.org. Here, we present the four films about social studies teachers and the cultures that support them. The website is organized around the four films and the questions they raise:

Why inquiry?
What makes inquiry possible?
What does inquiry look like?
How do you build an inquiry culture?

In each of these sections, we feature the film, access to the DDL modules and other relevant content for exploring the questions in more depth. For schools and school districts who are ready to take the plunge into inquiry, http://makinginquirypossible.org is a first-stop shop to build your inquiry community and strengthen your inquiry culture.

The MIP Project is indeed a starting place for professional development on teaching with inquiry, but it should certainly not be the only stop for teachers and schools who want to engage with inquiry for the long haul. The MIP Project connects with the C3 Teachers Network and inquiry-based resources that are helping educators make inquiry possible every day. C3 Teachers began in 2013 with the publication of the C3 Framework and today is a network of over 16,000 teachers sharing inquiry-based curriculum resources and learning more about how to bring inquiry to life in their classrooms.[8] There are over 350 inquiries available on http://C3teachers.org along with an active collection of bloggers sharing stories from their inquiry classrooms. The site is organized around hubs of educators in states and organizations who are building up their own inquiry cultures to enliven social studies and to sustain inquiry as the core of the curriculum.

Looking Ahead for the Making Inquiry Possible Project

This MIP Project began during the 2020 pandemic. The original concept included films featuring elementary and middle school classrooms, as well as the high school and districts featured in the current films. But Kentucky schools went to virtual instruction when the shutdowns began in March of 2020 and we were unable to start filming in the K–8 settings. Inquiry is hard; 2020 seemed impossible for an on-location film project!

What you see in the MIP Project is the very best of our social studies teaching profession fueled by true inquiry grit. Behind the scenes footage during the winter shoot reveals boom microphones, multiple cameras, and extensive lighting packages invading classrooms and meeting spaces. Without flinching, this MIP all-star educator cast walked right into the spotlight and articulated the why, the what, and the how of meaningful, inquiry-based instruction.

Our fingers are crossed that the pandemic will end in the coming year and we set out our directors' chairs once again to capture additional stories of inquiry in K–12 classrooms and districts. So, stay tuned: More films coming soon to the MIP website!

Notes

1. C3 Framework, https://www.socialstudies.org/standards/c3
2. Kentucky Department of Education, *Kentucky Academic Standards for Social Studies*, https://education.ky.gov/curriculum/conpro/socstud/Pages/default.aspx
3. C3 Framework, https://www.socialstudies.org/standards/c3
4. C3 Teachers, "Can the Civics Test Make You a Good Citizen?" inquiry, http://www.c3teachers.org/inquiries/civics-test/
5. Jennifer Fraker, Carly Muetterties, Gerry Swan, and Kathy Swan, "Can the Civics Test Make You a Good Citizen? Reconciling the Civics Test with Inquiry-based Instruction," Social Education 83, no. 6 (2019), 343–349.
6. www.raptlex.com/
7. http://idrivedigital.com
8. www.c3teachers.org

Social Education **85, no. 6 (2021): 382–386.**

Inquiry-Based Core Practices for Social Studies Teacher Education

Alexander Cuenca

Since the introduction of the *College, Career, and Civic Life (C3) Framework for Social Studies State Standards* in 2013, several states across the country have incorporated into their standards the idea that high-quality social studies instruction is characterized by active student engagement with inquiry. Although the notion that inquiry drives learning in social studies classrooms is not new or particularly provocative, the C3 Framework has enabled states to embrace inquiry as policy, which is a distinct turn in the history of social studies standards. The most recent iteration of the "social studies wars" has focused on curricular policymaking through content-based standards and turned mostly on the question of "whose" knowledge is included or excluded in social studies standards.[1] However, the C3 Framework bypasses content prescriptions, and instead, seeks to codify inquiry as the pedagogical modality that distinguishes quality social studies education.

In a recent study of the impact of the C3 Framework on state policy, at least 32 states cited, endorsed, framed, modeled, or adopted the C3 Framework in their social studies standards. Consequently, the expectation for almost 30 million students is that social studies teachers deliver inquiry-based social studies education.[2] Because teaching and teacher education are inextricably linked, as more and more states expect inquiry-based learning in social studies classrooms, social studies teacher education must find ways to respond and support the instructional shift toward inquiry in schools.

In this article, I sketch the merits of core practices as an organizing tool for social studies teacher education in the wake of the widespread adoption of the C3 Framework. The emerging scholarship on core practices argues that developing the professional knowledge and skills of teachers requires teacher education to coalesce its efforts around classroom-based practices that, among other conditions, demonstrate the potential to improve student achievement.[3] As inquiry-based education becomes a viable policy outcome for social studies education, it is incumbent on social studies teacher education programs to organize themselves around the preparation of social studies teachers for inquiry-based teaching.

Seven Core Practices for Social Studies Teacher Education

Social studies teacher education in the United States has numerous components. Features such as institutional or program mission, licensure pathway, certification regulations, and program location create a multiplicity of social studies teacher education experiences for prospective teachers across the country. The diversity among preparation programs often engenders robust discussions about the aims and purposes of social studies teacher education, such as social justice, disciplinary literacy, global citizenship, and student activism. Yet, these discussions often parallel those in the broader social studies education reform community by prioritizing content and curriculum over method. As Stephen Thornton noted, "there appears to be a long-standing prejudice against what educational reformers apparently see as the mundane matters of methods. Convinced that only subject matter is educationally worth talking about, reformers have generally been more intrigued by systemic curriculum development than classroom instruction." Thornton adds, however, that curricula are, "but a point of departure for instruction."4 For social studies teacher education, conversations about its functions and operations have also privileged curriculum. Although the overt focus on curriculum in social studies teacher education is perhaps a justified response to prepare teachers to identify and redress the distortions, gaps, effacements, and erasures, curriculum nevertheless remains a point of departure *for* instruction.

Given the diverse array of social studies teacher education programs, we may differ on the curriculum we ask preservice teachers to consider, but we share responsibility to prepare prospective teachers to deliver curriculum through instruction. What the C3 Framework provides is a policy pathway for social studies teacher education programs to coalesce around inquiry as an instructional modality to help prospective teachers deliver curriculum. If inquiry-based education is a viable policy *and* an empirically established end for social studies instruction, how do social studies teacher education programs prepare inquiry-based teachers?

Organizing social studies teacher education programs around a set of core practices provides one possible answer to the question above. According to Pam Grossman and colleagues,5 core practices are those practices that:

- Occur with high frequency in the classroom;
- Can be used in classrooms with different curricular or instructional approaches;
- Are capable of being mastered by novices;
- Allow novices to learn more about students and teaching;
- Preserve the integrity and complexity of teaching; and
- Demonstrate the potential to improve student achievement

Core practices are not meant to be exhaustive, nor reductionist representations of the knowledge, skills, and attitudes needed to teach. Instead, core practices serve as conversation points to help reorient the overt focus on curriculum toward a more appropriate balance with teaching method.

In 2017, I embarked on a research project to identify a set of core practices for middle and high school social studies teacher education based on the grades 6–12 inquiries published on the C3 Teachers website, which all followed the Inquiry Design Model (IDM).6 These inquiries served as a suitable source to identify social studies core practices because the IDM approach respects social studies as a school subject that intertwines disciplines together and recognizes that learning in social studies classrooms occurs when students engage in powerful and authentic acts of inquiry. Within these inquiries, I looked for repeated expressions of practice that met the normative criteria for core practices suggested by Pam Grossman and colleagues and could serve as a starting point to conceptualize the practice-based preparation of social studies teachers.

My analysis yielded seven core practices: (1) establishing social studies academic language; (2) helping students recognize the interdisciplinary nature of social studies phenomenon; (3) using interpretive questions; (4) helping students organize inquiries; (5) connecting inquiry to students' lives; (6) structuring opportunities for discussion; and (7) expanding inquiry into civic life. These seven practices are not meant to exclude the existence of other kinds of inquiry-based practices important for the preparation of social studies teachers. Instead, my hope was to identify a starting point to discuss the instructional organization of social studies teacher education given the policy avenues created by the C3 Framework to situate inquiry as quality social studies instruction.

Revolution of Ideas: A Decade of C3 Inquiry | 213

Establishing Social Studies Academic Language

A key practice across the IDM inquiries is helping students establish the terminology, language, and academic register required to pursue the tasks associated with compelling and supporting questions. Teachers are asked to establish social studies academic language in one of two ways. First, teachers can provide students with a common conceptual foundation to help them engage with the inquiry process. For example, in the Aztec inquiry, teachers are asked to help students establish the "absolute and relative location of Tenochtitlán as well as the unique geographic characteristics that contribute to our understanding about the city today." Likewise, in the Industrialization inquiry, teachers introduce key concepts such as "urbanization, factory life, technological advance, and the problems facing the working class."

The second way that teachers can establish social studies academic language is by naming terms within sources. In the Gender Wage Gap inquiry, where students consider the degree to which economic inequality reflects social, political, or economic injustices, teachers are asked to have students read an article in *Forbes* and help students "understand that, beyond calculation differences, there are inherent philosophical differences over what contributes to the gender wage gap (i.e., discrimination versus jobs in different industries)." As these examples illustrate, establishing academic language helps learners communicate the conclusions of their inquiries.

Helping Students Recognize the Interdisciplinary Nature of Social Studies Phenomena

Social studies education relies on the ways of knowing within specific disciplines, which requires students to apply different disciplinary lenses to help them understand and assess complex social phenomena. Moreover, from a citizenship perspective, the historical, political, economic, and geographic complexity involved in many social issues is beyond the possible vantage point of a single discipline. As such, many IDM inquiries ask teachers to help students approach questions, tasks, and sources through an interdisciplinary lens. For example, in the Johnson and Reagan inquiry, where students investigate the government's role in fostering economic opportunity, teachers are asked to have students view "economic themed commercials from other presidential campaigns to obtain a broader sense of the economic issues and arguments that have persisted over the past half-century." The analysis of a political commercial for economic issues requires students to see the confluence between political data sources and economic concepts and understandings.

Another common approach to foster interdisciplinarity is to consider the same phenomenon from different disciplinary perspectives. The French Revolution inquiry, for example, asks students to analyze the revolution from a social, economic, and political perspective. The Silk Road inquiry urges teachers to engage in a similar form of disciplinary analysis by having students, "consider the sociocultural and economic impact of silk for both Western and Eastern societies." By repeating the analysis through different disciplinary lenses, students can see how different disciplines yield different answers to the same phenomena, and perhaps more importantly how phenomena such as revolutions are complex bundled ideas. By teaching students how to analyze the politics of economics, the economics of geography, and the historical, social, and political commonalities of revolutions, teachers help their students see the value of examining social situations through different disciplinary perspectives.

Using Interpretive Questions

Asking and answering questions are essential to powerful social studies learning. Although the IDM features compelling and supporting questions that anchor the instructional design process, teachers are also asked to use interpretive questions that further elicit the interpretive capacities of students in response to compelling and supporting questions. Frequently, interpretive questions were used to explore the possibility of multiple "right" answers. For example, in the Roman Empire inquiry, which leads students through an investigation of the fall of the Roman Empire, students first read articles about whether or not history can predict the fall of empires. Teachers are then asked to engage students in a conversation featuring questions such as "What makes an empire?" "Can the fall of an empire be predicted?" and "What does it mean when an empire falls?"

Similarly, in the Campaign Finance inquiry, students investigate election costs, expenditures, and the complex relationships between candidates and political-action committees. Teachers are asked to have students analyze a sample of political correspondence between representatives of the two major U.S. political parties and their financiers by considering questions such as "What do both sides hope to get out of the agreement?" and "Is the funding tied to favors?" Interpretive questions are also used to help students broadly generalize social studies concepts and issues.

In the First Amendment inquiry, an investigation of students' rights and the First Amendment of the Constitution, teachers are asked to share a *Washington Post* article about the expulsion of students who posted a homemade rap video in Ohio, and then ask students questions such as "Did the rap video cause a distraction for other students?" "Does the school have a right to expel students for their activities on social media?" By eliciting multiple evidentiary answers and helping students generalize, the practice of using interpretive questions not only serves the immediate purpose of learning about specific content, but also helps develop students' capacities for interpretive reasoning.

Helping Students Organize Inquiries

Student performance within the IDM occurs during the formative, summative, extension, and taking informed action tasks. Tasks range from simple (e.g., create a T chart) to complex (making an evidence-based argument with counterclaims). Regardless of the purpose of the tasks, teachers' guidance consistently features scaffolding tasks to ensure that students are able to address the compelling question they are pursuing. In short, teachers are asked to facilitate how students organize disciplinary sources to help them progressively become more skilled and independent enquirers. To help students organize an inquiry, teachers are encouraged to use tools such as graphic organizers and adjunct displays.

For example, in the Immigration inquiry, where students examine whether there is anything new about current immigration debates, one of the formative tasks requires students to "write a paragraph using evidence from the sources that compares and contrasts the arguments made in support of the three historical approaches to immigration policy." In other lessons, teachers are expected to help students organize their inquiries by identifying important elements and features of sources. For example, in the Affordable Care Act (ACA) inquiry, where students investigate the public policy debate about the Affordable Care Act, after students read a series of five charts about the effects of the ACA from a blog on the *Washington Post* website, teachers can "point students to the sources of this data (e.g., Kaiser Family Foundation, Pew Research Center, and ABC) and have them consider the validity of each provider as well as the nature of blog posts versus news articles." As the examples above illustrate, by helping students organize inquiries, teachers support and scaffold the different ways that students engage in inquiry.

Connecting Inquiries to Students' Lives

A pervasive problem in social studies education is its lack of relevance to students' lives. Because the disciplines that constitute social studies in schools are often taught as ends unto themselves, studies reveal that students often fail to recognize the contemporary relevance of social studies subject matter.[7] As such, IDM inquiries ask teachers to make connections between the content and their students' lives. One approach is through situational connections. For example, in the Westward Migration inquiry, where students investigate the factors, conditions, and conflicts related to westward expansion in the United States before the Civil War, teachers may have students "reflect on an action they have taken from which they have benefitted at the expense of another individual or group." Similarly, the Japanese American Internment inquiry, where students investigate the tradeoff between freedom and national security, teachers can have students examine policies in their everyday lives, not in a manner to make those events equivalent, but to better understand the tradeoffs between personal freedom and the greater good. These situational connections help students bound the temporal distance between today and past events.

Another way that the inquiries help teachers connect the content to students' civic lives is by incorporating the home/community into lessons. In the Religious Freedom inquiry, where students examine sources about the practices and geographic distribution of world religions to develop a comparative understanding of major religions, teachers are encouraged to "incorporate information about belief systems found in their local community...." Prospectively, the practice of connecting inquiries to students' civic lives can help them contextualize social studies lessons in ways that inspire curiosity and interest in the topics.

Structuring Opportunities for Discussion

A common feature of social studies classrooms is discussion. Using classroom discussion to prepare students for democratic life is well established in the social studies education literature. Not surprisingly then, the IDM inquiries prominently feature opportunities for students to engage in discussions as part of the inquiry process. Although "discussion" was often used as a synonym for the act of questioning a whole classroom, the IDM inquiries promote sustained interaction among students through structured discussion formats. Across the inquiries, teachers can use protocols such as Fishbowl, Found Poem, Four Corners, Big Paper, and Structured Academic Controversy. These discussion formats help prompt a variety of skills such as discussing a text, encouraging turn-taking, and highlighting different perspectives. For example, in the Johnson and Reagan inquiry, teachers can facilitate discussion through a Structured Academic Controversy to help students "engage with the legacies of the Johnson administration and its impact on today's economy and political discourse." The Structured Academic Controversy format features sources that offer "modern political interpretations of Johnson's policies from liberal and conservative perspectives." Students are to "take an initial side on the issue, look at the evidence supporting that side, and then come to consensus after looking at all the evidence." Because discussion is often considered a proxy for democratic participation, structuring opportunities for discussion through common formats provides an important scaffold for rehearsing the habits of public participation in social studies classrooms.

Extending Inquiry into Civic Life

One of the distinguishing features of the C3 Inquiry Arc is the expectation that students publicly communicate the outcomes of their inquiries. In the IDM blueprint, the "taking informed action" section asks teachers to help students extend inquiry skills into real-world contexts. Applying the skills of inquiry to contemporary issues serves as an opportunity to practice inquiry as a habit of citizenship and helps frame the utility of social studies education for civic life. In some cases, teachers are guided to help students directly apply the knowledge yielded during an inquiry into a contemporary problem or issue. For example, in the Internet inquiry, which focuses on the compelling question "Is the internet good for democracy?" teachers can help students investigate the impact of Twitter on democratic processes. In other cases, extensions into civic lives are less directive; teachers can encourage students to follow their own curiosities about possible applications to their civic lives. For example, in the New Deal inquiry, where students investigate how the New Deal stimulated the economy and supported citizens in need, teachers are asked to follow students' curiosity about the proper role of government and the "extent to which government should take care of its people." These direct and indirect extensions of inquiry into the civic lives of students require teachers to help learners translate inquiries of disciplinary knowledge into relevant civic contexts.

Practices, Not Pedagogies for Social Studies Teacher Education

With so many states adopting inquiry as the defining characteristic of high-quality social studies instruction, the seven core practices outlined above can serve as an organizational heuristic for social studies teacher educators to respond to these emerging policy imperatives. Of course, this list is neither exhaustive nor conclusive, and requires a commitment by faculty to engage in both course-level and program-level conversations about how to structure learning opportunities within teacher education programs. As such, implementing core practices requires teacher educators to orchestrate intentional pedagogical moments that allow novices to work toward mastery of these practices. A list of core practices, for example, does not solve the problem of how teacher educators might go about helping prospective social studies teachers engage in the principled selection of instructional scaffolds that are most effective to help students pursue specific kinds of compelling or supporting questions. That work remains within the pedagogical purview of the social studies teacher educator.

Because core practices do not replace the pedagogical moments that teacher educators cultivate with prospective teachers, moving toward core practices does not mean abandoning critical views of the social studies curriculum. In this sense, the curricular agnosticism of core practices provides teacher educators with a fertile space to orchestrate program experiences with curricular perspectives that leverage content to accentuate justice, racial literacy, global citizenship, or activism. Indeed, core practices provide an opportunity to prepare social studies teachers with instructional practices that can help increase the probability that students will learn about critically oriented curriculum.

Learning how to conduct discussions, use organizational tools, and extend inquiry into the civic lives of students may look pedagogically different in social studies teacher education programs focused on ecological justice, critical media literacy, or global citizenship education because those curricular perspectives serve as different departure points for instruction. The language of core practices merely provides the instructional approaches most likely to help students inquire into different dimensions of the social studies curriculum. Given the significant and positive instructional shift that the C3 Framework has created for social studies education through policy, social studies teacher educators should embrace the opportunity to examine our practices and pedagogies and move toward frameworks that prepare teachers for inquiry-based learning.

Notes

1. Alexander Cuenca and Andrea Hawkman, "Reifying Common Sense: Writing the Missouri 6-12 Social Studies Standards," *Journal of Social Studies Research* 43, no 1 (2019): 57–68.

2. Ryan New, Kathy Swan, John Lee, and S. G. Grant, "The State of Social Studies Standards: What is the Impact of the C3 Framework?" *Social Education* 85, no. 4 (2021): 239–246.

3. Pam Grossman, Karen Hammerness, and Morva McDonald, "Redefining Teaching, Re-imagining Teacher Education," *Teachers and Teaching: Theory and Practice* 79, no. 5 (2009).

4. Stephen Thornton, *Teaching Social Studies That Matters* (New York, NY: Teachers College Press, 2004), 73.

5. Grossman, 277.

6. Alexander Cuenca, "Proposing Core Practices for Social Studies Teacher Education: A Qualitative Content Analysis of Inquiry-Based Lessons," *Journal of Teacher Education*, 72, no. 3 (2021): 298-313; S.G. Grant, Kathy Swan, and John Lee, *Inquiry Based-Practice in Social Studies Education: The Inquiry Design Model* (New York, NY: Routledge); Kathy Swan, John Lee, and S.G. Grant, *Inquiry Design Model: Building Inquiries in Social Studies* (Silver Spring, MD: National Council for the Social Studies); https://c3teachers.org/

7. Richard Harris and Rosemary Reynolds, "The History Curriculum and Its Personal Connection to Students from Minority Ethnic Backgrounds," *Journal of Curriculum Studies* 46, no. 4 (2014).

Social Education (in press, 2024)

Turning Student Teachers into Claim Makers: Developing the Pedagogical Content Knowledge of Novice Teachers with the *Persuasive Claim Framework*

Ryan Lewis, Kathy Swan, and Ryan Crowley

The task of becoming a teacher is daunting. Even as preservice teachers navigate the emotional and physical stress that teaching demands, preservice social studies teachers face new pressures ranging from curriculum disputes to a revolving door of political and social policies that attempt to redefine social studies. As such, social studies educators and methods instructors have struggled to develop a common language and set of expectations around what it is that "we do" in the classroom.[1]

In response, educators have developed tools and rationales that pursue a common language around the "what" and "why" of social studies teaching. The *C3 Framework*[2] and instructional models like the *Inquiry Design Model* (IDM)[3] place inquiry and argumentation at the center of this conversation. Yet, there is often a disconnect between what teachers *say* is important and what they actually *do* in the classroom. This incongruity has left many methods instructors scratching their heads, as year-after-year, novice teachers leave preservice programs espousing one view of teaching, later to abandon those views for more teacher-centric direct instruction. In light of this situation, the call for methods instructors is to *challenge* the preconceived assumptions of preservice teachers[4] while helping novice teachers *develop* explicit practices that they will need in order to become expert teachers.[5]

To answer that call, we argue here that the use of inquiry-based tools like the *Persuasive Claim Framework*[6] represents an effective way to steer teachers toward inquiry-based pedagogies. This conclusion is born out of a semester-long study of preservice teachers who centered claim-writing at the heart of their instruction. The results reveal that the use of the *Persuasive Claim Framework* prompted student teachers (ST) to develop increasingly complex strategies and tasks to support student claim-writing and inquiry. Furthermore, the *Framework* led to new ways of conceptualizing the progress of preservice teachers.

The Problem

The challenges facing methods instructors are not new. In his work on teacher preparation, Lee Shulman[7] argues that the central purpose of any teacher preparation program is to instruct teachers in the process of knowledge transformation. Shulman defines *pedagogical content knowledge* (PCK) as the blending of both content knowledge with pedagogical strategies. PCK represents the very heart of what teachers do: create opportunities for students to access content knowledge, and by extension, the basic knowledge that scholars have generated through decades of research and learning.

Developing a social studies-centric PCK framework, however, has proven elusive.[8] The challenge of defining a social studies PCK should not deter teacher preparation programs from trying to find common ground on what constitutes social studies PCK. But how should this be done? One concrete step may be to identify the key differences between the way *expert* teachers and *novice* teachers understand content, present content in lessons, and visualize a course's curriculum. For instance, expert teachers are more likely to visualize multiple ways in which the curriculum could be oriented, whereas novice teachers tend to see curriculum from a lesson-by-lesson perspective.[9]

Novice teachers differ in other important ways.[10] By contrast, expert teachers focus on tasks that aid in the *gathering* of evidence, and they help students develop strategies that aid in the *synthesizing* of evidence into writing. Novices gravitate toward formulaic scaffolds to help students gather evidence but do not teach students how to synthesize competing sets of information into one claim or thesis.[11] Thus the picture of expert teaching is as follows:

1. a focus on *interpretive* versus *recall* argumentative writing,
2. a focus on the *synthesis* of evidence rather than the *gathering* of evidence, and
3. a robust view of *curriculum.*

In essence, expert teachers are more likely to engage in a pedagogy of inquiry[12] in which the student is placed at the center of learning. Novices are much more likely to engage in practices that align with a direct instruction approach, reflecting a teacher-centric framework whereby transmission of knowledge is controlled by the teacher.[13] Inquiry pedagogies emphasize student-centric instruction where knowledge is more likely to be constructed by the student with assistance from the teacher.

Of course, most teachers do not fall neatly into one way of teaching or the other. Rather, the more expert teachers become, the more likely they are to develop practices that align with an inquiry-based approach. Conversely, those teachers with less expertise are more likely to embrace "coping" instructional strategies that fall back on teacher-centric approaches, such as lecturing and direct instruction.[14]

It is at this pivot-point between expert and novice teaching that this study focuses. What if it was possible to develop new "coping" strategies for novice teachers that encourage and support a move toward inquiry-based teaching? In this paper, we argue that claim-writing represents one of these potential strategies. And, in conjunction with tools like the *Persuasive Claim Framework,* that strategy enables student teachers to adapt their teaching to a more student-centric and inquiry-based approach.

The Framework

The *Persuasive Claim Framework* was introduced as a tool to help classroom teachers better instruct students on the challenges of argumentation. As claims are constituent parts of arguments,[15] the *Framework* makes sense in the social studies classroom, where students are encouraged to use contested and conflicting sources to arrive at conclusions,[16] supporting both historical and civic inquiry.[17]

Unfortunately, new teachers often struggle to define argumentative tasks in their classrooms.[18] In response, the *Persuasive Claim Framework* identifies a "persuasive claim" as an assertion of 1–3 sentences "that is supported with factual information and evidence from sources." It describes four dimensions of a persuasive claim: clear, evidentiary, accurate, and reasoned. According to the *Framework,* a "clear" claim uses language that is objective and effectively communicates conclusions. An "evidentiary" claim is convincing, drawing from multiple, often contradictory, sources.

Together, these dimensions are intended to provide an active and flexible model for students and teachers to think about what necessitates persuasive claim-making.

The Study

Over the past two years, a large public university in the American southeast utilized the *Persuasive Claim Framework* as the basis of its social studies methods master's degree examination. The master's exam placed the *Framework* and claim-writing at the center of the exam, asking student teachers (STs) to use it to guide their teaching. The examination was structured in three progressing phases of assessment: In Phase I (Diagnose), STs diagnosed their own students' claim-writing abilities, asking them to write a claim answering a compelling question. The STs evaluated student claims using a single-point rubric[19] adapted from the dimensions of the *Persuasive Claim Framework* (see Table 1). STs reflected on the areas their students required the most support and growth.

Phase II (Design) asked STs to design instruction to address the weaknesses of students' claim-writing. Using the IDM structure, student teachers created unit plans, adding opportunities for students to improve.

In Phase III (Deliver), they delivered their units. At the end, they re-evaluated their students' claim-writing, noting the dimensions in which the students grew. In written reflections, STs described what kinds of tasks they used to address the weaknesses of their students and if those tasks impacted student growth. They also explained how the *Framework* impacted their current and future teaching.

Table 1. The Persuasive Claim Framework Conceptualized as a Single-Point Rubric.

Enhancers	Criteria/Dimension	Distractors
(Areas that show progress)	**Evidentiary** Claim is convincing. Author weights evidence by corroborating multiple sources in order to support the claim. **Reasoned** Claim is logical and valid. It answers all parts of the question or task and conclusions follow a logical chain of reasoning. **Clear** Claim communicates conclusions effectively by using unambiguous language. Claim can be understood by a wide audience and avoids vague language. **Accurate** Information presented in the claim is factual and verifiable. Claim represents plausible interpretation of evidence.	(Areas that need improvement)

Methodology

The written products generated in each of these phases (i.e., rubrics, lesson plans, student claims, and reflections) form the basis of this study. Eleven STs participated in the 2021–2022 school year's master's examination. This cohort formed the focus of a phenomenological case study[20] that specifically examined the experiences of STs as they used the

Persuasive Claim Framework in their placements. We were guided by the following questions:

1. What were the results of teaching claim-writing as a practice within a preservice setting?
2. To what extent does the *Persuasive Claim Framework* represent an effective tool in developing the pedagogical content knowledge of novice social studies teachers?

The study began with the student samples collected in Phases I, II, and III of the examination. In order to create an independent sense of what a persuasive claim looked like, we independently analyzed de-identified student claim samples using the *Framework*'s dimensions. We then compared our coding data, reaching consensus in order to create a sense of agreement around each of the dimensions. We followed this process with a detailed analysis of the ST lesson plans and reflections. We identified codes and themes as they emerged.[21] Using the categories of "novice" and "expert" teacher, we looked for ways that student teachers approached the claim-writing process, utilizing language from the literature (e.g., "gathering"), but also making room for new themes that presented themselves with regularity (e.g.,"organizing").

The Results

Table 2. Examples of Methods of Instruction in Increasing Complexity (read columns vertically).

Gathering	Organizing	Understanding	Writing	Source Uses	Future Use
- Directional (Find Evidence)	- IDM Structure	- Student questions	- Directive (Write a Claim)	- Content Identification	- Explicit Instruction
- Identify Evidence	- Supporting Question	- Answering Supporting Question	- Summarize	- Length	- Clearer Instructions
- Guided Notes	- Venn Diagram	- Learning Checks	- Fill-in-Blank Stems	- Difficulty Level	- Repetition
- Table/Chart	- T-Chart	- Small Group Discussion	- Sample Claim	- Purpose	- Regular Practice
- Reading (Individual)	- Graphic Organizer (Generic)	- Whole Group Discussion	- Example Claim		- Scaffolding
- Reading (Groups)	- Graphic Organizer (Parts of Claim)	- "Jigsaw" Activity	- Supporting Question		- Teacher Feedback
- Annotating (Generic)	- "Bucketing"	- Class Discussion (source based)	- "Modeling" Claim		- Modeling
- Annotating (using Supporting Question)	- "Chicken Foot"	- Debate/ Deliberation	- "Chicken Foot"		- "Chicken Foot"
- Guided Questions (Generic)	- Graphic Organizer (Perspective)				- Peer-to-Peer Feedback
- Content Acronym ("VLOP," etc.)					- "Harkness Discussion"
- Guided Questions (Source Specific)					

What were the results of teaching claim-writing within a preservice setting? While individual STs struggled to consistently apply the individual dimensions of the *Framework* to their own students' work, STs were able to make accurate evaluations of the strengths and weaknesses of their classes as a whole. More significantly, the interpretive demands of the *Framework* pushed STs to create new tasks and structures in order to coach their students. These strategies began to form common themes around the *kinds* of tasks utilized. We grouped these strategies into these categories: gathering, organizing, understanding, writing, source use, and future use. These categories are summarized in Table 2.

Task 1: Gathering. STs displayed the widest variation of use of evidence-gathering tasks. Gathering refers to a routine, structure, or task intended to facilitate student gathering and collection of information. Gathering tasks ranged from generic guided questions to the use of borrowed acronym methods (e.g., KWL or SPY) to more complex graphic organizers and source-specific questions. As novice teachers are far more likely than expert teachers to focus on evidence-gathering tasks,[22] we were not surprised that gathering tasks were used across the board.

Task 2: Organizing. Organizing tasks are any use of materials, routines, and structures to organize gathered data from multiple sources. While nearly all STs utilized some forms of organizing tasks, their complexity varied considerably. While some STs relied on the IDM's supporting and compelling questions, some STs found increasingly complex ways for students to organize their evidence, utilizing "bucketing" and perspective identification. The presence of an organizing task in all the STs' Phase III teaching suggests that, at the very least, STs recognized that claim-writing demands both the collection of evidence and its organization as part of the interpretive process.

Task 3: Understanding. Some STs designed tasks to help students understand the evidence. While fewer than other tasks, there was wide variety in the complexity of understanding tasks. Understanding tasks are fundamentally different from writing tasks. STs used understanding tasks after gathering and organizing so students could make sense of the sources prior to writing. For example, one ST spent time before the writing task to allow students to ask questions about sources. Understanding tasks also differed from organizing or gathering tasks in that they asked students to use evidence in new or connected ways. For example, the use of a structured historical debate or whole class discussion to ask questions reflect markedly different purposes from gathering or organizing. What is clear is that nine of the STs omitted understanding tasks in at least one phase of assessment, with a further five STs not using them at all.

Task 4: Writing. While all STs collected writing samples, not all of them implemented writing tasks. A writing task is any use of materials, routines, or structures designed to help students write and respond to a question or prompt. The specific purpose of a writing task is to turn a mental argument into written form.[23] For example, some STs created variations of the "chicken foot" outline to provide structure for claims. This approach contrasted with many of the STs use of a simple directive to "write a claim." Significantly, writing tasks were less likely than other tasks to be used, showing less variation in their implementation.

Task 5: Source Use. The master's examination required that STs utilize a variety of sources as part of the claim-writing process. Source use refers to a discussion about the nature of sources, reasons for inclusion, difficulty, or modification for classroom use. Most STs did not include discussions of the potential uses for the sources they selected in their instructional design. While some commented on the medium of sources, few STs described the content of the sources, how the sources related to each other, or the perspectives of the sources. One ST provided a brief description of each of their included sources along with a content rationale for why they were included but did not mention how inclusion of the source impacted the interpretive process. Furthermore, there were few opportunities for students to consider the background, reliability, or impact of certain sources as they wrote. This omission is significant, and perhaps a limitation of the *Framework*, as experienced teachers are more likely to place importance on both the selection and use of sources that help to enhance student learning.[24] This difference likely accounts for the multiple appearances of single-perspective claim structures in student writing.

Task 6: Future Use. Future use refers to any discussion of how lessons learned in the preservice context might impact future teaching and use of claim-writing. STs acknowledged that "scaffolding" was part of any successful attempt at claim-writing. Also widely cited was "a need for more writing experience." Some STs, however, painted a much more robust picture of what tasks they would use in their future instruction, including the "modeling" of claims and the use of class discussion on student understanding of sources prior to writing.

Together, these six themes create a working picture of the *Framework*'s impact on novice teachers' practices.

Developing Teacher Pedagogical Content Knowledge

What did these themes reveal about the development of novice teacher PCK? All of the STs displayed a progression in the use and complexity of the tasks they employed from Phases I to III. The requirements of the *Framework* pushed STs to develop increasingly complex tasks. However, not all STs developed in the same ways or to the same depth. The *Framework* revealed as much as it instructed, allowing methods teachers a window into the PCK development of each ST.

Here, we offer three pictures of PCK development, which we refer to as *emerging expertise*, *expert-facing*, and *progressing novice*. These categories, summarized in Table 3, were based on the depth to which some STs utilized these tasks.

Of the 11 STs in the study, only one ST displayed all tasks and themes in their planning and instruction. In addition, they made important instructional shifts throughout the process of their placement, increasing the complexity and use of tasks. We believe this example revealed an emerging expertise—a clear progression from *gathering* evidence to *synthesizing* evidence, an intentional use of organization and understanding tasks to support student learning, and the creation of structures to support student interpretive writing.

Many other STs displayed marked shifts in the way they implemented more complex tasks from Phases I to III. However, in the area of writing tasks we saw important limitations. While some STs effectively implemented organizing and understanding tasks, most did not use writing tasks or other methods to explicitly coach students. This lack of attention to writing and, for some, lack of detailed emphasis on understanding tasks revealed an expert-facing level of PCK. In other words, there is evidence to suggest that these STs have an understanding of the difference between the gathering of evidence and the synthesis of evidence, but their thinking around claim-writing seems unclear and in its infancy. This finding suggests they may not yet have the PCK required to fully coach students in their claim-writing now, but likely have the disposition to do so in the future.

Some STs differed importantly from the emerging expertise and expert-facing STs. While these STs made important strides throughout their placement to help students write persuasive claims, they often struggled to fully implement an inquiry-based pedagogy in their classrooms. For example, in order to boost students' understanding of difficult concepts, these STs employed a series of learning checks and guided notes in order to monitor understanding throughout their units. While these instructional strategies displayed a high level of knowledge of their students, their actions were a pivot away from inquiry-based pedagogy to direct-instruction pedagogy. This situation is common among novice teachers faced with unfamiliar content,[25] but it creates a context for claim-writing that is based on the *recall* of factual information rather than an *interpretation* of the sources. As these STs had not yet fully departed from traditional novice teaching dispositions, we argue that they are still in a progressing novice phase.

Table 3. *Summary of Stage of Potential Student Teacher Levels of Pedagogical Content Knowledge*

Progressing Novice	Expert-Facing	Emerging Expertise
• Focus on gathering and organizing tasks • Vague descriptions of claim-writing uses beyond current lesson • Lack of focus on understanding and writing tasks • Emphasis on writing for recall versus writing for interpretation	• Focus on gathering, organizing, and understanding tasks, but may lack emphasis on writing tasks • Sophisticated but non-specific descriptions of claim-writing use beyond current lesson • May discuss the importance of writing but may lack specific techniques to improve student writing • Emphasis on writing for interpretation	• Focus on understanding and writing tasks • Sophisticated and specific descriptions of claim-writing use beyond current lesson • Discusses the importance of writing, showcasing specific techniques to improve student writing • Emphasis on writing for interpretation and multi-perspective claim-writing

Taken together, these categories form a pattern of teaching behavior. Thus, we can compare the work of other teachers in the same program, and potentially, novice teachers in these same stages of their teacher journey in the future.

Conclusions

There is a clear connection between the level of teachers' expertise and the kinds of tasks they implement in their classrooms. The *Persuasive Claim Framework* represents an effective tool for developing inquiry-based tasks for preservice teachers. By centering the *Framework* at the heart of methods instruction, STs used increasingly complex tasks to help students gather, organize, understand, and write their claims. The shift to tasks that emphasize synthesis of evidence in claim-writing reflects a progressive growth in teacher PCK.

Another implication of this study was the emergence of three important categories or phases of teacher development: *progressing novice, expert-facing,* and *emerging expertise* These categories are not static representations. Rather, they represent useful ways of thinking about student teacher progress. These categories can better assist methods instructions in specifically coaching their own students in argumentative writing. As preservice teachers are rarely challenged on their preconceived assumptions about argumentation,[26] it falls on teacher educators to find ways of addressing them, with explicit instruction on what is and what is not argumentative writing. Centering the *Persuasive Claim Framework* provides this opportunity. By placing the dimensional demands of the *Framework* at the forefront of the master's assessment, student teachers were pushed to create methods and strategies to address those demands. The use of these tasks revealed a continuum of teacher development. As such, the process of claim instruction reveals as much as it supports teacher PCK development, as many STs eventually created tasks that promoted student understanding and writing. These tasks reflected a steady growth in social studies-specific PCK.

Most importantly, the *Framework* provides a useful "coping strategy" for novice teachers struggling with the demands of classroom teaching.[27] Claim-writing is both inherently interpretive and argumentative over the top, prompting more inquiry-based approaches rather than reverting to direct-instruction practices when confronted with the challenges of teaching. In order to help preservice teachers work toward this goal, structures must be developed in order to provide both the student and the teacher with a model of what claim-making requires. *The Persuasive Claim Framework* represents one important and potentially powerful structure that places inquiry back into the heart of the classroom.

Notes

1. Dave Powell, "Brother, Can You Paradigm? Toward a Theory of Pedagogical Content Knowledge in Social Studies," *Journal of Teacher Education*, 69, no. 3 (2018): 252–262.
2. National Council for the Social Studies, *College, Career, and Civic Life (C3) Framework for Social Studies State Standards* (Silver Spring, MD: NCSS, 2013).
3. S. G. Grant, Kathy Swan, and John Lee, *Inquiry-Based Practice in Social Studies Education: The Inquiry Design Model* (New York: Routledge, 2017).
4. Chauncy Monte-Sano and Kristen Harris, "Recitation and Reasoning in Novice History Teachers' Writing Instruction," *The Elementary School Journal*, 113, no. 1 (2012): 105–130.
5. Chauncy Monte-Sano and Amina Allen, "Historical Argument Writing: The Role of Interpretive Work, Argument Type, and Classroom Instruction," *Reading and Writing*, 32 (2019): 1383–1410.
6. Ryan Lewis, "What's in a Claim? A Framework for Helping Students Write Persuasive Claims," *Social Education*, 85, no. 2 (2021): 116–120.
7. Lee Shulman, "Those Who Understand: Knowledge Growth in Teaching," *Educational Researcher*, 15, no. 2 (1986): 4–14.
8. Powell, "Brother, Can You Paradigm?"
9. Sigrun Gudmundsdottir and Lee Shulman, "Pedagogical Content Knowledge in Social Studies," *Scandinavian Journal of Educational Research*, 31, no. 2 (1987): 59–70.
10. Chauncy Monte-Sano, "Learning to Open up History for Students: Preservice Teachers' Emerging Pedagogical Content Knowledge," *Journal of Teacher Education*, 62, no. 3 (2011): 260–272.
11. Monte-Sano and Harris, "Recitation and reasoning."
12. Lee Shulman, "Signature Pedagogies in the Professions," *Daedalus*, 134, no. 3 (2005): 52–59.
13. Dennis Beck and Jenni Eno, "Signature Pedagogy: A Literature Review of Social Studies and Technology Research," *Interdisciplinary Journal of Practice, Theory, and Applied Research*, 29, no. 1–2 (2012): 70–94.
14. Gudmundsdottir and Shulman, "Pedagogical content knowledge in social studies."
15. Stephen E. Toulmin, *The Uses of Argument* (New York: Cambridge University Press, 1958).
16. Louis Mink, "Philosophical Analysis and Historical Understanding," *The Review of Metaphysics*, 21, no. 4 (1968): 667–698.
17. Walter Parker, *Teaching Democracy: Unity and Diversity in Public Life* (New York and London: The Teachers College Press, 2005); Walter Parker, "Public Discourses in Schools: Purposes, Problems, and Possibilities," *Educational Researcher*, 35, no. 8 (2006): 11–15.
18. Chauncy Monte-Sano and Susan De La Paz, "Using Writing Tasks to Elicit Adolescents' Historical Reasoning," *Journal of Literacy Research*, 44, no. 3 (2012): 273–299.
19. Kathy Swan, S. G. Grant, and John Lee, *Blueprinting: An Inquiry-Based Curriculum* (National Council for the Social Studies and C3 Teachers: 2019).
20. Sharan B. Merriam, *Qualitative Research and Case Study Applications in Education* (San Francisco, CA: Jossey-Bass, John Wiley & Sons, 2005).
21. Robert E. Stake, *The Art of Case Study Research* (Thousand Oaks, CA: Sage Publications, 1995).
22. Monte-Sano and Harris, "Recitation and reasoning."
23. Joseph W. Wenzel, "Three Perspectives on Argument: Rhetoric, Dialectic, Logic," in *Perspectives on Argumentation: Essays in Honor of Wayne Brockriede*, ed. Robert Trapp and Janice Schuetz (New York: ID Press, 2006), 9–26.
24. Emma Thacker, John Lee, Paul G. Fitchett, and Wayne Journell, "Secondary Social Studies Teachers' Experiences Planning and Implementing Inquiry Using the Inquiry Design Model," *The Clearing House*, 91, no. 4–5 (2018): 193–200.
25. Beck and Eno, "Signature Pedagogy"; Gudmundsdottir and Shulman, "Pedagogical Content Knowledge in Social Studies."
26. Monte-Sano and Harris, "Recitation and Reasoning."
27. Gudmundsdottir and Shulman, "Pedagogical Content Knowledge in Social Studies."

Conclusion: Looking Forward

There's just something about a ten-year anniversary. Maybe it is our cultural obsession with decades, or maybe it is the fact that we like making ten-year plans, or maybe it's just easy math. Whatever it is, a lot can happen in ten years. As we reflect back over the decade since the publication of the C3 Framework, we are tempted to put up a *Mission Accomplished* banner. But, we know better. A real revolution is not about the ends. This revolution of ideas is a means to an end.

To be sure, we can all agree that we accomplished much in the last ten years.[1] We opened this book highlighting some of those accomplishments including thirty-eight states that have revised their social studies standards with the C3 Framework in mind.[2] The New York Toolkit project, published in 2015, kicked off ten years of IDM-based curriculum inquiry that has led to the development of hundreds of inquiries published on C3Teachers.org and other open-source outlets. Educators around the world have been activated and inspired by the Inquiry Arc in the C3 Framework with tens of thousands of teachers plugged into classroom-based inquiry.[3]

We also opened this book with a recognition that revolutions need fuel. In reflecting back on the years since the publication of the C3 Framework, we feel that the inquiry revolution has indeed been well fueled. The twenty-seven chapters in this book represent just a few of the actions that have stoked the revolution. The question before us now is—what next? Being action-oriented social studies educators, we have a few ideas!

For starters, the social studies community needs to sustain and continue moving forward with the work to align social studies state standards with the C3 Framework and to articulate the social studies content that animates inquiry. This is no time to rest on our laurels. The reality that thirty-eight states and districts are actively using the C3 Framework in their standards is great, but let's aim for a clean sweep, one that gives students a chance to grapple with compelling questions and be empowered with the skills of inquiry. We owe no less to our students, to each other, and to our democracy.

We also need to continue growing and sustaining a robust network of social studies educators who develop inquiry materials and share lessons learned from teaching with inquiry. We have established something special with the existing network of social studies educators who are doing the meaningful work of building inquiry lessons with an open-source democratic ethos. Let's keep fueling the C3 Teachers movement.

Let's also continue to push the bounds of curriculum innovation around the C3 Framework Inquiry Arc. As is evident in the articles presented in this book, much good work has been done, but much work remains. We know some areas that are ripe for innovation—nurturing curiosity with new inquiry forms, connecting IDM with other forms of project-based learning, and building new assessment systems—to name a few.

So, how do we keep our focus and continue to fuel the inquiry revolution? We think the answer to that question hinges on *trust*.[4] Trust that develops as teachers and their students work with genuine questions, worthwhile tasks, and a range of sources that offer opportunities for teachers to reclaim what the vast majority assert as their reason to enter teaching from the beginning—the idea of helping students know and act as responsible citizens.

Instructional innovations that build trust are those that are built for the long run and are built on the deep relationships among teachers, students, and ideas. Trust demands that we are in community with each other. We see classroom teachers and their students as the rock upon which we can build the trust needed to continue the inquiry revolution of ideas.

We believe that we must commit to innovating new instructional practices that build trust, including ones that enable deliberation, collaboration, and production. We must be committed to innovating authentic assessment practices that scale from in-class formative tasks to large-scale reliable and valid assessments. We must be committed to trusting teacher educators who are carrying the inquiry revolution forward as they prepare the next generation of educators to teach with inquiry. Most importantly, we must be committed to C3-inspired teachers, who are blazing the inquiry trail, fueling the revolution, and delivering for their students learning experiences that respect and engage them for who they are and who they may become.

¡Viva la inquiry revolución!

Notes

1. S. G. Grant, John Lee, and Kathy Swan, "An Inquiry Revolution: 10 years after the C3 Framework." *Social Education* (2023).
2. S. G. Grant, John Lee, and Kathy Swan, "The State of the C3 Framework: An Inquiry Revolution in the Making," *Social Education* (2023).
3. John Lee, Alicia McCollum, and MaryBeth Yerdon, "C3 Teachers: The Heart of the Inquiry," *Social Education* (2023).
4. Kathy Swan, S. G. Grant, and John Lee, "Trusting Inquiry: Teaching with the Inquiry Design Model," *Social Education* 87, no. 5 (2023): 328–331.